SOLDIERS

LOST AT SEA

SOLDIERS
LOST AT SEA

A Chronicle of Troopship Disasters

James E. Wise Jr. and Scott Baron

Naval Institute Press
Annapolis, Maryland

Naval Institute Press
291 Wood Road
Annapolis, MD 21402

Library of Congress Cataloging-in-Publication Data
Wise, James E., 1930–
    Soldiers lost at sea : a chronicle of troopship disasters / James E. Wise Jr.
and Scott Baron.
        p.   cm.
    ISBN 1-59114-966-5 (alk. paper)
    1. Shipwrecks—History—20th century. 2. World War, 1939–1945—
Transportation. 3. Naval history, Modern—20th century. 4. World War,
1939–1945—Naval operations. I. Baron, Scott, 1954– II. Title.
    D810.T8W57 2003
    940.54'5—dc21

                                                        2003009755

Printed in the United States of America on acid-free paper ∞
11 10 9 8 7 6 5 4   9 8 7 6 5 4 3 2
First printing

For my shipmate, Capt. Frank Hantz, United States Navy, (Retired), a true gentleman and trusted friend for more than thirty years.

—James E. Wise Jr.

For my two Maris:
My wife Marisela—you deserved better. Thank you for two beautiful sons. My "Auntie" Marcella—always there. You inspired me to reach beyond my grasp.

—Scott Baron

Contents

Preface

Very little has been written about troopship operations and losses sustained throughout the course of naval warfare. With regard to U.S. publications, the Naval Historical Center Library, the largest of its kind in the world, holds but one book dedicated to the subject, *Troopships of World War II,* by Roland W. Charles, naval architect, published and distributed in 1947 by the Army Transportation Association, Washington, D.C. Another book published on the subject, *Troopships and Their Histories,* authored by Col. H. C. B. Rogers, O.B.E., and published in 1963, is devoted to British troopships. Other sources can be found that refer to troopship losses, such as *Lloyd's War Losses: The Second World War,* volumes 1 and 2; the Morison volumes; Capt. Arthur Moore's *A Careless Word, a Needless Sinking;* Peter Elphick's *Liberty: The Ships That Won the War;* Robert Browning's *U.S. Merchant Vessel War Casualties of World War II,* and a host of other books that briefly cover U.S. and British World War II troopship incidents. However, *Soldiers Lost at Sea: A Chronicle of Troopship Disasters,* while not all-inclusive, offers a history of international troopship casualties, both enemy and friendly, whose soldiers never made it to a distant shore to engage in combat. The first official recording of such a vessel was the loss of the British troopship *Birkenhead* in 1852.

It is our hope that this book will pay long overdue tribute to those brave soldiers who lost their lives in the vast oceans of the world far from home.

Acknowledgments

There are many to thank for assisting us in this comprehensive work; however, as in all of our written efforts, we must first recognize the exceptional research and administrative work done by our chief research assistant, Natalie Hall. She is an indispensable member of our team. Others who have rendered support in this effort include Jean Hort, Glenn Helm, Jack Green, James Arness, Hannah Cunliffe, Horst Schwenk, Dr. Edward J. Marolda, Kevin Reem, A. D. Lieber, Barry Whatton, Andy Carroll, Eric Voelz, George Toy, Rick Jevons, Debra Knox, Ward Garing, Stephen Rabson, and Roy Roberts, as well as Paul Wilderson, Kristin Wye-Rodney, Paul Stillwell, Ann Hassinger, and their colleagues at the U.S. Naval Institute.

SOLDIERS

LOST AT SEA

ONE

INTRODUCTION

The Evolution of Troopships

THE GREEK-ROMAN PERIOD

When man first went to sea it was for trading the products of his skill and toil. Discovering that streams and rivers were highways to open waters, many explorers and adventurers followed these early mariners to the Mediterranean basin, where traders from Asia, Europe, and Africa came together—not always in a friendly way.

Along with trading came the rise of piracy. To defend precious cargoes from these marauders, boats evolved that could house soldiers and escort merchant ships safely to port.[1] Early historians cite the round ship, a sailing cargo carrier, and the long ship, a combatant vessel propelled by oars, as examples. The round ships depended on the fighting long ships for protection, and together these teams became early navies. One early troopship was the Egyptian-oared war vessel, developed in c. 4700 B.C. Pharaoh Ramses III used a later version of it in 1194 B.C., when he defeated the Northerners of the Isles in the first recorded naval battle.

A keel eventually evolved, as represented in the Phoenician war boat of 750 B.C. Smaller and more practical than its Egyptian forerunner, this boat was armed with a ram, or metal beak. It had a fore and aft deck, with a high stockadelike bulwark to shelter soldiers and crewmen from spears, rocks, arrows, and Greek fire.

Grecian or Roman bireme troopship. *Naval Historical Center*

By the fifth century B.C. the Greeks had excluded the Phoenicians and the Carthaginians from the Black Sea and the Aegean Sea, gaining control of shipping in the eastern Mediterranean. Greek war galleys, built long and narrow for speed and easy rowing, roamed the seas protecting their commercial vessels. Preferred tactics were ramming and boarding, for which they carried marines, archers, and spearmen. Rather than destroying ships, they focused on killing the enemy.

During the Greco-Persian war amphibious assaults used troop carriers when, during the Persian expedition (494 B.C.), ten thousand soldiers crossed the Aegean and landed on the plain of Marathon. Eight thousand Athenian defenders engaged the invaders and pushed them back into the sea. With the subsequent defeat of the Persian fleet at the battle of Salamis (480 B.C.), the Greek victory ushered in the Golden Age of Athens. The Greeks had gained maritime and commercial superiority and, with their achievement of intellectual and artistic preeminence, they laid the foundation for Western Civilization.

In 275 B.C. the Romans conquered southern Italy, engulfing the Greek cities. The Romans borrowed designers and shipbuilders from their vassal Greek states and set about to build a large fleet of biremes, triremes, and quinqueremes. Their lack of seamanship proved disastrous as the Punic Wars began, with thousands lost in heavy seas off Sicily. Challenged by the elusive Carthaginian ships, which used sideswiping, ramming, flanking, and breaking-the-line tactics, the Romans found a way to turn a sea battle into an infantry engagement across decks with the corvus, an eighteen-foot gangway that housed a pointed iron beak under the outboard end. When an enemy ship closed or tried to sideswipe a Roman vessel, the corvus, which was pivoted from a mast by a topping lift, could be dropped on an unwary enemy, locking the vessels together. Legionnaires would then race across gangplanks to do battle.

The Romans became skilled seamen, steadily improving their tactics and weaponry, developing catapults to hurl stones, javelins, and combustibles at enemy ships. After winning the Punic Wars, Rome expanded into North Africa, Spain, Asia Minor, Egypt, and Europe. Under the leadership of Julius Caesar, Roman armies marched through Gaul and crossed the channel to Britain. Caesar's invasion fleet consisted of eighty transports, warship escorts, frigates, and cruisers. On board the transports were the Spanish legionnaires of the 10th and 7th Legions. Each troopship carried approximately 150 men. Setting up camp in Kent, Caesar's legionnaires were continually harassed by British tribesmen who proved to be formidable adversaries. In addition to fighting the tribesmen, the Romans had to contend with fierce weather that at one point heavily damaged their fleet. Upon the advice of his naval commanders who were concerned

Ancient Norse warship, or "dragon ship" with bow and stern ornamentation intended to resemble a dragon. *Naval Historical Center*

about the equinox—which would soon bring stormy weather down from the north—Caesar embarked his force and returned to France. It would take two more invasions of Britain to add the island fortress to the Roman Empire.[2]

Civil war at home eventually marked the decline of the Roman Empire, following four centuries of dominance. After splitting in two, the western empire was overrun by German invaders, the eastern by Muslim Arabs.

VIKINGS, CRUSADERS, AND THE OTTOMAN EMPIRE

Far to the north, the Vikings had been wreaking havoc. Norse noblemen fought continuously, not only abroad but also among themselves. The battles between the Norsemen were probably the first naval engagements in the history of northern Europe. Thirty-ton Oseberg troopships carried hoards of fierce warriors wielding spears, battle axes, swords, and bows and arrows.

Importantly, the Vikings were unrivaled shipbuilders. The sides of their ships were made from long, thin, overlapping wooden planks, nailed together with iron rivets, each perfectly shaped to fit the curves of the hull. Animal hair, dipped in tar, was wedged between planks to make the ship watertight. Bright colored shields along the sides kept the crews dry. The single Norse rudder hung over the right side, and because of this was dubbed the steer board side; to this day, the right side of a ship is the starboard side.

Initially raiders, the Norsemen were also famed explorers, pushing to the horizons of their known world and beyond. Aside from the British Isles and Ireland, they established themselves in Germany, Iceland, Greenland, Labrador, Latvia, Russia, and the eastern Mediterranean. In November 885 A.D. a fleet of seven hundred Viking vessels sailed up the Seine River and laid siege to Paris.[3] The Parisians fought off the Vikings for a year before being reinforced. The Vikings gave up their quest and retreated up the Seine.

Writings about early Viking engagements offer few clues as to how many troopships were lost in battle. Yet because the fighting was fierce and the sea and weather unforgiving, we can only assume that the toll was high.

The Crusades that pitched Christians against Muslims over control of the Holy Land were bloody endeavors with countless Christian knights and foot soldiers lost on land and sea. Traveling to the Holy Land by sea was in itself a danger-

Engraving of a medieval troop carrier during the reign of Henry III (circa 1260). Note the ship with hull door and ramp for offloading horses. *Naval Historical Center*

ous journey for the crusaders. Many of the expeditions sailed directly to the Middle East from the English ports of Southampton, Hastings, Dover, London, and Ipswich—as well as Vlerdingen, in the Netherlands. French and German crusaders made their way to the Italian ports of Lucca, Pisa, and Genoa. From there, ships took them to the Middle East. It is interesting to note that crusaders used landing craft with a bow ramp to land men and horses. These vessels could be considered forerunners of the LCTs used by the U.S. Navy in World War II.[4]

In *Anatomy of a Crusade* 1213–1221, author James M. Powell relates the sea hazards experienced by crusaders:

> Some three hundred ships departed from Vlerdingen in the Netherlands on May 29, 1217. This was the first contingent of the Fifth Crusade to actually get underway. It would not be the first to arrive in the east . . .
>
> The sea route chosen by the crusaders was perilous. There was no way to document fully how many of the ships that left Vlerdingen were lost at sea, but the number must have been substantial. Only a few days out, in the sea of Brittany, a ship from Monheim was wrecked on the rocks, and the fleet had to slow while its men were rescued from the rocks onto which they had climbed. Three more ships were

Naval battle between crusaders and Saracens. *Library of Congress*

wrecked in a storm off the Portuguese coast. Bishop James of Vitry, who had earlier traveled from Genoa to Acre, left a vivid description of the perils of travel on the treacherous waters of the Mediterranean. He described his fear during a storm in which the water was breaking over the ship, and this was despite the fact that he was traveling on a newly constructed ship and arrangements on board were suited to his episcopal rank. . . . Still the trip was far from comfortable. Contrary winds impeded their progress. They ran into a storm of such magnitude that fifteen anchors could hardly hold the ship back as the prow of the vessel rose to the stars and sank into the abyss. During the two days and nights that the storm lasted, many had nothing to eat, and James himself ate nothing cooked, because it was too dangerous to light a fire on the ship. Many on board took the opportunity to confess their sins and prepare for death. But, finally, the seas calmed and, with dolphins in their wake, they sailed toward Acre. Many travelers to the East were not so fortunate, however, and for them their crusade ended at sea.[5]

The crusade expeditions lasted into the thirteenth century. When the Christian sword and the Islam scimitar crossed for the last time, it was the scimitar that was sheathed in victory.

Political and religious feuds among Arabs provided an opening for the Turks to invade the Holy Land from the hills of Central Asia. The Turks swept across the Dardanelles and advanced to the Danube. Constantinople fell to Turkish hoards in 1453 whereupon the Turks expanded their rule and began to dominate the Mediterranean.

The Mediterranean showdown between the Christians and Muslims took place at the battle of Lepanto in 1571, with troop-laden galley fleets from Spain and Italy arrayed against the Turks. The Christians won the battle, with heavy losses of lives and ships levied by the Turks. Approximately thirty thousand Turkish soldiers were killed, and they lost all but 60 of their 250 galleys. Some seventy-seven hundred Christians lost their lives, and twelve ships were destroyed.[6]

EARLY BRITISH TROOP TRANSPORTS

Beginning in the fifteenth century, countries such as England, France, and Spain began construction of full-rigged ships that could transport explorers in their search for gold and other riches. The conquest of new lands resulted from such forays, and global empires were gradually formed.

It was during this period that British sea power gained ascendancy. England constructed a fleet of sailing vessels that could carry vast amounts of commercial goods, and it also built ships-of-the-line to protect its cargo carriers. Powerful nations transported their soldiers on these ships for foreign campaigns, but British cannon firepower ruled the day in its wars with France and Spain.[7]

Life aboard early British troop transports was just as uncomfortable as it was for those who sailed the globe in U.S. troop carriers during World War II. In both eras, troops were tightly packed into ships' holds in which they encountered rough seas and fierce storms and often suffered from severe seasickness.

The first convoy to carry regular army troops set forth in 1662 when some three thousand British soldiers in twenty-seven ships were transported from England to

The paddle-wheel steamer *Birkenhead* was Britain's first designated troopship.
The Naval and Military Press

Tangier to ward off besieging Moors. British soldiers at the time of the country's Restoration in 1660 and for years afterward were carried in warships, merchant ships, and convoy escort vessels. Detachments of Foot Guards and various regiments fought in the sea battles of the Second and Third Dutch Wars (Anglo-Dutch wars of 1665–67 and 1672–74). These detachments were eventually replaced by marines, and the need for an at-sea marine force was recognized by the British government in 1702; later, in 1753, the British Marine Corps was established, after years of bickering between the government and military.[8]

THE EIGHTEENTH AND NINETEENTH CENTURIES

British expeditionary forces were ordered to battle enemies at sea and on foreign soil throughout the 1700s. The longest conflict—the Napoleonic Wars—lasted for twenty-two years (1793–1815). Since France controlled most of the mainland of Western Europe, British military operations took the form of raids on the enemy coast and the landing of small forces—thus rose the need for troop transports. Spacious East Indian ships and nine-hundred-ton frigates (the most disliked ships by Royal Navy men) were converted to accommodate troops. These ships and others were used throughout the war. The conflict was hastened to an end by Nelson's defeat of the combined French and Spanish fleet at Trafalgar in 1805. Ten years later British Brigadier General Wellington (Arthur Wellesley, the Duke of Wellington) routed the French at Waterloo, and the Napoleonic Empire crumbled.[9]

During the years 1815–60 there were few military operations of any major consequence, although it was a period of momentous change in naval history. After two thousand years of oared propulsion and three hundred years of sail propulsion, the navies of the world shifted to steam power. Ship's armor and the iron hull were adopted, and rifled built-in guns with percussion-fused shells were introduced. And ships were designed and outfitted as troopships. The British paddle steamer *Birkenhead* was launched in 1846 and carried troops to Ireland and the Channel Islands. She had been converted for troop carrying and rigged for long-distance trooping. In 1850 she was officially commissioned as a troopship and sailed in succession to Ireland, Gibraltar, Canada, and Cape Town. Loaded with soldiers from eight different regiments in December 1851, the *Birkenhead* headed for South Africa, where her men were to reinforce the local garrison fighting in the Kaffir War. The ship and 1,200 troops were later lost, and because *Birkenhead* was the first loss of a designated troopship, an extensive investigation was conducted in England.[10] (The tragic loss of HMS *Birkenhead* is described in chapter 2.)

The first large-scale movement of troops since the introduction of steam occurred during the Crimean War in 1854. British steamship companies that had been subsidized by the government were required to release their ships for military use should the need arise. Steamships and big sailing ships transported approximately sixty-two thousand men and fifteen thousand horses during the war. Troopships were in continuous use during the last half of the nineteenth century, reinforcing overseas garrisons where soldiers faced unrest in various parts of the British Empire. The occupation of Cyprus was carried out in 1878, and a year later troops had to be rushed to South Africa to put down an uprising by Zulus, who were fierce warriors. There followed the Boer War (1899–1902) during which trooping was carried out entirely by engine-driven ships. Among those vessels acquisitioned for trooping was *Dunottar Castle,* which departed the Southampton docks on 14 October 1899. Amid the troops was a young man

The British troopship *Dunottar Castle* transported British soldiers to South Africa during the Boer War (1899–1902). When she departed the Southampton docks on 14 October 1899, a correspondent for the *London Morning Post,* Mr. Winston Churchill, was aboard. *Steamship Historical Society of America*

U.S. Nebraska Volunteers embark an inter-island troop carrier at Pasig, Manila, 23 June 1899. *U.S. National Archives II*

who had served in the 4th Queen's Own Hussars and was now a correspondent for the *London Morning Post,* Mr. Winston Churchill.[11]

Halfway around the world, American soldiers were engaged in the Philippine insurrection (1898–1900), which was precipitated by the Spanish American War. The Philippine people expected to gain their independence, but after two years of guerrilla warfare the insurgents were finally defeated by U.S. Army forces.

WORLD WAR I

When the First World War erupted, the British battle fleet was the most formidable force in the world. Ninety battleships and battle cruisers fought German forces during the war. At the start of the conflict HMS *Gloucestershire* was converted into a troopship and eventually fitted out as an auxiliary cruiser in 1915. HMS *Leicestershire* served as a trooper, and HMS *Worcestershire* transported troops until she was sunk by a German-laid mine off Colombo in 1917. Thousands of soldiers were transported to the middle and far east to shore up regiments in those areas. Troops were also brought to England from far-flung colonies to join British expeditionary forces destined for France. Steamships of shipping companies such as the Bibby Line, the Union-Castle Line, the

The British troopship *Aquitania* served in both world wars. *Steamship Historical Society of America*

The World War I British troopship *Mauretania*, the sister ship to *Lusitania*. *Steamship Historical Society of America*

Peninsular & Oriental Steam Navigation Line (P&O), and the British India Steam Navigation Line (B.I.) became the backbone of the troopship fleet. During the four years of the war the Bibby Line alone transported two hundred thousand British soldiers and twenty-five thousand American troops though it had only seven ships.[12]

Of particular note among the British ships that transported troops during World War I was the Cunard liner *Aquitania.* This forty-five-thousand-ton ship held the distinction of being the only major pre-1914 passenger vessel to serve in both world wars. In addition to her distinguished service as a "trooper," she briefly saw action as an armed auxiliary cruiser and toward the end of the war was converted into a hospital ship. *Aquitania, Lusitania,* and *Mauretania* were among the last of the great four-funnel liners. Collectively, these ships were known as Cunard's Superliner Trio.

In May 1915, *Aquitania* and *Mauretania* were ordered into shipyards for troopship conversion. These ships and other troop transports were needed to support Britain's campaign in the Dardanelles. With the Australian and New Zealand Army Corps (ANZAC) stalled on the beaches of Gallipoli, there was a desperate need for reinforcements. Ready for duty by early June, *Aquitania* and *Mauretania* could each carry six or seven battalions. During the next three months the two ships transported thousands of troops to the Dardanelles. Between May and August 1915, *Aquitania* carried thirty thousand soldiers to various sites in the Aegean Sea. By mid-August a staggering number of casualties had to be removed from the beaches at Gallipoli and transported to hospitals on Lemnos, Malta, and Egypt. As a result, *Aquitania* underwent another conversion to a hospital ship, which was completed in August. She then sailed for the Dardanelles in company with two other converted hospital ships, *Mauretania* and *Britannic.* Even though the Allies had abandoned Gallipoli by January 1916, casualties from the ill-fated operation filled hospitals around the Mediterranean for a year afterward. The *Mauretania* was laid up in March 1916, and the *Aquitania* was left to carry the troops home alone. By mid-1917 she had transported more than twenty-five thousand wounded soldiers back to the United Kingdom.

Just when it appeared that the two ships might have remained tied up at Liverpool for the remainder of the war, U.S. Army Gen. Frank T. Hines, chief of embarkation, convinced the British that he needed the two ships and the *Olympic* to carry U.S. expeditionary forces to France. The three liners arrived

The British troopship *Olympic* transported American Expeditionary forces to France during World War I. *Steamship Historical Society of America*

in New York in December 1917 and began transporting U.S. troops across the Atlantic for the next ten months. On each crossing *Aquitania* carried six thousand soldiers. Following the end of the war the ship made three repatriating trips from Liverpool to New York. *Aquitania* was returned to Cunard and resumed her commercial duty by June 1919. But her war journey was not over; *Aquitania* was once again requisitioned in 1939 by the British government to serve as a troopship during World War II.[13]

Perhaps one of the most gallant trooper ventures of the war occurred on board *River Clyde,* a converted collier, which carried ANZAC soldiers to a disastrous end on the beaches of Gallipoli in the Mediterranean.[14] The story of the ship and her misadventure is related in chapter 3.

The United States declared war on Germany on 6 April 1917. From that date through the end of the war more than two million doughboys were transported

U.S. soldiers embarked for France in 1917. *U.S. National Archives*

across the Atlantic to France, mostly on British and French vessels since the United States had only a limited number of large transport ships in its fleet inventory at the time. However, the United States provided almost all of the convoy escort ships.

Beginning in June 1917, fifty thousand U.S. troops were carried across the Atlantic to England and France each month. This number rose to two hundred thousand within a year. The U.S. Shipping Board seized all interned enemy ships when the United States entered the war, including the 54,282-ton German passenger liner *Vaterland.* After she was converted to a troopship and renamed USS *Leviathan,* she operated between Hoboken, Brest, and Liverpool from September 1917 to the signing of the armistice. Two weeks after the end of the war, a young sailor with a coxswain rating reported aboard the ship; future movie legend Humphrey Bogart made several trips across the Atlantic on *Leviathan* bringing American soldiers home.

The troopship USS *Leviathan* (SP-1326). As the former German passenger liner *Vaterland* she appears in camouflage during World War I. *Naval Historical Center*

Other German liners interned by the United States and converted into troop carriers included the 14,908-ton liner *Kron Prinz Wilhelm,* a former auxiliary cruiser. The ship was commandeered after it took refuge in the Chesapeake Bay while avoiding two British cruisers that were patrolling off Cape Henry. On 11 April 1915, the ship was denied its request to return to Germany and was interned for two years at the Naval Shipyard in Philadelphia. With the entry of the United States into World War I, it was seized along with the liners *Prinz Eitel Friedrich, Kaiser Wilhelm II, Kron Prinzessen Cecilie* and numerous other ships interned in various east coast ports. *Kron Prinz Wilhelm* was renamed USS *Von Steuben* and *Prinz Eitel Friedrich* became USS *DeKalb. Von Steuben* made nine transatlantic trooping voyages. She made her first crossing in October 1917 when she sailed from New York to Brest, France, with 1,223 doughboys aboard. Three other former German ships converted into troopships accompanied her, USS *Agamemnon* (ex–*Kaiser Wilhelm II*), USS *Mount Vernon* (ex–*Kron Prinzessen Cecilie*), and USS *America* (ex–HAPAG *Amerika*). During her two months of U.S. service *Von Steuben* transported 36,347 American soldiers across the Atlantic (22,000 of whom she brought home following the end of the war). *Von Steuben* was decommissioned on 13 October 1919 and struck from the Navy List. She was eventually sold to the Boston Metal Company for scrapping.

The troopship USS *Von Steuben* (former German *Kron Prinz Wilhelm*) made nine transatlantic troop-carrying voyages during World War I. *Steamship Historical Society of America*

Troops arriving home to Hoboken, New Jersey, from France, ca. 1919, aboard USS *Agamemnon. U.S. National Archives*

Members of the famous 369th Colored Infantry, formerly the 15th New York regulars, arrive in New York City, circa 1919. *U.S. National Archives*

DeKalb boasted a similar record: she was assigned to the Cruiser and Transport Force, Atlantic, and on 14 June 1917 made her first Atlantic crossing with U.S. expeditionary soldiers on board destined for France. During the next eighteen months, *DeKalb* made eleven such voyages, carrying 11,334 troops. With the end of the war she continued transport duty returning 20,332 troops from France in eight voyages. She was decommissioned in September 1919 and returned to the U.S. Shipping Board for disposal.[15]

When the war ended, Allied ships that were requisitioned for troopship use were returned to their respective shipping agencies and other former owners. However, Britain still required a fleet of troopers to move soldiers and their families to various outposts throughout its empire. Two companies, B.I. and Bibby, monopolized this service. Troopers such as *Lancashire, Dorsetshire, Somersetshire, Nevasa, Neura, Dunera,* and *Dilwara* (the first B.I. ship ever designed as a troop transport) plied the oceans on a regular basis making calls in India, Burma, East

Africa, Malaya, and Canada. Former German vessels appropriated by the United States for troopship conversion were retained in the Reserve Fleet. The ships were laid up in various bays and rivers along the east coast and redesignated U.S. Army transports. However, by the outbreak of World War II most had deteriorated and been scrapped. Other transports used to carry doughboys across the Atlantic were subsequently sold to various shipping companies at bargain prices for use as commercial carriers and passenger ships. However, the Army Transport Services and the Navy retained a number of ships for carrying military personnel and their dependents, rotating to bases in the Philippines, Cuba, Haiti, Hawaii, and the Panama Canal.[16]

THE 1920S AND 1930S

During the 1920s and 1930s, British, German, French, and Italian shipyards built or refurbished a number of lavish passenger liners leading to a fierce competition. British liners such as the *Aquitania, Mauretania, Berengaria, Titanic,* and *Queen Mary;* the Dutch cruise liner *Nieuw Amsterdam;* German steamships *Bremen, Europa,* and *Columbus;* the French liners *Ile de France, Normandie,* and *France,* which was known as the "Chateau of the Atlantic"; the Italian line's premier luxury liner *Rex,* known as the "Riviera Afloat," and its forty-eight-thousand-ton *Conte di Savoia* sailed from Liverpool, Southampton, Hamburg, Rotterdam, Le Havre, and Genoa to New York on a regular basis. A cover of *Life* magazine in the 1920s displayed several German liners docked in New York almost side by side scheduled to take passengers to Europe and the Caribbean. Tours of the Caribbean by German liners were scheduled by the New York office of the Cook Travel Agency. With the advent of World War II, most of these ships were requisitioned by their respective governments for use as troopships.[17]

Following her last crossing as a troop carrier, *Leviathan* was converted to a passenger liner. Her final trip was memorable in that she carried seven thousand doughboys of the famed Rainbow Division and the hero of the hour, Gen. John J. Pershing, commander of the U.S. Expeditionary Force in Europe. It took three years to complete the designs to convert the ship and obtain approval from the United States Shipping Board before *Leviathan* steamed to Newport News, Virginia, to be rebuilt as the flagship of the United States Lines.

During *Leviathan*'s maiden voyage on 4 July 1923, she carried little more

The Danish motorship *Europa* performed war duties for the Allies during World War II. She was sunk during a German air raid while berthed in Liverpool, England. *Steamship Historical Society of America*

Italian liner *Conte di Savoia. Steamship Historical Society of America*

than half a passenger load. Her first three voyages were profitable, but the next five were losses. A steady flow of emigrant passengers kept the liner from experiencing deeper financial troubles. More important, this factor allowed wealthy patrons the same luxuries enjoyed aboard competitive foreign liners. Even so, when this migration lessened the following year, the ship could hardly make ends meet. Prohibition was also a problem; while *Leviathan* remained a "dry" ship, its competitors were virtual floating bars, a luxury much more appealing to ocean traveling Americans. To make matters worse, a series of accidents at sea dogged the ship. On what turned out to be her last crossing, she was severely damaged during a midocean storm and barely made it to England. Returning to New York in a state of temporary repair, the United States Line owners decided that the ship was not worth salvaging. In January 1938 *Leviathan* sailed to Rosyth, Scotland, where she was cut up for scrap.[18]

In 1936 the United States Congress passed the Shipping Act, which established the Maritime Commission and initiated a program of subsidies for ship design and construction. To qualify for a government subsidy, two thirds of the crew were required to be U.S. citizens and had to undergo comprehensive background checks.[19] Two years later the commission established a replacement program which retired obsolete vessels at the rate of fifty ships a year. This number was increased the following year, and under the forced draft of wartime new construction was vastly increased. Yard capacity and availability of shipyard workers were the only limiting factors after the Japanese attack on Pearl Harbor. By September 1942 three hundred tankers and two thousand standard design Liberty and Victory ships had been contracted.[20]

WORLD WAR II

When the Second World War broke out, the British Army soon found that it would become much more dependent on the sea. Unlike World War I where there were only channel crossings to contend with, now with France occupied from 1940 to mid-1944 and the Mediterranean closed to convoys, troops had to be transported around the Cape of Good Hope to reach British forces fighting in Egypt, Crete, and Greece. Once again the British Merchant Navy was called upon to assume troopship duty. Foremost among the ships requisitioned

The German cruise liner *Columbus* is scuttled east of New Jersey by its crew to avoid capture by British naval forces. *Otto Giese Collection*

for carrier use were the two "Queens" of the Cunard Line, *Queen Mary* and *Queen Elizabeth*. Both ships were built for speed and that factor prevented successful attacks by German U-boats throughout the war.[21]

When the United States entered the war, *Normandie* was seized by the U.S. War Shipping Administration, renamed USS *Lafayette,* and transferred to the U.S. Navy. While being converted into a troopship in February 1942, she caught fire. It took four hours to bring the fire under control , and much of the water pumped aboard froze in her upper superstructure causing *Lafayette* to begin listing to port. At 2:45 A.M. as the tide rose in the Hudson River, she rolled over on her side and rested half submerged at her berth between *Mauritania* and *Queen Elizabeth*. *Lafayette* was salvaged the following year, but the expenses to right the ship and the costs estimated to put her into active service were deemed prohibitive. She was sold for scrap in October 1946.[22]

The German liner *Bremen,* flagship of the German Merchant Marine, was in New York just before war was declared. She quickly put to sea and managed to elude British pursuers as she crossed the Atlantic and arrived safely in Bremerhaven. When war was declared the German liner *Columbus* was caught in Veracruz, Mexico, but the ship was safe because she was in a U.S.–imposed Western Hemisphere neutrality zone. Capt. Willibald Dähne, skipper of *Columbus,* tried to sell the ship to German business interests in Mexico but to no avail. She eventually received orders to return to Germany. The ship sailed on 13 December 1939 and headed north through the Florida Straits trailed by U.S. destroyers who were relaying her progress to a British warship patrolling waters outside the neutrality zone. When abreast of New Jersey *Columbus* headed east and as she crossed the boundary of the neutrality zone was met by the British destroyer *Hyperion,* which fired a shot across her bow. Rather than risk British capture and subsequent conversion into a troopship, the crew scuttled the ship. Six hundred members of the crew were rescued by U.S. Navy ships and taken to Ellis Island as displaced seamen.[23]

Europa and *Bremen* were partially converted into troopships to support Operation Sea Lion, a planned German invasion of Britain. Sea Lion was later canceled and the ships were sent to Bremerhaven and refurbished for use as accommodation vessels. *Bremen* caught fire while docked and sank in March 1941, and *Europa* was captured intact by the Allies in May 1945. Neither saw active service as troopships. At the end of the war *Europa* sailed to the United States and was converted into a troop transport (AP 177) later used to repatriate U.S. servicemen from Europe. Following this duty she was given to France as reparation and joined the only French prewar liner survivor, *Ile de France,* as a member of the French Line. Renamed the *Liberté,* she and the Transat French Liner fleet soon regained their splendid prewar reputation. Thus, the German liner fleet contributed little to the German war effort. For the most part Germany had to depend on troop carrying merchant vessels when it invaded Norway in April 1940.[24] With regard to Baltic waters three large transport ships, *Wilhelm Gustloff, Goya,* and *Steuben,* and numerous other smaller passenger ships and merchantmen supported German operations in that theater. As a part of Operation Hannibal (the German codename for evacuation of German troops and civilians from advancing Russian forces that threatened to cross the Vistula peninsula and encircle the Gulf of Danzig in early 1945), more than five hundred German vessels, including 127 passenger ships and boats of all sizes, were ordered to the area to evacuate the endangered personnel. Disaster struck when *Wilhelm Gustloff, Goya,* and *Steuben* were sunk by Allied attacks. The result was the worst loss of human life in maritime history; *Wilhelm Gustloff* was torpedoed by a Russian submarine on 30 January 1945 and eight thousand to ten thousand lives were lost. On 10 February 1945 *Steuben* suffered approximately three thousand casualties, and on 16 April 1945 *Goya* went down with more than six thousand personnel on board.

The Italian liners *Rex* and *Conte de Savoia* didn't fare much better than the German liners; both ships were laid up in early 1940. A plan to convert the vessels into aircraft carriers was never executed. *Conte de Savoia* made a short troop-carrying voyage in 1943, but neither ship contributed significantly to the Italian war effort. *Conte de Savoia* was sunk later that year at Mallamocco, near Venice, by Allied forces while disguised as an island. *Rex* was sunk by RAF fighter-bombers on 8 December 1944. However, the ship was salvaged and rejoined the Italian liner fleet at the end of the war.[25]

In the Mediterranean

Throughout the early years of the war, control of the Mediterranean Sea became critical for the Allies and Axis powers. When Italy declared war on France and Britain, its combat fleet consisted of 190 warships, which included 85 black-hulled submarines.[26] Adm. Sir Andrew Browne Cunningham, commander in chief of Great Britain's Mediterranean Fleet, moved his headquarters and ships to Alexandria, Egypt, from the Island of Malta, which was only seventy miles from Italian air bases in Sicily. In addition to his own forces, which were bolstered by French warships, Cunningham could depend on the Gibraltar-based Force H, which operated in the Atlantic and the Mediterranean.[27]

Frustrated with his lack of success in North Africa, Benito Mussolini looked for another field of action and invaded Greece in October 1940 thinking that the campaign would be a walkover. It was not, and Hitler had to intervene. He started sending troops and armor through Yugoslavia, Romania, and Bulgaria to the Axis forces in Greece. When the Italians invaded, the British, fulfilling earlier assurances, sent air and ground forces to support the Greek effort. However, the Greeks needed little help as they pushed the invaders back to the Albanian border within a few weeks. This was only a temporary victory because eventually the British had to be evacuated.[28]

On 11 November the British made a devastating air attack against the Italian fleet at Taranto. Two waves of dowager aircraft, Fairey *Swordfish* planes flying from the carrier HMS *Illustrious,* attacked and severely damaged three Italian battleships, *Littorio, Cavour,* and *Duilo. Littorio* and *Duilo* were back in service within several months, but *Cavour* was still under repair when the war ended. The result was that the Italians moved their major combatants to Naples, where they would provide little hindrance to British convoys now sailing through the Mediterranean to resupply Malta and Alexandria.[29]

At the same time Hitler decided to rescue the defeated Italian force in Libya by sending a mechanized force under Maj. Gen. Erwin Rommel, known later as the "Desert Fox." Hitler also sent five hundred planes of the Luftwaffe's *Fliegerkorps X* to air bases in Calabria and Sicily to stop passage of British convoys to Malta and Alexandria, protect Axis shipping transiting to North Africa, and neutralize Malta. The first two tasks were carried out successfully but the Luftwaffe could not neutralize Malta and its tenacious defenders. In the late fall of 1940, British bombers flying from the island's battered airfields attacked the Italian fleet at Naples, damaging the battleship *Giulio Cesare* and forcing *Cesare* and the battleship *Vittorio Veneto* to sail to Spezia, a base well away from the battle area. This left only one serviceable Italian battleship, *Vittorio Veneto,* in the Italian Navy.

Pressured by the Germans, the remnants of the Italian fleet went to sea on 28 March 1941 to intercept British convoys en route to Greece. The forces met off Cape Matapan, and when the smoke cleared the Italians had lost three cruisers and two destroyers. Though able to escape, *Vittorio Veneto* was heavily damaged.

When the German forces reached Greece they quickly routed the British and Greek fighters. The British who survived the encounter made their way to the nearby island of Crete to await a German assault. That assault came on 20 May through the use of air power with a primary attack effected by thirteen thousand parachutists and glider troops and nine thousand mountain soldiers brought in by JU-52 transports. Had the Germans attempted an amphibious assault, the British might have been able to hold on to the island. The following night, a British cruiser force swept around the west end of the island and met a German invasion flotilla of *caiques* (small troop-carrying craft) en route to Crete. In the ensuing battle the Germans lost fifteen ships and more than four thousand troops.

By 27 May the situation for the thirty-two thousand British troops on the island was critical as the German airborne forces advanced. The Royal Navy was called upon to rescue the men by sea with very limited air cover. Since there were few suitable port facilities available, the men faced being evacuated from open beaches

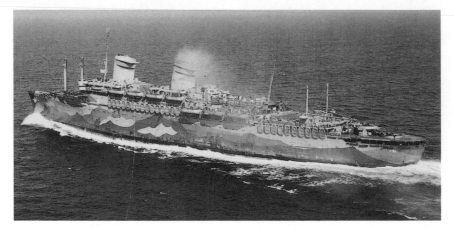

The U.S. troopship *West Point* (AP 23). *U.S. National Archives*

that would expose them to the Luftwaffe. The thought of another Dunkirk ran through the minds of Admiral Cunningham and his staff. It was planned to bring them out between midnight and 3 A.M. Between 28 May and 1 June, 18,600 of the 32,000 troopers were rescued. The cost was heavy; under constant attack by enemy bombers, one aircraft carrier and two cruisers were damaged; three cruisers and six destroyers were sunk; and six cruisers and seven destroyers were damaged. But the effort of the fleet was deemed magnificent. Admiral Cunningham stated in his dispatch that "his men had started the evacuation already overtired and . . . had to carry it through under savage air attack . . . it is perhaps even now not realized how nearly the breaking point was reached. But that these men struggled through is the measure of their achievement."[30]

The Near East

In the fall of 1941 Allied forces faced a dire situation in the Mediterranean. Russia was hard-pressed, Greece and Crete had been occupied by the Germans and Rommel was enjoying success in his desert campaign. Reinforcements were needed by the British if they were to maintain control of the three gates into the Mediterranean: the Straits of Gibraltar, the Dardanelles, and the Suez Canal. The British could not spare ships to transport troops to these vital areas and asked the United States to provide a task group to carry the necessary men and materials to these strategic points. The U.S. Navy agreed to provide its largest trans-

U.S. Marines aboard the troopship *Wakefield* at Norfolk, Virginia, 19 May 1942. *U.S. National Archives*

ports and best escort vessels to carry twenty thousand officers and men from Halifax to the Near East. The task group consisted of a carrier, *Ranger;* two cruisers and six transports: USS *Mount Vernon* (AP-22), USS *Leonard Wood* (AP-25), USS *Joseph T. Dickman* (AP-26), USS *Orizaba* (AP-24), USS *Wakefield* (AP-21), and USS *West Point* (AP-23), the only troopship in the U.S. inventory that grossed more than 26,000 tons. *Mount Vernon, West Point,* and *Wakefield* (formerly the United States Lines' ships *Washington, America, and Manhattan*) had recently been converted into troopships.

The convoy sailed from Halifax on 10 November 1941 bound for Trinidad, where the ships refueled. Since the destroyer escorts did not have the capacity to make the long journey ahead, the tanker USS *Cimarron* (AO-22) was added to the convoy. At latitude 17 degrees south and longitude 20 degrees west, *Ranger* and two destroyers, *Rhind* and *Trippe,* left the convoy and returned to Trinidad. By the time the convoy had reached Africa, the United States and the British Empire were at war with Japan. When the convoy arrived at Capetown on 9 December, the situation had once again changed; Germany and Italy had declared war on the United States. At this point the American escorts were urgently needed elsewhere and they departed the convoy. *Mount Vernon* subsequently landed her troops at Singapore and was then ordered to Suez to transport Australian troops from Egypt to Colombo and Fremantle. In Australia she picked up some refugees from Corregidor, Battle of Java survivors and personnel that were withdrawn from the Netherlands, East Indies, and sailed for San Francisco, where she arrived in March 1942. The main convoy reached Bombay on 27 December, and *Wakefield* and *West Point* were ordered to transport troops to Singapore. While at Singapore *Wakefield* was damaged by a direct hit from an attacking Japanese aircraft. She was then temporarily repaired at Bombay and ordered to San Francisco via New Zealand. *West Point,* having sailed with *Wakefield* to Bombay, embarked 5,333 Australian troops, which she transported to Adelaide, Australia. During the war, *West Point* made fifteen Pacific and forty-one Atlantic crossings. She carried 505,000 passengers (American, British, and ANZAC troops, WACs, WAVES, wounded soldiers, diplomats, entertainers, refugees, and prisoners of war) across 436,144 nautical miles, earning the nickname "Grey Ghost" from her habit of operating unescorted.[31]

Besides *Westpoint* and *Wakefield* there was a dearth of medium-sized U.S. passenger liners suitable for conversion to troop transports, certainly nothing tonnage-wise to match the seventeen-knot Japanese tankers and motor ships. Prior to World War II, troopships were under the jurisdiction of the quartermaster general and operated by the Transportation Corps of the U.S. Army. In addition to these, other army troopships used during the war came by way of bareboat charter (the charter of a boat from the owner, without crew, fuel, stores, etc.) or on a loan basis (vessels that were owned by the Maritime Commission and released to the War or Navy Departments for service without charter hire, to be returned on a mutually agreeable date). All of these vessels were manned by civilian crews. Of the sixty-five large army-operated troopships, eight served in both world wars. Many of the army troopships were retained in the Transportation Corps after the war but in time most were scrapped. Navy troopships during much of the war transported Army personnel. Army troops along with thousands of Marines, Seabees, and support personnel were also carried aboard Navy transports (APs) and attack transports (APAs).[32]

Malta and Africa

Returning to the Mediterranean war in 1941, the British formed a new attack group that became known as the Malta Striking Forces. Using a combination of newly arrived aircraft, and cruisers, destroyers, and submarines, the group concentrated on attacking nearly every convoy that sailed for Rommel's supply ports. In early April 1941 an Axis convoy was sighted off the Tunisian coast by aircraft from Malta. Four destroyers of the Malta Striking Forces engaged the convoy's five transports and three destroyer escorts and, in two hours of battle, four of the enemy ships were sunk and the others crippled. Two sank the following day, and later the Italians were able to salvage a destroyer. One merchant ship survived the attack. Seventeen hundred troops and thirty-four thousand tons of military materiel desperately needed by Rommel were lost.[33]

German U-boats and British submarines were operating in the Mediterranean early in the war with both forces enjoying multiple successes. U-boats successfully attacked and sank British merchant ships attempting to relieve Malta and also torpedoed major combatants such as HMS *Eagle,* HMS *Ark Royal,* and HMS *Barham.* The most successful of the British subs was HMS *Upholder,* a small U-class boat well suited to the shallow waters of the Mediterranean. She was part of the Royal Navy's 10th Flotilla based at Malta in 1941–42. British submarines that became part of the Malta Striking Forces represented a significant

The Italian transport *Neptunia. Steamship Historical Society of America*

threat to Rommel's supply lines to North Africa. *Upholder,* skippered by Lt. Comdr. Malcolm Wanklyn, sank more than 128,353 tons of Axis shipping between 6 September 1941 and 14 April 1942. She was subsequently sunk by an Italian motor torpedo boat (MTB) while trying to attack a convoy off Tripoli. Wanklyn was known in the Allied underwater community as the "ultimate submariner." Among the many Axis vessels he sank were three fully loaded Axis troopships: the Italian liner *Conte Rosso* in May 1941 (for which he was awarded the Victoria Cross) and the Italian transports, *Oceania* and *Neptunia,* in September 1942, both sailing in the same convoy.[34]

By April 1941 General Rommel rapidly pushed the British eastward in Africa and soon crossed into Egypt. British Gen. Sir Archibald Wavell had sent his most experienced troops to Greece, and he was left with raw recruits from home to meet the German Afrika Corps and Luftwaffe. A British convoy arrived in Alexandria from Gibraltar with much needed war supplies, troops, and more than two hundred tanks. Although this strengthening of British forces slowed the German advance, Rommel began to run into serious supply problems. Aside from the successes of the previously mentioned Malta Striking Forces, Rommel faced additional shortages when Hitler began to divert supplies destined for North Africa to the Russian campaign. Of the sixty thousand tons of supplies

Rommel requested for June, only three thousand made it into port. General Montgomery relieved Wavell that same month and Montgomery set about to reorganize and retrain his forces while building up supplies. Maltese-based long-range torpedo planes continued to rain havoc on Axis convoys. With limited supplies and the knowledge that the British were to receive heavy reinforcements by September 1942, Rommel took the risk of attempting a breakthrough at El Alamein in August and failed to dislodge the British "Desert Rats" while the RAF made devastating attacks on German tanks and supplies. With the defeat at El Alamein, loss of tanks and military equipment, and the receipt of less than promised fuel supplies from the Italians, Rommel called off his offensive. By now the United States had entered the war, and Rommel wrote, "From the moment that the overwhelming industrial capacity of the United States could make itself felt in any theatre of the war, there was no longer a chance of ultimate victory there. Even if we had overrun the whole African continent as long as a small bridgehead remained offering good operational possibilities, and provided the Americans were able to bring in their material—we were bound to lose it in the end. Tactical skill could only postpone the collapse, it could not avert the ultimate fate of this theatre of war."[35]

Between June 1940 and February 1943, some seventeen hundred Axis convoys transported more than 280,000 Italian and German troops to Libya and Tunisia. Of that number, twenty thousand soldiers did not reach their destinations; however, convoy ships and escorts saved a great number of these men after their ships had been attacked and sunk by British air and sea forces.[36]

The United States Enters the War

Following the outbreak of war in Europe and the fall of France, many in Washington doubted that Britain could withstand the German onslaught. There was deep concern that the British fleet might be defeated and that Royal Navy ships could be used against the United States. With this in mind Congress passed legislation which provided for a two-ocean navy and the first peacetime draft in the nation's history. When the war started, Britain was desperately short of escort vessels. This led to a deal between the United States and Britain whereby fifty World War I Navy destroyers would be turned over to the Royal Navy for ninety-nine-year leases for U.S. bases at six sites from the Bahamas to British Guiana. Britain offered a similar agreement for bases in Bermuda and

Newfoundland; in return, the United States gave the British ten antisubmarine-equipped Coast Guard cutters.

Despite strong sentiment within the United States that the nation remain neutral, the country gradually began to drift into an undeclared war with Germany. In December 1940 Roosevelt extended a lend-lease program to the British whereby a "cash and carry" policy established early in the war that allowed British and French ships to visit the United States and pick up vitally needed war materials was amended by eliminating the "cash" requirement. Approved by Congress, this allowed the United States to provide munitions to Britain and later the Soviet Union on a loan basis, thus averting the problem of war debts.

Early the following year the United States agreed to provide escort support for convoys crossing the Atlantic. British and U.S. military strategists at the same time agreed that if war broke out, the British–U.S. alliance would adopt a policy of defeating Germany first because Germany with its industrial might, proximity to Britain, and military successes posed the greater threat. Roosevelt and Churchill met in Newfoundland and forged the Atlantic Charter, which defined the use of U.S. escort vessels, the U.S. policy of all aid short of war, and postwar goals.

In September 1941 the U.S. destroyer USS *Greer* was fired upon by a U-boat. A month later the destroyer *Kearney* was torpedoed by *U568,* and two weeks later the U.S. destroyer *Reuben Jones* was attacked and sunk by *U552.* On 7 December 1941 Japanese carrier aircraft attacked Pearl Harbor and the United States was suddenly at war.[37]

When Roosevelt proposed his Lend-Lease program, he also ordered the Maritime Commission to organize a new shipbuilding program that would mass-produce relatively uncomplicated vessels to carry war materials and troopers. The commission selected a design patterned after the British Sutherland tramp steamers—sixty of which were then under construction for the British. The War Shipping Administration, which had enveloped the Maritime Commission and been given command of all seaborne transportation, launched the first Liberty ship, *Patrick Henry,* on 27 September 1941. (Roosevelt called it a Liberty ship in his Fleet Day address as the ship slid down the ways at the Bethlehem-Fairchild Shipyard in Baltimore.) By any standard the ship had its flaws. It was slow, the quarters were cramped, and the ventilation was poor, but it could carry ten thousand tons of freight stowed in five holds and lashed top-

The first Liberty ship, *Patrick Henry. The Mariners' Museum*

side on long flushed decks. The ship was simple to build, operate, and repair. Its boom and mast fittings could be worked by stevedores throughout the world. In addition to carrying cargo, holds could be converted to carry troops, though soldiers who were transported in these vessels found such sea journeys difficult to endure.[38] One such soldier, 6'7" Pvt. James K. Aurness, U.S. Army, remembers his voyage to North Africa quite well.

They loaded us right onto the ship, with duffel bags slung over our shoulders. We were directed to the hold, just forward of the bridge, then down two stairways to the bottom of the hold, which had been converted for transporting troops. There were vertical rows of bunk-like hammocks, consisting of two poles with a piece of canvas stretched between them. They were about two feet apart and 500 men were jammed into this space. Because of my size I couldn't get comfortable, so I spent most of my time on deck.

As we left the dock and moved up the channel, other ships joined us. When we were out at sea and darkness fell, I went below and ate chow, listening to others talk about where we were going and when we would see combat. Soon we bunked out for the night, though unfamiliar ship noises and the sway of the sea interrupted our slumber.

Pvt. James K. Aurness, U.S. Army, 2nd Platoon, E Company, 2nd Battalion, 7th Regiment ("Cotton Balers"), 3rd Infantry Division, in 1945. He changed his last name to Arness after he entered the entertainment business. *James Arness Collection*

Next morning, we found ourselves in the middle of a huge convoy steaming along at about 10 knots. That was the top speed designated for the convoy, but destroyers ripped up and down its edges at about 30 knots, searching for German U-boats. They told us the next morning we'd have to go on limited rations, because our stores had been left on the dock inadvertently. We grumbled over this news, of course, but it wasn't long before food was the least of our concerns. Far out to sea, the ship ran into a violent storm. Practically everyone became seasick, and within a day or so the hold was a stinking mess. Everything was plugged up, and the deck below was covered with the retching of hundreds of men.

Aurness and the rest of the troops made it safely to their destination. He was assigned to the 3d Infantry Division, was later severely wounded at Anzio, and subsequently awarded the Bronze Star and Purple Heart. After the war he chose

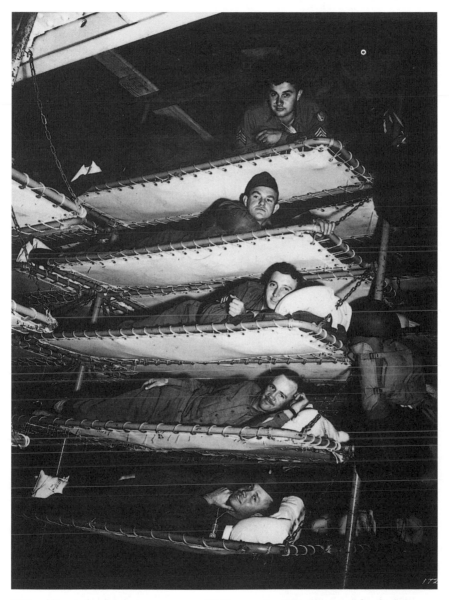

U.S. soldiers in bunks on army transport SS *Pennant*, San Francisco port of embarkation,
1 November 1942. *U.S. National Archives*

an acting career, changed his last name to Arness, and readers will remember him as Sheriff Matt Dillon in the long-running television series, *Gunsmoke*.[39]

During World War II some two hundred standard Liberty ships were partially converted to carry troops. Thirty-four Liberty ships were fully converted as troopships, and these were operated by steamship companies and crewed by merchant seamen.

The first convoy to include Liberties with troops on board was UGS11, which departed Hampton Roads on 26 June 1943. Included in the convoy were eight Liberty ships carrying 1,542 soldiers. A month later a second convoy transporting 3,400 men departed the Chesapeake. Two more convoys departed in August. By the end of the year, 77,000 soldiers had sailed on Liberties from the Chesapeake. Between June 1943 and May 1944, 454,360 military personnel embarked on ships at Hampton Roads. Of this number some two hundred thousand troopers sailed on board 562 Liberty ships. Millions of other soldiers sailed from other ports during that period; many were transported on Liberty ships. Of the hundreds of thousands of troops that crossed the Atlantic for Europe and Africa, approximately thirty-six hundred were lost in incidents at sea. Most of these casualties were lost aboard three ships, the British liner *Rohna*, the Belgian ship *Leopoldville*, and the Liberty ship *Paul Hamilton*.[40]

Allied Losses and Success

The British India passenger liner *Rohna* was sunk in the Mediterranean Sea on 26 November 1943. The ship had the distinction of being the first transport to be sunk by a radio-guided missile during World War II. While sailing in convoy KMF26, *Rohna* was struck by a glider bomb launched from an attacking German aircraft. Ablaze, the ship sank within thirty minutes after being hit. The eight-thousand-ton ship carried 2,200 American troops and 1,015 were lost. Rescue work was seriously hampered by darkness and a heavy sea swell. This incident remained one of the great Allied troop transport tragedies of the war.[41]

In December 1944 U.S. troops of the 66th Infantry Division (Black Panthers) began loading aboard the Belgian liner SS *Leopoldville* at Pier No. 38 in Southampton for a nine-hour voyage to Cherbourg, France. The troops largely comprised the 262nd and 264th Infantry Regiments, and although they believed they were on their way to reinforce units at the Battle of the Bulge, they

U.S. troops returning to the United States following World War II on *Queen Mary.*
Steamship Historical Society of America

were in fact on their way to the Lorient-Saint Nazaire sector of Brittany to relieve the 94th Infantry Division so that the veteran division could be sent to the Bulge.

As *Leopoldville* was loaded with troops, German *U486* lay submerged five and a half miles off Cherbourg waiting for a target. Troops on board the overcrowded *Leopoldville* numbered 2,235. There were fourteen lifeboats, mostly assigned to the ship's crew, and a gross shortage of preservers that were to be used by the troops if the ship ran into trouble. No instruction was given to the men on how to lower the ship's rafts.

U486 fired a torpedo that struck the ship on the starboard side aft. It exploded instantly killing between three hundred and five hundred men who could not escape the flooding compartments once the stairwells were destroyed in the explosion. The ship finally went down at 8:05 P.M., and the soldiers struggled in the icy forty-eight-degree water. Many of them died entering the water, never advised to unfasten their helmets or tie their life jackets tightly, resulting in broken necks. Approximately eight hundred U.S. soldiers lost their lives in the tragedy.[42]

The Liberty ship *Paul Hamilton* was en route to Anzio in the fifty-ship convoy USG38 when the convoy came under attack by German aircraft east of Oran in the Mediterranean Sea on 20 April 1944. Struck by an aerial torpedo, the ship, which was carrying 504 troops, 47 crewmen, and 29 armed guards, was loaded with ammunition and explosives. The ship disintegrated, sending bodies and flames high into the evening sky. When the smoke had cleared, only pieces of timber could be seen floating in the sea. All 580 men perished.[43]

The "Queens" (*Queen Mary* and *Queen Elizabeth*) along with the British liner *Aquitania* did most of the "heavy lifting" during the war. During her six and a half years of troopship service, *Queen Mary* traveled more than six hundred thousand miles transporting some eight hundred thousand military and civilian personnel. She played a major role in every Allied campaign of World War II. *Queen Elizabeth,* during her five years of service, carried nearly 750,000 people— troops, wounded, diplomats, and prisoners—steaming nearly a half-million miles. *Aquitania,* which served as a troopship during World War I, was called upon once again to provide trooper services when the Second World War broke out. Her conversion back into a troopship was completed in November 1939, and she operated in both Atlantic and Pacific waters. She transported Canadian troops from Halifax to Southampton, Australian and New Zealand troops to England via Cape Town and the Middle East, and eventually for the next few years circled the globe carrying Allied troops to various destinations. Axis forces never attacked the ship during the war; only heat stroke and dehydration took the lives of several men during the ship's transits of the South Pacific and Indian Oceans. At the close of the war *Aquitania* had traveled more than 526,000 miles and transported close to 400,000 passengers.[44] Between 1942 and 1945 these three huge liners carried almost two million men to war without losing a single passenger to enemy fire.

During the early years of the Battle of the Atlantic, German U-boats attacked and sank a vast number of merchantmen carrying critical war supplies to Europe. When the war ended, the Allies had lost three thousand ships—amounting to approximately fourteen million tons—to Nazi U-boats. Nine hundred U-boats were destroyed and seven thousand German submariners remained of an original thirty-nine thousand. The Allied success can be attributed to the overwhelming industrial might of the United States and its accelerated shipbuilding programs, the use of the convoy system, aggressive antisubmarine warfare tactics, new technologies, the employment of carrier-supported "hunter-killer" groups, the breaking of the German Ultra communications system by the Allied code-breakers, and finally the bravery and courage of Allied seamen who battled a determined undersea enemy and the often fierce waters and weather of the Atlantic.[45]

The Allied invasion of North Africa in November 1942, the victorious resistance of the Russians at Stalingrad, and the defeat of the Afrika Corps at El Alamein marked the turning point in the war for the Germans. The long retreat back to the fatherland began, and soon the Allied forces were forging forward up through Italy, the "soft underbelly" of the Mediterranean. By now Allied air power dominated Europe and with the invasion of Normandy on 6 June 1944 the beginning of the war's end was in sight. Germany capitulated on 7 May 1945.

The Pacific Theater

Hours before the attack on Pearl Harbor, a Japanese expeditionary force that had been sighted off Formosa and Indochina began landing troops on the Malay Peninsula. The troops were transported on board an assortment of vessels, including steam passenger ships, transports, and merchant vessels. At the same time the Japanese also captured Guam and Hong Kong. In January they invaded Thailand, the Philippines, and Borneo. Wake Island fell, British forces surrendered Singapore on 15 February 1941, and the Stars and Stripes were hauled down in the Philippines on 6 May 1942. Within two months the Japanese had conquered the oil-rich islands of the Dutch East Indies, their primary goal in Southeast Asia. Despite the efforts of the combined Allied naval forces that tried to stop Japanese advances, they found themselves outnumbered and out-gunned in early encounters such as the Battle of the Java Sea (27 February 1941) where a combined allied force of American, British, Dutch, and Australian (ABDA) warships was destroyed.[46]

Although the Pearl Harbor attack dealt a serious blow to the Pacific Fleet, a few bright spots emerged. None of the shore facilities was seriously damaged,

U.S. Marines aboard SS *Republic* (AP-33) in Pacific Convoy, 1 April 1942.
U.S. National Archives

the Japanese had failed to destroy the fleet's fuel storage areas, and the navy's fast carriers and their support ships escaped harm since they were at sea at the time of the attack. The *Lexington* fast-carrier striking group was southeast of Midway Island with three heavy cruisers and five destroyers; the cruiser *Indianapolis* was at Johnston Island with five converted destroyer-minesweepers; the carrier *Enterprise* was returning to Pearl after delivering Marine fighter aircraft to Wake Island; and the heavy cruiser *Minneapolis* with three light cruisers and a dozen destroyers was maneuvering south of Oahu. Also, the heavy cruiser *Pensacola* was passing through the Phoenix Islands escorting navy transports *Chaumont* and *Republic,* two army transports, and three freighters. The transports carried thousands of soldiers, hundreds of aviators, replacement aircraft, and vital war materials bound for the Philippines. The force was joined by the heavy cruiser

Louisville, which was escorting army transports *Hugh L. Scott* and *President Coolidge* returning from Manila.[47] On the west coast were the carrier *Saratoga,* a light cruiser, three World War I destroyers, and four submarines. The submarine *Gar* was off the coast of Mexico, the cruiser *Trenton* was at Panama, and the cruiser *Richmond* was operating off Peru. U.S. submarines which were to play a vital role in the Pacific campaign were deployed as follows: Wake Island—*Tambor* and *Triton;* Midway—*Trout;* off Oahu—*Thresher, Plunger, Pollack,* and *Pompano.* Within hours after the attack Adm. Ernest J. King, Commander in Chief Atlantic Fleet, ordered the carrier *Yorktown,* battleships *New Mexico, Mississippi,* and *Idaho,* three squadron of patrol bombers, and a destroyer squadron transferred to the Pacific fleet.[48]

With rapid victories in their drive through the Southwest Pacific, the Japanese suddenly faced an enormous problem: what to do with the vast number of captured Allied prisoners of war. After suffering from the brutality and wanton killing by Japanese military guards, the prisoners were moved to various bases within their newly gained empire to act as laborers constructing administration buildings, roads, runways, and housing facilities for Japanese occupation forces. They were transported on Japanese passenger ships, transports, and freighters living under the most hellish conditions. In fact, these ships became known as "hellships." During the war, of the 126,064 prisoners moved by sea, more than 20,000 were killed by friendly fire from U.S. submarines and attacking aircraft. The Americans had no knowledge that Allied POWs were on board these ships.

In April 1943 *Suez Maru* was en route from Ambon to Haruku carrying 546 POWs, mostly British, when it was torpedoed by USS *Bonefish* (SS 223). Prior to the sailing, Lieutenant Colonel Anami, in charge of loading the POWs, gave orders that should the ship be torpedoed, all POWs who survived the attack were to be shot. The order was subsequently carried out by the crewmen of the ship prior to its sinking.[49]

Probably the worst case of such incidents was the sinking of the forty-five-hundred-ton *Junyo Maru.* On 16 September 1944 she sailed with two escorts from Batavia (now Jakarta) to Padang, Sumatra, carrying twenty-two hundred POWs (British, U.S., Dutch, Australian, and Indonesian) and approximately forty-two hundred Javanese slave laborers. The captives were to provide labor for the Sumatran railway that was being built to run coal from the west to the east coast of the island and then to Singapore. Halfway to its destination the ship was torpedoed by HMS *Tradewind,* which fired four torpedoes at the plodding merchant ship and then dived to the safety of the depths below. An hour later the submarine rose to periscope depth, and Lt. Comdr. S. L. C. Maydon, skipper of the boat, scanned the waters where the ship had been. The sea was clear except for a Japanese escort that was some three miles away. When night fell Maydon surfaced the boat and headed east, not realizing that the sea behind him was full of dying men. Following the attack Japanese escorts rushed to the stricken ship and started rescuing survivors. However, most of those saved were Japanese crewmen and sentries. Each waved a small Japanese flag that they carried to identify themselves. The following day a Japanese corvette returned and rescued those still alive. Of the seventeen hundred western POWs, fifteen hundred were lost. Only a few of the five hundred Indonesians survived. All of the Javanese laborers were lost.[50]

Unlike the troopship tragedies that occurred in Atlantic and Mediterranean waters, there were no major troopship disasters in the Pacific during the war. Of those sunk, losses were kept to a minimum due to their gallant crews and the rescue efforts of escort ships. In November 1943 the troopship *Cape San Juan* was torpedoed by the Japanese submarine I21 some 1,500 miles from Brisbane, Australia. Aboard the ship were sixty crewmen, forty-two armed guards and 1,348 Army troops. Allied combatants came on the scene quickly and saved all but 130 soldiers. Eighteen days later, I21 was sunk off the Marshall Islands by VC-35 aircraft flying from the carrier *Chemanago* (CVE-28). On 3 January 1945 the Liberty ship *Kyle Johnson* sailed from Hollandia, New Guinea, for Lingayen Gulf in the Philippines with a convoy of one hundred ships. As the convoy passed Subic Bay off the western shore of the Philippine province of Luzon, it was attacked by eight Japanese aircraft. Though taken under intense fire by ships of the convoy, one plane managed to penetrate the antiaircraft barrage and crash into the starboard side of the *Johnson* causing an explosion in the No. 3 hold and setting the ship on fire. The stricken vessel dropped out of the convoy as the crew fought to save the damaged ship. The fire was eventually brought under control, and the ship made it to Lingayen Gulf. However, of 506 troopers on board, 129 were lost in the initial attack on the ship. APs and APAs were the most common transports used in the Pacific to carry assault troops and war materials for invasion of Japanese-held islands. Though a number were damaged and sunk by Japanese submarines and aircraft, only small numbers of troops were lost. The Japanese continued their primary strategy of striking U.S. combatants rather than support ships. This was especially true when they started their "divine wind" (kamikaze) attacks.[51]

The turning point in the Pacific war was the U.S. victory at the Battle of Midway (4 June 1942), where U.S. carrier forces sank four Japanese carriers and a heavy cruiser and destroyed 322 aircraft. Thirty-five hundred Japanese Navy men were lost; among them were experienced and skillful pilots who could never be replaced.[52]

This victory opened the door for the Allied counteroffensive beginning with the invasion of Guadalcanal. Although Marines landed to relatively light opposition, the Japanese reacted immediately, launching raids from Rabaul on the U.S. invading force. These raids were followed by a Japanese night naval attack—the Battle of Savo Island—that destroyed three heavy U.S. cruisers. As the Marines inched their way forward on Guadalcanal, the Japanese used small craft to support Japanese troops because any ship larger than a thousand tons or more became subject to Allied air attack. When the Japanese attempted to reinforce the island with these large ships, U.S. aircraft sank seven of eleven transports and forced the others to beach themselves. Eventually, they used destroyers to make night forays with troops using launches, cutters, and collapsible boats to reach the jungle shorelines.[53]

Several factors hindered the Japanese in their attempt to slow Allied advances. The Japanese minesweeping capability provided minimal protection for their ships. More than one hundred Japanese warships struck mines during the war. Forty-nine were sunk. Japanese antisubmarine forces were unskilled and unaggressive, which led to devastating shipping losses caused by Allied submarines. Also, the Japanese had not developed a convoy system, and failures in cryptanalysis resulted in flawed intelligence on the movement of Allied warships and merchantmen.[54]

Beginning in mid-1943, the Allies began a strategic dual advance across the Pacific retaking islands in the Central Pacific while driving up the so-called New Guinea–Mindanao Axis. The Fifth Fleet that drove through the Central Pacific used a force of six large carriers, five light carriers, eight escort carriers, five new and eight old battleships, nine heavy and five light cruisers, fifty-six destroyers, twenty-nine transports and cargo vessels, and a vast number of landing craft. The New Guinea–Mindanao Axis was an army offensive that advanced by a series of amphibious operations supported by land-based air in bypassing enemy concentrations.[55]

As the war progressed, the number of U.S. submarines patrolling enemy waters increased to more than 180 boats. Although combatants and tankers were their primary targets, the submarines were constantly on the prowl for troopships. Of the 1,241 Japanese ships (5,161,559 tons) sunk during the war by U.S. submarines, more than 250 were passenger-cargo ships or transports, vessels used to carry troops. Operational patrol reports record the incidents of these sinkings and the tremendous loss of Japanese soldiers that went down with these ships.[56]

In February 1944 the Japanese sent Imperial Army units to the Marianas Islands in anticipation of a U.S. invasion to retake formerly held bases. Soldiers were embarked aboard four transports that aggregated between five thousand and ten thousand tons. After departing port they formed a convoy that included a destroyer screen and air escort. The convoy arrived at Ujina, the principal Army shipping depot, the following day. Another transport, *Sakito Maru,* carrying the 18th Regiment from Manchuria, joined the convoy at that point. The force departed for the Marianas on 26 February. Three days later with their destination less than a week away the ships were attacked by U.S. submarines, which included USS *Trout. Sakito* was hit, and *Aki Maru* took a torpedo in a passenger-loaded hold that killed approximately five hundred soldiers. When it appeared to those aboard the remaining transports that the attack had ended, *Tozan Maru* was sent to the bottom after being struck by two torpedoes. By the following day some two thousand troops had been lost and hundreds of soldiers had to be treated for shock, exposure, and wounds. Although *Aki Maru* survived the ordeal and was able to limp into Guam on 4 March, she was sunk a few days later after disembarking the remainder of her troops.[57]

In late April of that same year, two Japanese divisions were loaded and sailed for New Guinea with numerous escorts to relieve beleaguered garrisons. The convoy, designated Take Ichi (Bamboo No. 1), departed Shanghai and soon encountered disaster. It sailed into the path of the submarine USS *Jack,* which was patrolling northwest of Luzon. *Jack* carefully positioned itself for an attack and sank a fifty-four-hundred-ton transport. All of the men on board, an Army regiment of three thousand, were lost. The crippled convoy put into Manila to reorganize, and Bamboo No. 1 was again at sea headed for New Guinea. Standing in their way was another U.S. submarine, USS *Gurnard*. On 6 May she quickly dispatched three Japanese ships in the convoy, passenger-cargo ships *Aden Maru* and *Taijima Maru,* and the seven-thousand-ton cargo ship, *Tenshinzan Maru.* After this attack the remaining ships of Bamboo No. 1 gave up their efforts to reach New Guinea, landed their troops in Halmahera in the Moluccas, and then dispersed. When the troops were eventually ferried in launches to New Guinea, they joined an army on the brink of defeat and either fled into jungle or were captured.[58]

British and Dutch submarines complemented the U.S. submarine campaign during the Pacific war. Though their contributions were limited, they did enjoy some spectacular success. One of the best examples was the sinking of the thirteen-thousand-ton Japanese heavy cruiser *Ashigara* off Sumatra in 1944 by HMS *Trenchant.* Pressed into service as a troop transport, *Ashigara* sank with five thousand troops aboard after *Trenchant* scored hits with five torpedoes.[59]

By the end of 1944 U.S. submariners had effectively cleared the seas. The Japanese merchant fleet was practically nonexistent. What ships remained stayed in the Yellow Sea and the Sea of Japan. Three events involved the "Silent Service" in 1945. Adm. Charles A. Lockwood sent nine submarines into the Sea of Japan to attack whatever Japanese ships could be found. Some twenty-eight enemy ships were sunk in fifteen days; however, USS *Bonefish* was lost during the operation. Next, the last U.S. submarine to be lost in the war, USS *Bonehead,* failed to return to its home base. It was the fifty-second U.S. boat lost in the war. Finally, USS *Torsk* sank a small Japanese frigate off the coast of Honshu. It was the last Japanese ship sunk during World War II.[60]

The value of the Silent Service was best summed up by Fleet Admiral Chester W. Nimitz when, following the war, he wrote, "As British airmen are credited with saving Britain in those critical days after Dunkirk, so our gallant submarine personnel filled the breach after Pearl Harbor, and can claim credit, not only for holding the line, but also for carrying the war to the enemy."[61]

As MacArthur's Southwest Pacific forces recaptured Borneo and the Philippines, the Central Forces successfully invaded Iwo Jima and Okinawa. B-29 bombers conducted devastating fire raids on Japanese homeland cities. All Japanese oil from its southern resources area and bound for its home islands was

Second Division high pointers in Nagasaki, Japan, October 1945, on their way home.
U.S. National Archives

cut off by U.S. submarines and aircraft flying out of Luzon. The submarines also prevented coal and iron from entering the continent. Russia's entry into the war and the dropping of atomic bombs on Hiroshima and Nagasaki finally forced Japan to surrender, which they did formally on board the American battleship USS *Missouri* in Tokyo Bay on 2 September 1945.[62]

TWO

TROOPSHIP DISASTERS

The Nineteenth Century

BIRKENHEAD

HMS *Birkenhead* was the first naval vessel to be built and designated as a troop-ship.[1] It was constructed during a period when the British Admiralty was in the midst of debating whether to convert its wooden warships to iron ships. Doubtful that iron ships would be of value, the Admiralty decided in 1845 to award a contract to shipbuilder John Laird of Birkenhead for the construction of one ship. The vessel was to be a second-class steam paddle frigate. Many other iron frigates were ordered while shooting tests continued in an attempt to measure the effect of gunfire on iron plating. The tests were not reassuring since cannon balls readily passed through iron plating, causing large holes with jagged edges making any plugging extremely difficult. If the shots landed near the waterline of a warship, the effect would be disastrous. The results of these tests led to more controversy, and many in the Admiralty were of the opinion that iron could not be beneficially employed as a material for the construction of vessels of war. Finally, on the orders of the First Lord, the Earl of Auckland, George Eaton, all work on iron frigates was to stop. Seventeen other iron frigates under construction were scrapped or converted into troopships, the largest being the two-thousand-ton *Simoom*. Since the *Birkenhead* was well

The *Birkenhead* wreck. *The Naval and Military Press*

along in her construction, she was the first to be fitted out as a troopship. The Royal Navy and the Mercantile Marine would remain wooden-hulled for another ten years.

Birkenhead was launched on 30 December 1845, and completed in 1846. During the following year, she transported troops to Ireland and the Channel Islands. For the next few years she was removed from trooping duties and laid up for alterations, which included expanding her internal spaces, cutting doorways for the troops (thus negating the protection of watertight bulkheads that would later prove disastrous), adding a third mast, and rigging her as a barque to make her more suitable for long-distance trooping since she only carried coal for twelve days. In 1850 she was commissioned as a troopship and made voyages to Canada, Gibraltar, Ireland, and Cape Town.

Birkenhead in her status as a commissioned troopship carried a crew of 130 officers and men. These included seamen, stokers, petty officers, engineers, boy ratings, stewards, a paymaster's clerk and a sick-bay steward, and six Royal Marines to act as sentries and man four small broadside guns. There were no commissioned officers in her complement, but she was commanded by a naval

Lt. Col. Alexander Seton, the heroic officer who commanded the troops on *Birkenhead*. *The Naval and Military Press*

master, Mr. Robert Salmond, an experienced warrant officer. He was known as one of the most skillful masters in the Royal Navy.

In December 1851 *Birkenhead* docked at Spithead and the following month boarded one officer and sixty-nine other ranks of the 12th Foot (the future Suffolk Regiment) and two officers and six other ranks of the 12th Lancers. Proceeding to Queenstown, she picked up 494 men of all ranks from different regiments, including the 2nd, 6th, 43rd, 45th, 73rd, 74th, and 91st. Wives and children of the troopers were also taken on board to accompany their husbands.

These troopers were reinforcements for ten regiments already fighting in the African Kaffir campaign. They were young, new recruits who received little training and were put in uniform and sent to a far-off war shortly after their enlistment. Most were of Irish and Scottish descent. At the time the British Army was swamped with Irish recruits who were escaping the destitution of their homeland brought on by the potato blight of the 1840s. More than a million people died in Ireland from starvation and disease during that period.

On 7 January 1852, the ship departed Queenstown in a driving snow storm and met with tumultuous seas, plunging the ship into valleys and peaks of raging water that poured over the vessel. All the ship's hatches were locked shut, and the troops and passengers sealed below became terrified as the ship's crew struggled to keep her afloat. Many were either seasick or injured by being thrown about in their accommodation spaces. Two women died and were buried at sea when the gale subsided ten days out of port. Another two died later in childbirth. As *Birkenhead* passed abeam of Gibraltar the seas quieted, and the crew set about cleaning up the ship. Fortunately little damage was done, and within a few days the senior military officer on board, Maj. Alexander Seton of the 74th Highlanders, established a rigid routine and began to drill and exercise the recruits. The soldiers responded to Seton's inspired leadership and within weeks they evolved into a disciplined and controlled body that took pride in their sense of unity and loyalty, elements that were usually only found in long-established, combat experienced regiments. Seton demanded obedience and received it twofold from his soldiers, who admired and respected him. He was dedicated, fair to all, and compassionate to the women and children who accompanied the troopers. The troopers worked hard to win his approval as they continued toward their destination, and Seton was satisfied that they would perform well when tested in battle.

Birkenhead reached Simonstown, the naval base at Cape Town, on 23 February and disembarked twenty sick men and thirty-six women and children. Upon reporting to the senior naval officer on the base, Commo. Christopher Wyvill, Seton found out that the Kaffir campaign was going badly for the British and that his troops were urgently needed. During the next two days soldiers and sailors worked together to quickly bunker the ship, bring on board stores, and stow provisions. More personnel, including soldiers of the 91st Regiment and a number of colonial volunteers, boarded the already crowded ship. Counting the crew, the original complement of officers, soldiers, women and children, and newcomers, the number of souls on board was approximated at 638. Several horses were purchased and loaded on board, making a total of thirty horses haltered amidships. Fodder and bales of hay were stacked on the upper deck and the foredeck.

Birkenhead sailed at 6 P.M. the evening of 26 February 1852 and headed for its final destination, Port Elizabeth. As the ship passed Cape Hanglip that night, land was clearly visible and native campfires could be seen along the shore. At 1 A.M. the lookouts on the forecastle called out "All's well." Second Master J.

Monument to the 74th Highlanders in St. Giles Cathedral, Edinburgh.
The Naval and Military Press

O'Davis answered with an "Aye aye." At 2 A.M. there came a shout of "By the deep twelve," indicating that the ship was in just twelve fathoms of water and that they had come upon a shoal. Before another sounding could be made, the ship's forward motion came to an abrupt halt. The early morning air was filled with a grinding and tearing sound as men were flung to the deck by the sudden impact. *Birkenhead* had struck a reef off Danger Point and a pinnacle rock broke through her bottom. When Master Salmond ordered reverse engines, hoping to loosen the ship from the reef, the hull was torn open. Water rushed quickly through the holed ship and shut down the coal-burning engines. Most of the troops in the overcrowded lower deck were drowned as they slept in their hammocks.

Seton immediately arrived on deck and conveyed to his officers the importance of discipline and silence to avoid panic among the troops. He then ordered the soldiers to fall in on deck. The troopers smartly formed orderly ranks and remained steadfast as the ship began to list. Parties were detailed off to man the ship's pumps and launch eight lifeboats. Three of the boats were eventually lowered loaded with about thirty crewmen and all the women and children. The scene was heart-wrenching as wives clung to their husbands standing steady in the ranks. The horses were blindfolded and driven into the sea. They were immediately set upon by sharks that gathered around the ship.

The three lifeboats had barely got clear of the ship when it broke in two near the foremast. Seton was tempted to allow those who could swim to jump overboard but fearful that they might try to board the lifeboats and capsize them he asked the troops to remain in formation. The officers shook hands with each other and resumed their posts in front of their men. Twenty-five minutes after *Birkenhead* struck the reef she sank with her troops still holding fast. Although land was near, few of the men could reach it. Most could not swim, and although they held on to wreckage they were attacked by sharks and became mired in dense seaweed. Only the strongest and perhaps the luckiest were able to survive. Seton and Salmond and most of their men went down with the ship. Fifty men clung to a mast, which was the only part of the ship that remained above water. Forty were rescued by the cutter *Lioness*. Of the 638 on board the ship, 193 were saved, including all the women and children; 445 were lost.

The names of *Birkenhead*'s lost men were inscribed on a brass plate and placed in the Chelsea Hospital by command of Queen Victoria, "to record heroic constancy and unbroken discipline." A monument was also erected in St. Giles Cathedral in Edinburgh to honor the fallen of the 74th Highlanders. King William IV of Prussia was so impressed by the heroic behavior of *Birkenhead*'s troopers that he ordered that all his regiments be read the story of their bravery.

To this day the story of *Birkenhead* and its gallant men is considered to be the proudest moment in the annals of the British Army.

SULTANA

A side-wheel steamship, *Sultana* plied the waters of the Mississippi during the latter part of the Civil War to take advantage of the lucrative cotton trade when the Union opened the river to commercial vessels. Built at Cincinnati, Ohio, in February 1863, she was constructed with an extra-wide second deck to carry more bales of cotton. She also housed two very tall smokestacks to prevent sparks from dropping onto her valuable and very flammable cargo. By 1864 *Sultana* was making routine runs between St. Louis and New Orleans. Capt. J. Cass Mason, skipper of *Sultana,* was considered to be a hot shot by other riverboat captains since he often took unnecessary risks, especially when it came to steamboat races. In early 1865 he set a record for the fastest New Orleans to St. Louis run, four days and seven hours. When the war ended, he and other government contract-approved boats vied for carrying loads of Union prisoners of war home.

Early in the Civil War, exchanges of prisoners were routine. However, the process was often complicated because of Federal refusal to recognize the Confederacy. Exchanges were initiated in July 1862, and a prisoner exchange agreement was reached that was based on a process that had been established with the British during the War of 1812. The system was implemented whereby an officer had to be exchanged for an officer of equal rank or a specified number of enlisted soldiers. As the war continued, the system became a nightmare of paperwork and bookkeeping to ensure that neither side was shortchanged. Bickering erupted on both sides over violations of the original agreement.

The South, which desperately needed its men back to shore up its dwindling forces and could not meet the housing needs of large numbers of Union POWs, pushed an issue that brought an end to the prisoner of war exchange. It concerned the use of black troops by the Union. The Confederates threatened to execute any white officer found in command of black soldiers and to sell all

Steamboats at the public landing, Vicksburg, Mississippi, February 1864.
Collection of the Public Library of Cincinnati and Hamilton County

captured black soldiers into slavery. Under no circumstance would the South ever consider exchanging black soldiers.

Gen. Ulysses S. Grant, knowing that the enlistment of many Union prisoners would expire after their release and that they would go home, saw no reason to continue the exchange since he would be allowing Confederate soldiers to rejoin their units and fight to the end. Grant issued an order in July 1863 to end all prisoner exchanges. Although the order was backed by Union Secretary of War Edwin M. Stanton, it was not completely carried out because Union officers still had the option to exchange prisoners under unusual circumstances; hence field exchanges took place until the end of the war.[2] Even so, the Confederates gradually found that they could not cope with the tens of thousands of Union prisoners that overwhelmed their existing camps, with more arriving every day. There was no space, food, or medicine for the prisoners, who were transferred to tobacco warehouses and other facilities. The Confederates were also concerned that a large Union cavalry force might sweep down on one of the camps and free the prisoners. Because Grant had an abundance of manpower he could leave Union soldiers where they were, thus burdening the enemy but also extending the misery of his soldiers. The Confederates finally proposed several new plans, and in January 1865, with the war winding down, the North accepted a man-for-man prisoner-exchange arrangement.

The plan called for Union and Confederate prisoners "under parole" to be moved to mutual exchange camps and then released once man-for-man swaps had been arranged. Most of the Confederate prison camps were vastly over-crowded, and Union soldiers suffered from disease and malnutrition. Those held at the prisons in Cahaba (Alabama) and Andersonville (Georgia) were to be moved to little-used Camp Fisk, situated on neutral ground four miles west of the Mississippi port of Vicksburg. From there they would be transported north on riverboats.

The prisoners were to remain under the control of the Confederacy until the exchanges could be made. To ensure neutrality, the "parole camp" at Fisk was guarded by Union soldiers, but Confederates accompanied the prisoners and remained with them until the proper number of Confederate prisoners could be placed in their custody.

The first contingent of eight hundred Union soldiers from Cahaba made their way through enemy territory by riverboat and rail to Jackson, Mississippi, and then forty miles on foot to the Big Black River and Union-held territory. They were skeletal in appearance, some on rough wooden crutches, others carried by their comrades on makeshift stretchers.

The soldiers emerged from the woods to a clearing at the Big Black River and stopped, stunned by what they saw ahead. In the distance "Old Glory," their flag for which they had fought so intensely, was flapping in the breeze above a Union camp site. Yelling as one they moved toward it, a ragged group who had suffered the ravages of sickness and starvation after years in a Confederate prison camp.

The prisoners camped for the night on rebel ground; then, at first light they lined up near the end of a pontoon bridge. As a Confederate officer checked off a roster of names, one by one they crossed over into the Federal territory accompanied by Confederate escort soldiers.

Shortly thereafter, other Union prisoners and their Confederate guards flooded in from Cahaba, and five thousand more Union soldiers were on their way to Vicksburg from Andersonville. All were scheduled to journey home on the waters of the Mississippi. The men were transported on railroad flatcars to

J. Cass Mason, master of *Sultana*. *Ohio Historical Society*

nearby Camp Fisk, where the Union prisoners were clothed, fed, and assigned sleeping tents.[3]

By early April, Fisk's expatriated community had grown to several thousand, and the camp was a mix of Union prisoners and a small number of Confederate soldiers. Confederate Lt. Col. Howard A. M. Henderson, commanding the Confederate contingent from Cahaba, and Col. N. G. Watts, Confederate

Commissioner of Exchange at Vicksburg, would not turn over the Union prisoners until an equal swap was made.

At the time, though, few Confederate prisoners were being sent to Vicksburg; thus, the two sides were at an impasse. Hordes of Union prisoners continued to arrive at Fisk, and the Union found itself hard-pressed to contain the restless men. Most of the Union parolees were sickly, but at the same time feverishly enthusiastic because they were going home to their loved ones.[4]

Meanwhile, Union General N. J. T. Dana waited at the river port of Vicksburg, assuming that arrangements had been completed for the exchange and that Union men would soon be arriving. Reportedly they would be destined for western states, to be taken on board Mississippi River paddle wheelers to Benton Barracks, Illinois, or to Camp Chase, Ohio. Dana was commander of the Department of Mississippi, encompassing both Vicksburg and the District of West Tennessee. It was an area of some eighty thousand square miles.

At his post, Dana had been living a life of tranquility. A West Point graduate, he had seen combat in the Mexican War, been wounded at Telegraph Hill, and then severely disabled by an artillery shell while leading a brigade at Antietam. When he received the War Department telegram informing him that the prisoners would be heading his way, he had no concept of how many were involved, nor the state of their health, nor from where they would be coming.

With insufficient information about the background and thus the precise nature of his assignment, it was Dana who decided that Camp Fisk would be the best holding place before the Vicksburg wharfs. He thought the prisoners would arrive in small groups and be gone before another group arrived, and he planned the billet arrangements accordingly. By mid-March he was shocked to hear that more than one thousand prisoners were at the Black River pontoon bridge ready to be transported to Camp Fisk.

In what was normal army fashion at the time, Dana decided to turn over the whole confusing situation to a subordinate, Capt. George A. Williams of the 1st U.S. Infantry Division. Dana expected that Williams would keep an accurate count of the men at Fisk and prepare them for shipment north. The young officer was given the title of assistant commissioner of exchange, and Dana sent him off to negotiate with the Confederate officers. Williams traveled to Mobile to procure a copy of the prisoner-exchange agreement. Unable to find such an agreement, he was ordered next to Cairo, Illinois, to consult with General Grant about the mess.

When Williams left Vicksburg, volunteer Union officer Capt. Fredric Speed took his place. Dana readily approved Speed's offer to take responsibility for the problems that seemed to mount daily. On 13 April Colonel Watts received a telegram: "Confederate Officer Having Charge of Prisoners, Vicksburg. All Federal officers and men who are held as prisoners" were to be paroled without the usual man-for-man exchange. "By agreement with General Grant, equivalents are to be given on the James River [Virginia]." Watts was to let the prisoners go. When Williams returned to Vicksburg he noted that Speed had things well in hand and elected not to request his old job back but to assist his replacement instead.[5]

Dana's order to Speed was to prepare the prisoner rolls as quickly as possible and send them north, so that at least one thousand men could be loaded on board ships stopping at Vicksburg. Accurate rolls were impossible to produce, but Speed was able to muster thirteen hundred men to be shipped. They were loaded into boxcars at Fisk and taken to the wharf at Vicksburg, where they boarded *Henry Ames*.

By 22 April Speed was able to enroll and make ready for transportation seven hundred more Union soldiers, who were shipped out on the noncontract packet *Olive Branch*. Shortly thereafter another steamer had docked at Vicksburg—*Sultana*. This handsome paddle wheeler, launched on 4 February 1863, looked every bit the part of her regal name.[6] On 14 April 1865, she tied up at Cairo, Illinois. That same night, President Abraham Lincoln finished some paperwork in the Executive Mansion in Washington, D.C., then joined his wife at Ford's Theater. Within twelve hours he would be dead, assassinated by actor John Wilkes Booth.

By the following day, news of the murder had not reached as far west as Cairo, and newspapers carried the story that the war was almost over, Lee having surrendered to Grant. The front page of the *Cairo Eagle* devoted several columns to the comings and going of passenger steamboats along the river, while the back included long lists of Civil War casualties. The devastating news about the president did reach the *Cairo Eagle* before *Sultana* left to travel downriver, and the new headline read "National Calamity." As the first ship to leave Cairo, *Sultana,* would be the one carrying the tragic news to ports in the south. When she arrived at Memphis and distributed copies of the *Cairo Eagle,* the city went into an uproar. It was the same scene at every port, all the way down to New Orleans.

Overloaded with troops, *Sultana* is shown departing Helena, Arkansas, at 8 A.M. on 26 April 1865. *Naval Historical Center*

On her return upriver, *Sultana* was plagued by a boiler in need of repair. Vicksburg was chosen as the site for the work.[7]

Business was light along the Mississippi at that time, and any delays in a ship's schedule could upset the delicate balance between profit and loss. The pressure was on for a speedy fix. Once docked, *Sultana* engineers raced to Klein's Foundry and requested the services of a boiler mechanic and rivet hammer. As they ran up the roadway toward the foundry, they passed *Sultana*'s local business agent. Reaching the ship, the agent immediately sought out the master of the vessel, Captain Mason, and delivered some exciting news: a neutral exchange camp near Vicksburg held hundreds of Federal prisoners, waiting to be transported north. *Sultana*, he suggested, would likely be selected to transport troops up to Cairo. Captain Mason quickly saw the profit in filling his ship with these men. General Grant had established a standard price for moving Union troops from point to point: five dollars for each enlisted soldier, ten for officers. *Sultana* was a government contract ship, authorized to carry Union troops.[8]

Speed informed General Dana that the remainder of the prisoners would be put on board *Sultana*, and that he estimated this would be thirteen hundred men. Dana agreed to the decision, and Speed hurried back to Fisk and ordered the men to prepare for transport to Vicksburg. Meanwhile, Captain Williams went to the Vicksburg wharf, and over the loud ringing of metallic hammering that came from the ship's engine room, he told Captain Mason to expect a full load. The foundry men were working on the leaky boiler: two damaged plates on the larboard side of the middle-larboard tank were badly bulged and needed to be replaced. But Mason decided to hold off major repairs until they reached St. Louis. Patchwork maintenance was completed, and the ship was made ready to receive the Camp Fisk parolees.

The first contingent of six hundred soldiers soon reached the wharf by rail and streamed aboard the *Sultana*. Mason told Williams that the ship would leave in two hours. But then no more prisoners came into sight. Williams charged into Dana's office and accused Captain Speed of accepting bribes, delaying the prisoners at Camp Fisk, and being in cahoots with agents of the Atlantic and Mississippi to send prisoners later, on board their noncontracted packets.

Dana sent a dispatch to Speed at Camp Fisk asking if Speed intended to send any more prisoners to sail with *Sultana,* since she would soon be leaving port. Speed replied in the affirmative and later, when Williams and Speed began to share information, they were convinced that other Union officers were involved in a kickback scheme, and they became determined to load all remaining prisoners at Camp Fisk aboard *Sultana*.

Speed immediately began loading railcars with parolees and, once they were rolling, organized small marching parties to make the four-mile trek to Vicksburg on foot. As the men boarded the ship, Williams tried to group them by state, regiment, and company, but the units became so mixed and the numbers so overwhelming that it was impossible to sort everyone and assign them to their proper sections. Prisoners from Alabama, Missouri, Nebraska, Pennsylvania, Illinois, Indiana, Iowa, Kentucky, Michigan, Ohio, Tennessee, Virginia, and West Virginia were loaded onto the paddle wheeler.

Near the middle of the night, Speed left Fort Fisk and returned to Vicksburg reporting to Dana that all prisoners had been cleared out of the camp. There were now no fewer than 196 regiments on the pages of *Sultana*'s roster. Under a black velvet sky, Speed and Williams finally looked up at the crowded decks and realized that the ship was vastly overloaded. It was still not too late to transfer some of the men to the two near-empty packets docked next to *Sultana,* but the two men decided it would be too difficult to divide the load at this point.

Explosion of *Sultana*. *Naval Historical Center*

Sultana cast off her lines shortly after 9 P.M. on 24 April 1865, and slowly disappeared into the darkness of the swirling, swollen Mississippi. On board were approximately two thousand soldiers, one hundred civilian passengers, eighty-five crewmen, a guard unit of twenty-two, and mules, horses, and hogs. *Sultana's* legal maximum load was 376 persons, including the crew.

As the ship began her journey north, she was jammed from stem to stern and packed from rail to rail. There was not a foot of unoccupied space available. All the soldiers were joyous to be going home; even the sick and wounded were in good spirits. Hardly anyone slept the first night out: talk of home dominated every conversation.

But all were not so carefree. Mason worried whether his overloaded ship could survive the trip, and then there were the fractious boilers. Chief engineer Nathan Wintringer nursed them carefully, watching for indications of trouble. The vessel was so top-heavy that she rolled with every turn. Chief Mate William Rowberry took every measure to keep her balanced, but *Sultana* lacked adequate bulk freight to provide the ballast that would ensure safety. To add to the crew's anxiety, the highly experienced helmsmen, George Kayton and Henry Ingraham, were faced with keeping her on a steady course against a swirling torrent of debris-filled water. Because of one of the worst spring floods in the river's history, the shores of the Mississippi had spread back into swamplands, making it difficult for the helmsmen to steer down the main channel.

Thirty-six hours after leaving Vicksburg, *Sultana* docked at Helena, Arkansas. It was 7 A.M. on Wednesday, 26 April. The town, normally bustling with a population of five thousand, was awash in river mud. The men were not allowed to depart the ship during the brief stop, so the town's citizens crowded the shoreline, waving to the troops and shouting warm greetings. It was here that photographer T. W. Bankes made a picture of the overloaded steamboat. Anxious to be in it, soldiers rushed to the shore side of the boat and nearly capsized the vessel before order was restored. Bankes's picture is the only known photo of the ship that was taken before disaster struck, a few days later.

Sultana departed Helena an hour after she docked. The helmsmen were able to navigate the main channel steadily, steering against strong currents all the way to Memphis, which they reached at 7 P.M. on 26 April. Here the boat unloaded 230 hogsheads of sugar, 97 boxes of wine, and the lot of hogs she was carrying. This new absence of freight made the ship even more top-heavy, setting her up for sure disaster.

Though ordered to remain on board, hundreds of paroled prisoners slipped off the vessel and roamed the dusty streets of Memphis. Many found a Soldier's Home where they were treated to a hot meal; others with cash found pleasures of a different sort. The riverfront saloons were soon filled with frail men enjoying their first drink in years. A number of passengers disembarked and several came aboard, including U.S. Congressman–elect W. D. Snow of Arkansas. When the last casks of sugar were unloaded, at about 11 P.M., Mason had the brass bell sounded, signaling that the ship would soon depart.

Shortly before midnight on 26 April, *Sultana* departed Memphis. It was a pitch-black night; clouds hid the moon and stars. A slight drizzle swept over the ship and her sleeping occupants. George Kayton was at the helm and took the vessel out to mainstream, and steered her for a safe center passage among several islands known as the Hen and Chickens. Captain Mason had retired for the night, and Chief Mate Rowberry kept Kayton company in the pilothouse. They were prepared for a long and lonely watch ahead.

Below, the assistant engineer, Wes Clemens, stood checking his straining boilers. Despite the heavy weight and the head-on current, Clemens was able to maintain enough steam to push the ship forward at the usual nine knots. The four stoke holds were open, and sweating men heaved coal into the fireboxes, ensuring that each shovelful was spread evenly over the glowing embers. At 1:41 A.M. the ship passed Island 41, near the Arkansas side; fifteen minutes later, Tangleman's Landing on the Tennessee bank. Usually at this point the stream was three miles from edge to edge, but this night it was swollen to at least three times its normal width, flooding the forest along the Tennessee highland and extending deep into the Arkansas flats.[9]

At 2 A.M., without warning, *Sultana*'s boilers burst. The thunderous explosion was heard in Memphis, seven miles away. The eruption split the boat in two, and hundreds were killed instantly or fatally injured. Soldiers sleeping above the boilers were hurtled into the air, their mangled bodies landing on the now-fiery inferno or cast into the darkened river waters. Many were scalded and buried under falling wreckage. The smokestacks toppled over, and as the ship came to a sudden halt many soldiers jumped into the river. But few could swim, and when others who could jumped after them they were grabbed and pulled under, drowning with the desperate souls who clutched their legs. Some found pieces of wreckage to cling to, but they had to fight off others frantically trying to save themselves.

Smoke and hissing steam blinded those still on board, so they stumbled over bodies as they tried to find a way off the ship. Doomed, they screamed, cursed, and prayed as flames engulfed *Sultana*. Some stood on railings with their clothes on fire, too afraid to jump into the water.

Many of the soldiers were heroes. Men who had been through years of torture and imprisonment, thinking only of going home, forgot everything but assisting the dying and injured. Many lost their own lives in doing so. Hundreds of heads bobbed in the water as everyone tried to get as far away as possible from the boat. Thinking that the bushes nearby marked a shoreline, people swam for them. But when they reached the branches, they found that the water was still deep and the brush not strong enough to hold them above water. Many perished, not realizing that because of the swollen river the twigs were actually treetops.

The only boat close enough to offer rescue service was *Bostonia No. 2*, twelve miles upriver and unaware of the blast or the fire that lit up the night sky. Those on the sinking *Sultana* and in the water were left to save themselves. Unfortunately, the packet carried no lifeboats, only cork life belts racked under each stateroom bed. But the sudden destruction had made it impossible to use these lifesaving devices. Captain Mason worked tirelessly to save his passengers, and he was last seen on the burning deck. It was assumed that he went down with the *Sultana*'s remains.

Finally *Bostonia* rounded a bend and turned downriver above the Hen and Chickens. Not more than a mile ahead, the horrified helmsman saw a huge fireball. It was the floating funeral pyre of *Sultana*. By the time *Bostonia*'s master, Capt. Jonathan T. Watson, reached the main deck, his ship was forging through *Sultana*'s victims. Desperately trying to stay above water, they clung to any debris they could find. Watson quickly ordered his crew to throw everything over the side that could float, and proceeded forward at half-speed until he passed the flaming wreck and could see no more bobbing heads in the water. He then turned his ship around and dropped anchor on the Arkansas side of the river. A yawl was lowered and crewmen began pulling people out of the water. An hour later, with one hundred survivors on board, *Bostonia* raced for Memphis.[10]

When rescue boats arrived from Memphis, they stayed clear of the burning hulk. John Fogleman and his neighbors watched the disaster from a high vantage point at Mound City, Arkansas. They could clearly make out men clinging to trees. Noting that the Memphis boats were not seeing these men, Fogleman and his two sons decided to take the matter into their own hands. Within an hour they had built a raft of two-foot logs, which they dragged down to the muddy bank and cast off to rescue whomever they could. They saved a few dozen people, then watched as the smoldering hulk of the ship turned slightly into an eddy. There was a knot of people clearly visible, still on *Sultana*. Immediately the Foglemans headed for them. They could only take six men at a time, and they had to move fast because the flames were dangerously close to the people who remained on board.

After taking the first load of six halfway to the shore, Fogleman decided to deposit them onto the trees on the flooded bank, and headed back to the wreck. Speed was critical. He got a second load and then a third. However, when he returned for the fourth, he found that the weakened parolees were unable to hang onto the trees for any length of time. He had to take these struggling soldiers to the shore. There were still thirteen men on *Sultana*. Two more trips were made, one taking seven men and the last the remaining six. At 9 A.M. on 27 April 1865, seven hours after the ship had exploded, Mississippi waters closed over *Sultana*.

Wesley Lee of the 102nd Ohio Infantry Division was the first to inform authorities of the *Sultana* disaster. Surviving the boiler explosion, he shed his outer clothing and tore some planks from a stairway, then threw himself into the river. He managed to stay afloat down the Tennessee side of the river and reach Memphis. By now, some ninety minutes after the explosion, about fifteen hundred survivors were scattered across five thousand acres of the flooded Mississippi.

Near the center of the Memphis landing was a wharf boat, a floating office for conducting port business. Two men, one of whom was a telegrapher, heard cries coming from the water and jumped into a skiff. With one holding a kerosene lantern high and the other rowing, they soon came upon Lee and hauled him into the skiff. The telegrapher immediately sent out the alert. Captain Curtis, master of river transportation, gave orders to the commander of the river guard to notify every vessel at the wharf. Three steamers, *Jenny Lind, Pocahontas,* and a ferry named *Rosadella,* were ordered to fire up and proceed upstream to *Sultana*. The ironclad *Essex,* the tin-clad USS *Grosbeak,* and the gunboat USS *Tyler* joined in the rescue operation along with yawls, riverfront skiffs, and other small craft. All were soon out on the river pulling survivors to safety.

In Memphis word spread, and the city rushed to the levee. The wharf was crowded with medical personnel, members of the Sisters of Charity, and citizens wanting to help however they could. Ambulances and omnibuses were loaded with injured and driven to one of the city's six hospitals.

At dawn, the three steamers passed *Bostonia* with her survivors. Rescue boats continued the grim task of searching for anyone, dead or alive. Lifeless bodies were uncovered clinging to boards wedged under their arms. Other bodies were found in trees for more than a month after the disaster, many popping to the surface near the wreck. Packets sailing downriver spotted them on the banks or lodged in driftwood.[11]

On 29 April Maj. Gen. Cadwallader C. Washburn, commanding the District of West Tennessee, sent a telegram to Secretary of War Stanton with the following request:

> Will you please order an inquiry to be made at Vicksburg to ascertain why 2,000 released Federal prisoners were crowded on board the ill-fated steamer *Sultana,* against the remonstrance of the captain of the boat and when two other large steamers were in port at the same time bound up river, with very few passengers? The loss of life is known to exceed 1,400.[12]

Stanton handed the initial investigation over to Gen. E. A. Hitchcock, commissioner for exchange of prisoners, who promptly opted out of his appointment. He said he knew nothing about the affair except what he read in the papers and turned the matter over to Brig. Gen. William Hoffman, commissioner general of prisoners, whom he ordered to Memphis and Vicksburg "to inquire into the circumstance of the destruction of the steamer *Sultana* in the Mississippi River."

Hoffman was tasked with answering three questions: how many had been lost, what had caused the disaster, and who was to blame. When Hoffman reached Memphis, he found that two other inquiries were already under way, one by Washburn and the other by Dana. Hoffman requested and received transcripts of the proceedings of these investigations. According to Dana's account of the roles of Col. R. B. Hatch (chief quartermaster at Vicksburg), Williams, Speed, and Capt. W. F. Kerns (officer in charge of river transportation), the latter two were jointly responsible for the disaster.[13] With regard to how many men had been lost, Dana stated that there was no list of Federal prisoners who had been on board the ship. There was only the Confederate roster of prisoners from Indiana, Kentucky, Michigan, Ohio, Tennessee, and Virginia who had been delivered to Camp Fisk.

When Hoffman returned to Washington to analyze the documentation he had gathered, he received a telegram from General Washburn: "Twelve commissioned officers and 757 enlisted . . . were saved from the steamer *Sultana.*"[14] Five days later, on 19 May, he wrote the following in his report to Secretary Stanton: "I am of the opinion that the shipment of so large a number of troops on one boat was, under the circumstances, unnecessary, unjustifiable, and a great outrage on the troops."

Regarding the four officers under Dana who were directly and indirectly involved in the loading (Speed, Kerns, Williams, and Hatch), he found that Colonel Hatch and Captain Speed appeared to be the most censurable. "Captain Speed was intrusted with the transfer and shipment of the prisoners, and active management and control of it, and I therefore considered him fully responsible," wrote Hoffman. Dana was exonerated, and Hoffman concluded that Kerns had rightfully informed higher authority, whereas Hatch had taken no action after being informed that *Sultana* was overloaded. Williams was discounted, because he had no direct responsibility concerning the matter.

Turning to the question of what had caused the catastrophe, Hoffman commented: "What is usually understood as the explosion of a boiler is caused by the sudden development of an intense steam by the water coming into contact with red-hot iron, which produces an effect like the firing of gunpowder in a mine, and the destruction of the boilers and the boat which carries them is the consequence." Hoffman remarked that there were two fundamental causes of most boiler explosions: first, the sudden development of runaway steam pressure by the water coming into contact with red-hot iron; and second, a normal pressure of steam acting on some weak or defective part of the metal. *Sultana* had been destroyed by one or the other, but Hoffman could only speculate on which.[15]

J. J. Witzig, supervising steamboat inspector, Fourth District, went further in his annual report for 1865. He pointed to the patchwork that was done while the ship was in Vicksburg, noting that the iron plate riveted onto one of the boilers was only one-quarter of an inch thick. His report stated:

This was on the part of the engineer a gross violation of the law, the body of the boiler being made of iron $^{17}/_{48}$ of one inch, and inspected, and the safety valves regulated for iron of that thickness and the pressure allowed (145 pounds to the square inch) was the extreme limit. Had the boiler been inspected after the repairs, the pressure allowed by law would have been 100.43 pounds of working pressure per square inch, as prescribed for boilers 46 inches in diameter, made of iron $^1/_4$ inch thick. From Vicksburg to Memphis *Sultana* traveled at her usual speed, which shows that the usual pressure steam was used. The foregoing is sufficient to explain the cause or causes of the explosion.[16]

Hoffman concluded his report with an estimate of casualties. The reports and testimony show that there were 1,866 troops, seventy cabin passengers, and eighty-five crewmen on board the boat, or 2,021 total. Of the troops, 765 were saved and 1,101 were lost. Of the seventy cabin passengers and eighty-five crew, approximately eighteen were saved, giving a loss of 137, making the total loss 1,238.[17]

In an effort to minimize the numbers, the government set the death toll much too low. However, in sworn testimony before the Memphis court of inquiry, several survivors and those involved in the transport of the parolees agreed that there had been 1,966 paroled soldiers and twenty-two military guards on board the ship, placing the total at 1,988 men.[18]

Prior to the disaster, parolee Capt. A. C. Brown, Company I, 2nd Ohio Infantry, gave testimony that *Sultana's* first clerk, William J. Gambrel, told him that the ship carried twenty-four hundred soldiers, one hundred civilian passengers, and a crew of eighty men and women—a total of 2,580 people.[19] Other figures were mentioned that continued to increase the numbers of those on *Sultana* that night, but no one could accurately testify as to just how many were on board and how many had died. After several years of investigations, the final tally listed below seemed the most accurate:

Paroled Prisoners	2,015
Passengers	100
Crew	85
Guard Unit	22
Total	2,222[20]

But the number of parolees was probably higher, and passengers and crew an approximation. The total on *Sultana* that fateful night was probably closer to between 2,250 and 2,300.

By the time Secretary Stanton reviewed Hoffman's report, two of the players had left the stage. Col. R. B. Hatch had retired, and Maj. Gen. N. J. T. Dana had resigned his commission. Captain Speed subsequently faced a court-martial for "neglect of duty, to the prejudice of good order and military discipline." He was found guilty and sentenced to a dishonorable discharge from the service.[21]

But the record of the court-martial proceedings and verdict were forwarded for final action to Gen. Joseph Holt, judge advocate general of the army, who found the verdict too severe and correctly pointed the finger at other officers. He wrote in his report: "It is recommended that the sentence be disapproved and that Captain Speed be publicly exonerated from the charges which have been made against his character as an officer." With Holt's official review of the incident, all were now cleared of accountability, while each shared some measure of guilt for the *Sultana* transgression.[22]

The rest of the country learned little of one of the greatest maritime tragedies of its time. The *New York Times* ran a story on it, a five-inch item on page 4 of the 29 April 1865 issue. Subsequent coverage amounted to a total of two columns, before the *Times* dropped the story completely. *Harper's Weekly* published a woodcut of *Sultana* in flames, but failed to include a report on how it had happened. A National *Sultana* Survivors Association was eventually formed years later, and periodic meetings were held. But as survivors passed away one by one, the horror of their ordeal remained largely unknown. Today what is left of the once-proud *Sultana* lies deep under the fertile soil of the Arkansas flats, her fate as obscure as that of the passengers who boarded her more than 130 years ago. Later analyses of the tragedy placed the loss of life at approximately seventeen hundred people, soldiers and civilians.[23]

Comparisons have been made between the loss of *Sultana* and the loss of *Titanic,* which sank in 1912. Both carried about the same number of passengers, and survivors of each disaster numbered about the same, *Titanic,* 706, and *Sultana,* 785. However, 200 of the *Sultana* survivors died in hospitals following their rescue; thus, *Sultana* suffered greater loss of life. Interest in the *Sultana* tragedy quickly waned since there was little newspaper coverage and the public was in mourning over the assassination of President Lincoln. *Sultana's* casualties, soldiers who were nameless to the general public and went through living hell that dark night on the Mississippi so long ago, were quickly forgotten. Although at the time *Sultana* was considered to be the greatest maritime disaster in history, the enormous publicity surrounding the construction and maiden voyage of *Titanic,* considered to be "unsinkable," and the loss of some of its wealthy and famous passengers, established *Titanic* as the subject of books and movies for decades to come. In later years there were greater ship disasters, especially during World War II, when vessels carrying troops lost more than seven thousand men when they were sunk by enemy action.

Aftermath: Sultana *and Robert Loudon*
On 6 May 1888, the *St. Louis Democrat* ran an article which cited a St. Louis

resident, William Streetor, as having been told by a Confederate mail carrier and blockade runner, Robert Loudon, that he had sabotaged the paddle wheeler *Sultana* causing its destruction in 1865 just north of Memphis. Union investigations of the *Sultana* explosion and sinking held immediately following the event discounted such sinister activity and focused on a patchwork boiler repair that gave way as the ship moved up the Mississippi with its cargo of Union prisoners of war.

Robert Loudon was a nefarious character who had a criminal record at an early age. He was jailed in 1852 on a murder charge. Upon his release from Pennsylvania's Eastern State Penitentiary he befriended Absalom Grimes and together with Confederate Navy Comdr. Issac N. Brown destroyed the Union ship *Baron de Kalb*. Loudon soon joined a group that became known as the "Organized Boat Burners," which were contracted by the Confederate Secret Service. During the course of the war these men destroyed some sixty ships that plied the Mississippi. Loudon is credited with the burning of the steamer *Ruth* on 4 August 1863, after which he was captured and charged with spying, mail running, and boat-burning and sentenced to hang. He received a reprieve on 6 May 1864, thanks to the intervention of a St. Louis priest and nun and the efforts of his mother, who had gone to Washington and pleaded her son's case with President Lincoln.

Still in jail and facing a death sentence, Loudon was transferred to Alton prison and escaped. Federal agents stationed in ports and cities along the Mississippi were continuously on the alert to apprehend known boat-burners and Loudon was high on their list. When *Sultana* reached Memphis for a brief stop before continuing northward, she moved across the river to take on coal. This is where some believe sabotage took place. Coal bombs were being used by the Confederates and there was speculation that Loudon had laced the coal stores with these bombs. The devices looked like ordinary lumps of coal but in reality were cast iron blocks with cores containing ten pounds of powder.

It was never proven that *Sultana* met its demise by sabotage; it is more likely that a flawed boiler exploded and doomed the ship and its passengers. Loudon, a known drinker and storyteller, did have the capability and risk mentality to perform such a deed; however, there remains only his word regarding his action and no evidence exists to support it. Shortly after telling his tale to Streetor, Loudon left St. Louis, settled in New Orleans, and died there of yellow fever in the fall of 1888.[24]

World War I

ROYAL EDWARD

With the Allied and Central Powers stalled on the Western Front during World War I and the Russians pressuring the British and French governments for critical war materials, the Allied military leaders executed a major assault on the Dardanelles in 1915 with the object of capturing Constantinople, the capital of Turkey. Neutral during the early part of the war, Turkey eventually joined the Central Powers and welcomed into their ranks German officers, who proved to be brilliant tacticians during the Allied invasion.

Royal Edward (ex-*Cairo*) was built in 1908 by Fairfield Shipbuilding & Engineering Company in Glasgow, Scotland. The eleven-thousand-ton vessel along with her sister ship, *Royal George,* was originally built for the British-owned Egyptian Mail Steamship Company for fast service between Marseilles and Alexandria. The service was unsuccessful, and the vessels were laid up until sold to Canadian Northern Steamships, Ltd. (Royal Line) and then placed in the Avonmouth to Montreal service in 1910. They were subsequently converted into troopships at the start of World War I.[1]

On 28 July 1915, troops boarded *Royal Edward* at Avonmouth and sailed that day for Alexandria, Egypt. She carried 220 crewmen, thirty-one officers and 1,336 men, reinforcements for the famed British 29th Infantry and details of

Royal Edward. Steamship Historical Society of America

the Royal Army Medical Corps, destined for Gallipoli, Turkey. Within a few months many of these men would join in the battle for the Gallipoli Peninsula and suffer heavy losses. The disaster of the Gallipoli campaign would prove to be the undoing of the First Lord of the Admiralty, Winston Churchill.

Captained by Comdr. P. M. Watton, R.N.R., *Royal Edward* was reported off Lizard Point, fifty miles southwest of Portsmouth on the twenty-eighth. On that same day *Royal George* sailed with troops from Davenport, England, for Gallipoli. After calling at Malta, *Royal George* arrived safely at Alexandria, Egypt, on 9 August and departed Alexandria on the eleventh, reaching Mudros harbor, Lemnos Island, on 13 August. Mudros was the staging point for the Allied fleet and ground forces that attacked the Dardanelles in April 1915. *Royal Edward* was to follow a day behind her sister ship.

The 127-ton German coastal Unterseeboot *UB14,* under the command of Kapitänleutnant Heino von Heimburg, was ninety feet long and ten feet wide and carried a crew of fourteen. The boat had been completed in early 1915 in Bremen and was hauled overland by train to Pola, an Austro-Hungarian port on the Adriatic Sea, where she was reassembled and launched anew to intercede British and French shipping in the Mediterranean. Her first victory was secured

Oberleutnant zur See Heinz Adolf von Heimburg, commanding officer of *UB14*. *U-Boot-Archiv*

on 6 July 1915, when she torpedoed and sank the Italian armored cruiser *Amalfi*. A week later she sailed for the Dardanelles; however, since her range was limited, she had to be towed more than halfway to her operating area by an Austrian destroyer. She finally reached Bodrum, Turkey, on 24 July. Being in a state of disrepair, a maintenance team had to be dispatched from Constantinople to conduct repairs. The team had to travel by train and camel to reach the docked boat.

After departing Bodrum, *UB14* encountered the British hospital ship *Soudan* on her first patrol in the Aegean Sea on 13 August, but she did not attack the clearly marked hospital ship. However, shortly afterward she sighted the unescorted *Royal Edward* six miles west of the island of Kandeliusa sailing for Mudros Harbor. Heimburg fired one torpedo from a mile away and hit the ship in the stern. The ship sank within six minutes. Some 935 troops went down with the ship due in part to the fact that just before the attack the troops had carried out a boat drill so, when the torpedo struck, many were below decks stowing their gear. The hospital ship *Soudan,* two French destroyers, and some trawlers quickly arrived on the scene to commence rescue operations. Unfortunately, only 661 men could be saved. *Soudan* rescued 440 survivors while the destroyers and trawlers picked up the other 221.[2]

Dr. C. J. G. Taylor, a medic on the *Soudan,* remembered the incident quite well:

. . . We set sail for Alexandria. On the way down and halfway to our destination we were having breakfast when we passed close to a large transport, the *Royal Edward,* steaming in the opposite direction. Within the hour we picked up her SOS saying she had been torpedoed. Captain Gill at once turned the ship through 180 degrees and we were soon speeding back along the course we had come. We arrived on the

The German U-Boat *UB14. U-Boot-Archiv*

Survivors of *Royal Edward* aboard the British steamship *Soudan*. *Imperial War Museum*

scene of the disaster about 10 A.M. The sea was littered with wreckage and lifeboats, many of which were bottom upwards to which men could be seen clinging. Others we could see hanging on to anything which could float. We promptly lowered boats to go to the rescue. In my boat was Harry Reah, the Chaplain, the Rev. McDawson, Bainbridge and one or two other Doctors. We were soon busy pulling men out of the water. One I remember had a fractured dislocation of the ankle, the joint was completely laid open and exposed, the foot was simply attached to the leg by the tendon achilles. We kept up the search till four in the afternoon by which time my boat had picked up forty survivors. It was a terrifically hot day and my bottom began to get very sore from rowing. When we at last got back to the ship and were hoisted in, all I wanted was a long cold drink . . . *Soudan* rescued all together 440 men out of a total of 1,500 or so souls which the *Royal Edward* had been carrying . . . The ship had been already pretty well strained to the limit of her accommodation before we picked up those 440 extra mouths to feed. We had to dispose of them as best we could on the decks, fortunately the weather was fine and hot and it was no hardship to live a few days in the open. The problem of clothing them and feeding them was satisfactorily coped with and the rescued were all most grateful. Of course, red tape had to interfere with the satisfaction we felt with doing what we thought was a good job of work.

When the Captain reported to Alexandria by radio that we had 440 survivors on board there was no message of congratulations only a terse demand that we should radio a full nominal list of survivors including the names and next of kin and their religion. When we secured alongside at Alexandria we were able to send our casualties ashore but no arrangements had been made for the accommodation of the *Royal Edward* survivors. In fact we gained the impression that the High Military authorities thought we were a confounded nuisance for having done what we did and we had to keep our guests for another day or two until high command deigned to send instructions for their disposal.[3]

The survivors of the 29th Division would in time find themselves and other elements of their division engaged in a horrific fight on the Helles beaches at Gallipoli. (The following section, which details that battle and the use of the collier-converted troopship *River Clyde* to transport many of the division's soldiers to the beaches, is one of devastation and heroics.) Thirteen troopers of the 29th won Victoria Crosses (Britain's highest military award) during the Gallipoli campaign.[4]

SS RIVER CLYDE

In a little-known corner of the Mediterranean Sea, the Gallipoli Peninsula, in eight and a half months of fighting on dusty brown plains and grass speckled slopes, in suffocating heat and freezing cold, almost a quarter of a million men would perish in one of the most disastrous amphibious campaign assaults in the history of military warfare.

The Dardanelles-Gallipoli operation had its beginning in Western Europe, where by 1914 the war had come to a standstill. Allied and Central power military leaders found themselves pouring men and materials into the so-called Western Front with negligible results. Consequently, Allied strategists became vitally interested in opening a link to beleaguered Russia. Turkey remained neutral early in the war and through treaty agreements closed the Dardanelles to belligerent shipping. Thus, the Allies were unable to supply the Russians with much-needed munitions and draw in return from the vast quantities of excess grain that were piling up in Russian seaports.[5]

The situation changed in October 1914 when Turkey cast its lot with the Central Powers. Prior to this, Turkey and Germany had cemented closer ties, and it was no surprise to either adversary that a German Military Mission arrived in Turkey almost immediately tasked with reorganizing the Turkish Army. Germany sent one of its best tacticians, Gen. Liman von Sanders, to lead the mission. Allied leaders now looked to the capture of Constantinople (present-day Istanbul) as the only chance to open the waterway from the Mediterranean to the Black Sea. The situation came to a head when the Turks, in keeping with their new expansionist policy, invaded the Russian Caucasus. Russia quickly requested a diversionary action in the Aegean Sea to relieve the pressure of the fast-moving enemy offensive.[6]

The British initially turned their attention to a pure naval assault up the Dardanelles, with the capture of Constantinople as the final objective. After much argument among British military planners, the War Council gave Churchill, the First Lord of the Admiralty, the go-ahead on a naval operation that would destroy all forts at the mouth of the Dardanelles and sweep the enemy minefields as far upstream as the Narrows. The fleet was to move beyond this point only if the initial results were successful.[7]

In the meantime, Turkish officials knew that a forcing of the Dardanelles and an attack on Constantinople were imminent. The defense of the city was turned over to the German ambassador, who in turn placed Adm. Guido Von Usedom in command. Von Usedom acted quickly. He moved all available military resources below the Narrows and commenced building fortifications and positioning artillery. Minefields were carefully planned and laid to check the advance of Allied warships. At the same time, General Von Sanders took charge of the Turkish Fifth Army on the Gallipoli Peninsula. Von Sanders trained his army with one thought in mind: Meet the enemy in Asia Minor or on the shores of Gallipoli, not in the streets of Constantinople. He rushed the construction of bridges and roads to ensure lines of communications for reinforcement and supply of Turkish forces positioned along the straits.[8]

British intelligence on the enemy's preparations was lacking as the Allied fleet, under the command of Vice Adm. Stackville H. Carden, approached the straits in mid-February 1915. The first phase of the operation—the destruction of the forts at the mouth of the Dardanelles—proved to be impossible without ground support to silence Turkish guns. Although few personnel casualties were suffered by either side, the forts were severely damaged, and Allied ships were hit by Turkish return fire. After sixteen days of advance and retreat, the fleet came to

River Clyde at *V* Beach, Cape Helles, Gallipoli, April 1915. *Imperial War Museum*

a halt as Carden pressed Churchill for ground units. Agitated, Churchill barraged his reluctant admiral with cablegrams, calling for immediate continuance of the naval operation. An embittered Carden pressed onward, and by mid-March the fleet was ready to initiate the second phase of the operation: an attack on the Narrows. By this time Admiral Carden was near nervous collapse, and just forty-eight hours before the commencement of the attack he resigned his command, passing the helm to Rear Adm. John de Robeck.[9]

On the morning of 18 March 1915, a near score of British and French warships in line abreast formations moved toward the Narrows and opened fire. As the vessels shattered the fortress guns at Kilid Bahr and Chanak, they exercised planned maneuvers that called for the forward line of British ships (*Queen Elizabeth, Agamemnon. Lord Nelson, Inflexible, Prince George,* and *Triumph*) to initially bombard the Narrows forts; then six French battleships were ordered to the van, passing through the British ships that continued to fire. After two hours of shelling, de Robeck ordered the French ships to wheel about and retire as he moved up four more British battleships that had been waiting in the rear. An undetected minefield met the French ships as they moved in column down the Asian side of the straits, and the deadly field quickly began to take its toll. The French battleship *Bouvet* struck a mine and went down with a loss of nearly six hundred men. De Robeck immediately sent his minesweepers in to clear the way. As they advanced to start sweeping operations, they were caught in a deadly crossfire from field guns on both shores. Trapped in a devastating barrage, the small wooden craft took severe punishment before retreating. Ordered not to proceed up the channel until all minefields were cleared, de Robeck was ultimately forced to order a general retirement.

As the British warships began to retreat they ran into immediate trouble. *Ocean* and *Irresistible* struck mines and sank. *Inflexible,* heavily damaged by a mine, managed to limp from the straits. Nevertheless, many felt that the enemy was defeated and that victory was within the grasp of the fleet. However, Field Marshal Lord Horatio Kitchner, British secretary of state for war, decided that a ground assault would be necessary if the operation were to succeed. He ordered the Australian and New Zealand Army Corps (ANZAC) to proceed from Egypt to Lemnos, an island twenty miles west of Gallipoli. The 29th Division was later ordered from England to the island, and by the middle of March eighty-one thousand troops were at Lemnos preparing to invade the peninsula.

Kitchner had appointed Gen. Ian Hamilton as commander of the Mediterranean Expeditionary Force. Since the beginning of the campaign, Hamilton had begun planning for a ground assault on the Gallipoli Peninsula. The capture of the forts on the plateau at Kilid Bahr became the principal objective of his army. He planned to land his most experienced troops, the British 29th Army Division, at Cape Helles, designated *V* beach. The 29th consisted of three thousand soldiers (1st Royal Munster Fusiliers, two companies of the 2nd Hampshire Fusiliers, one of the 1st Royal Dublin Fusiliers, and a field company of Royal Engineers). While the 29th Division was landing at *V* beach, five thousand other soldiers, including ANZAC troops, were to go ashore at beaches *S, W, X,* and *Y,* flanking *V* beach. They were ordered to wait at their own beach positions until the 29th moved up the peninsula and then join them in a coordinated drive on Kilid Bahr. The flanking troops reached their beaches in small boats towed by steam trawlers. The landings at beaches *Y* and *X* had gone smoothly; however, as the 1st Lancashire Fusiliers went ashore at beach *W* they were mowed down by Turkish machine gunners. Six Victoria Crosses were awarded in this action, and despite heavy losses the fusiliers fought their way through barbed wire and gained a foothold on the beach. However, the landing at *V* beach proved to be a disaster.[10]

Men of the Australian and New Zealand divisions on the transport, the ex-German *Lutzow* from which they landed at dawn at Gallipoli Peninsula, 25 April 1915. *Imperial War Museum*

At dawn on 25 April 1915, Allied naval guns opened up on enemy positions along *V* beach. Without aerial spotting the barrage proved ineffective. The big guns ceased their firing at sunrise as picket boats loaded with soldiers moved toward the sandy beach line. During this brief lull, Turkish infantrymen, somewhat benumbed by the fierce shelling, scrambled back to their trenches and watched as the boats reached shore. At 6:30 A.M., as Royal Dublin Fusiliers of the 29th Army Division prepared to jump into the water and wade onto the beach, they were met with devastating gunfire. Of the initial landing party of approximately 240 men, only 40 made it ashore without being hit. The waters along the beach and around the boats began to turn red with the blood of wounded and dead Fusiliers.[11]

Shortly thereafter the Turks watched the four-thousand-ton SS *River Clyde,* a ten-year-old Glasgow-built collier converted into a troopship, approach the beach. Painted a dull brown color, she presented a peculiar sight. Four doors or salleyports had been cut in her sides from which wooden gangways extended forward to her bow. She towed a 150-foot steam hopper and three large lighters.

Two miles from the shore the steam hopper *Argyll* was to move forward of the collier and provide a jetty as the ships reached the beach. Any gaps were to be filled by the lighters. Two thousand Royal Munster Fusiliers and the Hampshire Regiment of the 29th Division were huddled in the holds of the collier waiting for the signal to race ashore. Armored and sandbagged casemates housing machine guns were positioned on the foredeck of the ship to provide covering fire for the troops. In command of the operation and collier was acting Capt. Edward Unwin. Unwin's number one was Midn. George Drewry. In addition, the ship carried a crew of six seamen, six engine room ratings, a carpenter, a reservist, Leading Seaman William Williams (who talked his way on board), and Lt. Col. Weir de Laney Williams, who manned the makeshift bridge with Unwin. Drewry was ordered to command the hopper that was crewed by Seaman George Samson and six Greek sailors.

As the first wave of fusiliers came under murderous fire at *V* beach, Unwin's plan began to unravel as his cadre of ships and barges headed for the shore with the second wave of troops. Having had to maneuver to avoid arriving before the initial wave, *River Clyde* beached further out than planned. To complicate matters, the hopper had also grounded on its port side. Watching the horrific losses experienced by the first wave, Drewry and Samson jumped over the side of the hopper and, swimming through frigid waters, hauled the lighters, which had been connected by a rope, to the stern of the hoppers. They successfully moved the lighters to the bow of *Clyde*. Unwin left the "bridge" with Seaman Williams, and they made their way down to one of the lighters. Using the steam pinnace that had towed the first wave of boats to the beach, they moved one of the lighters close to a spit of rocks just offshore. When the water became too shallow for the pinnace, the two men jumped into the water and pushed the lighter within a few yards of the beach. Drewry threw them a rope from the lighter, which they held taut keeping the bridge linkage in place while standing waist deep in water. All the while Unwin and Williams were engulfed in a hail of gunfire. Unwin finally gave the order for the troops to disembark.

Two companies of the fusiliers immediately exited the ship through the salleyports onto the gangways only to be met by gunfire from four Turkish machine-gun emplacements that overlooked the beach. Within minutes the Turkish fire decimated the fusiliers attempting to come ashore. Those that followed suffered the same fate. Dead and wounded lay on the gangways, on the lighters, and in the water. Air Commodore Samson came flying over the beach in a biplane at that moment and noted that the calm blue sea was red with blood for a distance of fifty yards from the shore. Those that made it ashore were shot while trying to dig themselves in. When soldiers stopped coming out of the ports, Drewry checked the holds where British soldiers had been transported and found many soldiers dead or wounded around the salleyports.

About the same time that the surviving 1st Royal Munster Fusiliers reached the beach, Williams was mortally wounded. Unwin dropped the line and went to the aid of his shipmate. With no one holding the line that kept the bridge to the shore intact, the link was broken and the lighter drifted out into deeper water. Drewry swung into action and took a line from another lighter that was closest to *Clyde* and pulled it back to the rock spit. He then carried Unwin back on board the ship where the captain could be treated for hypothermia brought on by his prolonged immersion in the frigid waters.

A third wave of four boats loaded with troops arrived from the fleet offshore and came alongside the starboard side of *Clyde*. Drewry went on board the third lighter where he met Lieutenant Morse, the senior member of the newly arrived troops. Morse's thirty-eight-man party was tasked with ferrying reinforcements ashore. His men knew about the situation on the beach because they had helped transport the wounded and dead back to fleet ships from the first two attempted landings. First they had to attempt to restore the bridge crucial to the landing operation. While leaving the boats and boarding the lighter, many more soldiers were lost to enemy fire. About all the remaining troops could do was lie low in the lighter. After about an hour of inaction, Drewry, though inflicted with a shrapnel wound to the head, and Morse attempted to join the lighters together. With the help of Midn. Wilfrid St. Aubyn Malleson, the steam hopper and lighters were positioned, and a new landing bridge was connected at 9 A.M. A half hour later another attempt to land troops was ordered, and as a company of the 2nd Hampshires raced through the salleyports and down the gangway they were immediately cut down by the enemy. The disembarkation was again halted. With the operation at a standstill, soldiers and seamen began to recover the dead and wounded, in the process exposing themselves to Turkish guns.

Numerous acts of bravery were displayed as wounded and dying fusiliers were retrieved and brought aboard *Clyde*. Among the most heroic was Captain

Unwin, who rescued many injured soldiers. Near collapse and wounded, he and other rescuers managed to climb aboard a pinnace and play dead until the craft could be pulled back to *Clyde* by rope.

A thousand troops still remained on *Clyde* as well as in boats carrying hundreds of troops some distance offshore. No one in charge seemed willing to order another landing for fear of sending men to certain destruction. When dusk fell and darkness concealed the landing forces, the surviving troops in *Clyde* and troops waiting in boats offshore managed to land and cling to a thin perimeter of the beach. Allied forces never did take Kilid Bahr or reach Achi Baba. Beachheads were established but advances were halted by the enemy, and soon there developed a stalemate much like that which occurred on the Western Front. By November 1915 it became obvious that the Allies could not gain their objective. The order to evacuate was given by Kitchner, and during the next few months some 115,000 men were removed from the beaches with remarkable efficiency. Turkish losses were placed at 300,000 dead and wounded. Allied dead numbered 46,000 while some 219,000 wounded were evacuated from the peninsula during the campaign. Of the 46,000 British, French, Australian, and New Zealand dead, only 17,000 have known graves.

Thirty-nine Victoria Crosses were awarded to men who fought at Gallipoli. Six were earned by those who heroically met the enemy at *V* beach. The six so honored were Acting Capt. E. Unwin, Midn. G. Drewry, Midn. W. Malleson, Sub.-Lt. A. Tisdall, Able Seaman W. Williams, and Seaman George Samson.[12]

Aftermath

George Leslie Drewry was promoted to acting lieutenant in November 1915 and appointed to HMS *Conqueror.* Two months later he was awarded the Victoria Cross by King George V at Buckingham Palace. Since he was the first RNR officer to receive the Cross, he was presented with a Sword of Honour by the Imperial Merchant Guild. By mid-1918 he commanded the decoy trawler HMT *William Jackson.* While serving on the *Jackson* a block fell from a derrick and struck him. His skull was fractured and his left arm broken; he died the day after the incident.

GALLIA

During World War I the loss of the French liners *Gallia, La Provence,* and *Amiral Magon* accounted for 24 percent of all passenger ship casualties during the war.[13]

Germany's leading U-Boat "ace" Kapitänleutnant Lothar von
Arnauld de la Periere, commanding officer of *U35*. *U-Boot-Archiv*

Converted to troopships to support the Gallipoli offense, their sinking represented the loss of 3,180 soldiers.[14] By far the greatest loss of men occurred when
the German U-boat *U35* sank *Gallia* in October 1916 off the coast of Sardinia
in the Mediterranean Sea. Commanding *U35* was Kapitänleutnant Lothar von
Arnauld de la Periere, Germany's leading U-boat ace.[15]

Gallia was built in 1913 to provide passenger service between Bordeaux and
the River Plate in South America. The three-masted, 14,966-ton ship, capable

U35, which sank *Gallia* in October 1916 in the Mediterranean. *Naval Historical Center*

of doing twenty knots, could carry 1,086 passengers in four classes. Following the onset of World War I, it was acquisitioned for military service.[16] During the first week of October 1916, the ship loaded twenty-seven hundred French and Serbian troops at Marseilles and sailed for Salonika (Thessalonika), Greece. The troops were destined to join British, Australian, and New Zealander forces already fighting the Turks at Gallipoli.[17]

Gallia was spotted by *U35* lookouts on 4 October zigzagging unescorted at eighteen knots off Cape Matapan. It took all of von Arnauld's skill to position his boat to make an attack. With only one torpedo in a stern tube, *Gallia* offered herself up to him when she turned unexpectedly, which enabled von Arnauld to close within nine hundred yards. Although he was faced with a difficult shooting angle, he decided to take a chance and fired. As the torpedo streaked away von Arnauld took *U35* deep. When he heard the roar of an explosion, he took the boat up to periscope depth to witness the stricken *Gallia* in her death throes. He recalled,

> The picture of that floundering vessel sticks in my mind with undiminished horror
> . . . there was a wild panic on the stricken vessel's crowded deck. Lifeboats were being

The French liner *Gallia*. *The Mariners' Museum*

lowered by men too much in a panic to let them down slowly and safely. Hundreds of soldiers were jumping into the water and swimming around. The sea became a terrible litter of overturned lifeboats, overcrowded and swamped lifeboats, rafts and struggling men. After what I had seen, I did not feel elated.

The torpedo explosion destroyed the ship's radio equipment; thus no SOS could be sent. The following day 1,362 troopers were picked up by the French cruiser *Chateaurenault*. The loss of life numbered 1,338 men. *Chateaurenault* was subsequently sunk in December 1917 off the Atlantic coast by the Austro-Hungarian submarine *U38*.[18]

Several months before he sank *Gallia*, von Arnauld intercepted and sank *La Provence* (*Provence II*), one of the Cie Generale fast liners that was en route from Toulon to Greece. Before the war *La Provence* provided transatlantic passenger service between La Havre and New York. The 13,753-ton ship could accommodate 1,354 passengers in three classes and was capable of making 21.5 knots. Following the outbreak of the war she served with the French navy as an auxiliary cruiser and troopship. On the day she was sunk she was carrying seventeen hundred troops to the battlefields of Gallipoli. As a result, close to one thousand of these men went down with the ship, which sank rapidly after being torpedoed.[19]

The French liner *La Provence. Steamship Historical Society of America*

The 5,566-ton *Amiral Magon* was torpedoed without warning by a German submarine on 25 January 1917 while she was en route to Salonika with nine hundred French soldiers aboard. The damage to the ship was so cataclysmic that the ship went down within ten minutes, taking the crew and troopers with her.[20]

It is interesting to note that Kapitänleutnant Lothar von Arnauld de la Periere still holds the record as the most successful submariner of all time. His achievements were unexcelled during the two world wars. By the time he returned to Germany in March 1918, he had sunk two warships, one armed merchant cruiser, five troopships, 125 steamers and sixty-two sailing vessels for a total of 453,716 tons.[21]

World War II, 1940–1943

ARANDORA STAR

Prior to the beginning of World War II, there was a large number of Germans, Austrians, and Italians residing in the British Isles, working in the hotel, restaurant, and engineering industries as well as other fields. Many were longtime residents, and even included expatriates and refugees from Nazi Germany. With war on the horizon, the British Home Office had already prepared a system to classify aliens living in the United Kingdom according to their potential danger to security in case of war.[1]

On the outbreak of war a certain number of Germans and Austrians were interned forthwith. Thereafter, all Germans and Austrians at liberty were examined by a tribunal and classified as follows: Category A, those ordered to be interned; Category B, those exempted from internment but subject to special restrictions; and Category C, those exempted from internment and from special restrictions.[2]

As early as October 1939, German aliens appeared before tribunals to determine if they constituted a security risk. Those so identified were removed to internment camps located across England.[3] During this time, there was great concern in England about the real possibility of invasion. In March 1940 the Germans had bombed the naval base at Scapa Flow. Denmark capitulated in

April, and the following month Norway was invaded although British naval forces continued to contest the occupation of key Norwegian ports until June. In May German blitzkrieg infantry and armored units swept across Belgium, Luxembourg, and the Netherlands, and France was on the verge of collapse as the Allied armies began evacuating the country on 27 May. However, that same month, Britain elected a new prime minister, Winston Churchill, and the nation's spirits were bolstered. "Winnie" was back!

There was real concern regarding the security risk large numbers of internees in a country in danger of "imminent" invasion presented. On 3 June Lord Swinton, on behalf of the Home Defense Executive, "represented to the Lord President the danger of retaining alien internees and prisoners of war in country."[4]

The fear of invasion was aggravated on 10 June, with Italy's declaration of war on Britain and France. Following Italy's declaration of war, Italians were added to the list of potentially dangerous aliens. On 11 June the minister of home defense reported to the War Cabinet that, with certain exceptions, Italian males between the ages of sixteen and seventy would be interned.[5] At that same time, the cabinet was informed of Canada's agreement to accept four thousand internees and three thousand POWs. A plan was devised to ship the internees to Canada and Australia, using three ships. The first ship to sail was *Duchess of York* with twenty-five hundred internees aboard.[6] The second ship, *Arandora Star,* was "placed at the disposal of the War Office on 19 June, the date of sailing given as 25 June" although actual embarkation didn't begin until the 30th.[7]

The Blue Star liner *Arandora Star* had enjoyed a glamorous prewar career as a hostess to royalty, celebrities, and the wealthy as she cruised to some of the world's most exotic ports: Sierra Leone, Cuba, Florida, and the Gold Coast in the winter; Germany and the Scandinavian fjords in the summer.[8]

Built and originally named *Arandora* by Cammel Laird and Company shipyard at Birkenhead on Merseyside, Liverpool, she was originally designed for fast passenger and refrigerated cargo service to South America. Launched on 4 January 1927,[9] she was refitted in 1929 as a cruise liner with a capacity of 354 first-class passengers and renamed *Arandora Star.*[10]

Her four steam turbine engines propelled her 14,694 gross tons at a speed of sixteen knots,[11] taking her on one winter cruise to South Africa, Java, Malaya, Ceylon, and Egypt. But in the 1930s, as *Arandora Star* sailed the world, the

Oberleutnant Günther Prien, commanding officer of *U47*.
U-Boot-Archiv

world headed toward war. *Arandora Star* was on a passage to New York when
Germany invaded Poland on 1 September. Two days later, England was at war.

After disembarking her passengers in New York, she sailed for England, docking at Falmouth, and after paying off her crew was put at the disposal of the
Admiralty and the Minister of Transportation. Deemed inappropriate for conversion into an armed merchant cruiser, she awaited other duties and was
ordered to Avonmouth in December 1939.[12]

Much thought and concern had been expressed over how to counter the
threat posed by German U-boats. One possible solution was to create a light,
but strong, obstruction to intercept torpedoes, an obstruction that was also
portable enough to be towed on the flanks of convoys.

Thus it was that *Arandora Star* was equipped with the experimental Admiralty
Net Defense, and a system of booms was installed. She next sailed to Portsmouth
where she was fitted with nets of various meshes. Each morning, *Arandora Star*
sailed into the channel and conducted her trials with the nets in place. Gear alterations were made at night for the following day's trials. Then for reasons known

only to the Admiralty, *Arandora Star* was ordered to Devonport in late May where the booms and other gear were removed.

The Admiralty Net Defense was subsequently installed on more than seven hundred ships by the end of the war. Although there were shortcomings (the nets only covered 60–75 percent of a ship) it was successful three out of four times. Of the twenty-one ships contacted by U-boat torpedoes, only six were lost, and the other fifteen torpedoes exploded in the net with minimal damage or became entangled in the net and failed to detonate.[13]

After the gear was removed, *Arandora Star* was ordered to Liverpool, where she narrowly missed being hit on a night attack by a single aircraft. Ordered to sea the next day, she was directed to rendezvous with the aircraft carrier HMS *Glorious* and the antiaircraft cruiser HMS *Coventry* off Narvik, Norway, as part of Operation Alphabet, the evacuation of British and Allied forces from Norway on 5–8 June.

Arandora Star entered the fjord on or about 4 June and began embarking sixteen hundred officers and men of the Royal Air Force, as well as some Polish and French troops. In sum, the operation rescued approximately twenty-five thousand men, but at the cost of the troopship *Orama,* the trawler HMS *Juniper,* the tanker *Oil Pioneer,* the carrier *Glorious,* and two destroyers, HMS *Acasta* and *Ardent.*[14]

After disembarking her troops at Glasgow, *Arandora Star* sailed to Swansea, where she was ordered to proceed to Brest and rescue as many troops or refugees as possible. The bombing was so severe that it prevented most from getting out, and only a few could be rescued. France was crumbling, and after disembarking the half dozen rescued refugees and refueling at Falmouth, *Arandora Star* returned to the French coast at Quiberon Bay, where she removed about three hundred troops and refugees without incident and carried them back to Falmouth. Next ordered to Bayonne, she was again greeted by large numbers of bombers, but overloaded small craft were able to carry about five hundred out to the ship. The task of transferring the refugees was complicated because the exchange had to be accomplished while the ship attempted to evade German bombers.[15]

Despite the chaotic conditions, *Arandora Star* returned one last time to the French coast, embarking seventeen hundred troops, including most of the Polish army staff and troops at St. Jean de Luz. Unmolested by bombers that appeared

U47 returning to base after patrol. *U-Boot-Archiv*

overhead, she sailed to Liverpool. It was in Liverpool on 29 June that the senior officers learned that they would be sailing to St. Johns, Newfoundland, in Canada with a cargo of German and Italian internees, as well as a small group of prisoners-of-war.[16]

Sources differ as to exactly how many internees boarded *Arandora Star* that morning, but the consensus seems to be 565 German internees (including 86 POWs) and 734 Italians, or almost 1,300 total.[17] To further complicate the political situation, the Germans included Austrians, Nazis, anti-Nazis, Jews, and a complement of merchant seamen.[18] Combined with a crew of 174 and two hundred guards and interpreters, the total on board when she weighed anchor numbered 1,673.

The internees continued to board the afternoon and evening of the thirtieth, and it was past midnight before all were settled in. *Arandora Star* departed early on the morning of 1 July, leaving without an escort in good weather at a speed of fifteen knots.

Arandora Star sailed past the Point of Ayre, then the Isle of Man, Kintyre, and Malin Head, which she passed at 3 A.M. on the morning of the 2 July. At about

6:15 A.M. she was seventy-five miles west of Bloody Foreland heading toward the Atlantic.[19] At the same time, the German U-boat *U47* was en route back to her home port of Kiel when an officer on watch spotted the ship.

U47 was a type VIIB submarine, built by Germaniawerft, Kiel, and launched on 17 December 1938 under the command of (then) Oberleutnant Günther Prien. Celebrated for his daring raid on Scapa Flow Naval Base, where he sank the battleship HMS *Royal Oak* on 14 October 1939, Prien had only one damaged torpedo left aboard when *Arandora Star* was sighted, and after some quick repair work it was launched.

The torpedo struck below the waterline on the starboard side near the after engine room, wrecking the turbines and knocking out the main and emergency generators, as well as damaging two of her fourteen lifeboats. However, the ship was still able to send out an SOS that was received and acknowledged at Marlin Head.

Victor Tolaini, an Italian internee, describing the sinking in his memoirs, remembered, "A torpedo struck home and the ship began to sink. A pronounced list to the right made the launching of lifeboats on the left deck impossible. The force of the explosion jammed most of the cabin doors, trapping many of the occupants. The lights went out and people had to grope their way out."[20]

Accounts differ as to the degree of panic on deck, but it is uncontested that more than half of the ninety rafts aboard made it into the water, that German merchant sailors assisted in the launching and manning of the lifeboats, and that many older Italians refused to leave the sinking ship. No instructions had been given regarding the procedures for abandoning ship, or in the use of life vests or life belts, which were available but not issued.[21]

At approximately 7:15 A.M., the ship's siren sounded seven short and one long blasts (the signal to abandon ship), and Capt. E. W. Moulton and his senior officers "walked over the side" into the rising water. As Fehle noted, "The ship was settling with an increasing lift, and it appeared that she broke in two by a second explosion [apparently a boiler explosion], before she finally sank. It was a dreadful sight as many people were still on the upper decks holding on to the railing." This was approximately five minutes later, at 7:20 A.M.[22]

Coastal Command, alerted by Marlin Head, responded quickly, and by late morning an RAF *Sunderland* flying boat appeared overhead and dropped food, medicine, and a message saying that help was on the way.

Sometime between 1 P.M. and 2 P.M., the Canadian destroyer HCMS *St. Laurent* (H83), under the command of Comdr. H. G. DeWolf, arrived and began picking up survivors, assisted later by the British destroyer HMS *Walker* (D27).

The search continued for five hours, and although many were pulled from the sea—often through the heroic efforts of the destroyers' crewmen—805 men were lost, including Captain Moulton, twelve officers, forty-two of the crew, thirty-seven guards, 470 Italians and 243 Germans.[23]

The survivors were landed at Glenrock, Scotland, early on the morning of 3 July. The sinking of *Arandora Star* led to a public outcry and a re-evaluation of the policy of deportation, resulting in the decision to intern enemy aliens only in Britain.[24] The name *Arandora Star* was never used again by the Blue Star Line.

Oberleutnant Günther Prien, "The Bull of Scapa Flow"
The first member of the Kriegsmarine to be awarded the coveted Knight's Cross during World War II, Günther Prien was born in the central German town of Osterfeld in Thuringia on 16 January 1908. The son of a judge and the oldest of three children, Prien went to sea as a merchant seaman in 1923, at age fifteen, to help support his mother.

After graduating from a three-month training course at the Seaman's College at Finkenwarder, near Hamburg, Prien was assigned to the sailing ship *Hamburg*. He spent the next eight years learning the craft of seamanship, working up from cabin boy, deckhand, and cook, to earn his master's certificate in 1931, at the age of twenty-four.

The nation's dire financial situation in 1932 led to reductions in all areas of the German economy, including the merchant marine, and Prien soon found himself out of a job. After working as a laborer on work gangs, Prien volunteered for the Reichsmarine, the successor to the old Imperial Navy, in January 1933, just as Adolf Hitler and the National Socialists were coming to power.

After a year as a Fahnrich zur See (officer candidate) aboard the light cruiser *Königsberg,* Prien, now a Leutnant zur See, transferred to U-boats. After training under (then) Kapitän zur See Karl Dönitz, he served aboard *U26* under Kapitänleutnant Werner Hartmann, patrolling Spanish waters during the Spanish Civil War.

Arandora Star. Steamship Historical Society of America

On 17 December 1938, Prien, now an Oberleutnant zur See, was given command of *U47*. A Kapitänleutnant at the start of World War II, he earned his first victory sinking the 2,407-ton British steamer *Bosnia* on 9 September 1939, only two days after the start of the war. It was his first war patrol, and two additional British freighters, *Rio Claro* and *Gartavon,* were sent to the bottom before he returned home on 15 September. For his actions, he was awarded the Iron Cross 2nd Class ten days later.

Prien achieved immortal fame when, on 14 October 1939, *U47* penetrated the heavily defended British Home Fleet naval base at Scapa Flow in the Orkney Islands and sank the 31,200-ton battleship HMS *Royal Oak* at her mooring. Commander Rear Adm. H. F. C. Blagrove and 833 of the crew were lost in the attack.

Early on the fifteenth, Prien returned to Wilhelmshaven, where Dönitz and Grossadmiral Erich Raeder met the ship, presenting Prien with the Iron Cross First Class, and the entire crew with Iron Crosses. That afternoon, Raeder, Dönitz, and Prien flew to Berlin aboard the Führer's personal plane, and the following day Hitler himself presented Prien with the *Ritterkreuz,* the coveted

Knight's Cross, calling the raid "the proudest deed that a German U-boat could possibly carry out." He later earned oak leaves for his Knight's Cross, receiving the award on 20 October 1940 after battling the Allied convoy HX79 the previous day and sinking four ships.

During ten patrols, *U47* sank thirty-one ships (191,918 tons) and damaged another eight (62,751 tons). On his sixth patrol, when he sank *Arandora Star,* seven additional ships were destroyed by Prien's torpedoes.

Departing St. Nazaire, France, on 20 February 1941, at the start of her tenth patrol, *U47* attacked convoy OB293 six days later, sinking four ships, *Kasongo, Diala, Rydboholm,* and *Borgland* (20,193 tons). The last radio transmission from *U47* was received on 7 March, after which she went missing, never to be heard from again.

British destroyer HMS *Wolverine* is credited in most historical sources with the sinking of *U47.* While the boat was maneuvering to get in position for another attack on the convoy, HMS *Verity* and HMS *Wolverine* detected *U47* on their type 286 radar equipment. Prien went deep and survived five hours of hunting by ASDIC, only to surface for some unknown reason a short distance from the *Wolverine.* Prien immediately dived while *Wolverine* raced to Prien's last position and dropped charges set for shallow depth. *Verity* followed dropping ten depth charges. Oil was sighted on the surface and the *Wolverine* hydrophone operator reported underwater breaking-up noises. *U47* suddenly surfaced once again only to disappear, apparently out of control. *Wolverine* went over the spot where the U-boat disappeared and dropped additional depth charges. The *Wolverine's* crew watched from the stern as the explosions broke the surface. They could see a bright orange glow beneath the sea, which seemed to last for ten seconds. Then pieces of wreckage began to bob to the surface. Prien and his entire crew were lost in the attack.

LANCASTRIA

When asked to name the greatest passenger ship disasters, many might respond with *Lusitania,* or perhaps *Titanic.* Few would answer with *Lancastria,* whose losses exceeded both ships combined. Despite being, what some have called, "the greatest maritime disaster in Britain's history," the circumstances of her sinking, largely unknown to the general public, have remained officially secret since 1940, a secret initiated at the personal instructions of Prime Minister Winston Churchill.[25]

By mid-June 1940 the situation in Europe was grim for the Allied forces. France was on the verge of collapse, and Italy entered the war on the side of the Axis powers on 10 June. For nine days (26 May–3 June), troops of the British Expeditionary Force and their allies scrambled to evacuate Dunkirk and escape to the safety of England.[26] With the route out of Dunkirk closed, Allied soldiers raced south toward St. Nazaire trying to stay ahead of the pursuing Wehrmacht. Waiting at dockside, or anchored outside the harbor, were seventeen vessels of varying types sent to rescue and evacuate the retreating troops and civilians.[27] Among those ships was the Cunard liner *Lancastria*.

Built as *Tyrrhenia* by William Beardmore and Company, Limited, at Dalmuir on the Clyde, Glasgow, Scotland, her keel was laid on 2 June 1919 and she was launched on 31 May 1920. She and her sister ship, *Cameronia,* were constructed during the building boom to replace shipping lost in the First World War. Her "fitting out" was delayed due to difficulties at the builder's yard, but by 13 June 1922 she was ready for her maiden voyage from Liverpool to Quebec and Montreal.[28]

Sailing for the Cunard/White Star Lines, her twin Brown-Curtis double reduction geared turbines propelled the 16,243-ton *Tyrrhenia* across the Atlantic at speeds of up to 16.5 knots. In February 1924 her name was changed to *Lancastria,* and she was refitted to carry 580 cabin and one thousand third-class passengers. In the years before the war, the ship sailed back and forth across the Atlantic from Liverpool and Glasgow to Quebec, Montreal, Halifax, Boston, and New York, as well as Gibraltar, Naples, Hamburg, and Genoa, with cruises to the Mediterranean, the Caribbean, the Bahamas, and Bermuda.[29]

Lancastria began a six-day cruise from New York to Nassau on 2 September 1939 and was at sea when war was declared the following day. The ship returned to New York, where after her portholes were blacked out and she was repainted a battleship grey she sailed unescorted for home with a stop to load cargo at Halifax on 21 September.

Upon her arrival at the Royal Victoria Dock in London at 4:30 P.M. on 5 October, she was requisitioned by His Majesty's government for use as a troop transport, and RMS *Lancastria* became HMT *Lancastria.* After the installation of defensive guns, she began a series of voyages back and forth across the Atlantic carrying Canadian civilians home on her westward voyage, and returning to England with vital war cargo, including crated aircraft on her decks.[30]

Lancastria. Steamship Historical Society of America

As early as 1 March, when Hitler ordered the invasion of Norway, the Scandinavian country was recognized by both sides as being of strategic importance. The Allies needed control of the coastline in order to strengthen its blockade. Germany needed the coastline for naval bases and to keep supply lines open for Norway's iron ore, vital to Germany's ability to wage war. On 9 April Germany launched Operation Weserubung, a pre-emptive air and sea strike against Norway, attacking Denmark at the same time.

Although *Lancastria* was ordered to Scapa Flow in the spring of 1940 in preparation for carrying troops to Norway, high command determined that large liners would be too vulnerable in the restricted waters of the Norwegian fjords, and the plan was canceled. British, French, and Polish troops were landed to assist the Norwegians, occupying the ports of Narvik, Namsos, and Trondheim on 15 April. *Lancastria* was utilized to help evacuate these same troops from 3 June to 8 June, when the port was recaptured by the Germans. Norway surrendered two days later, on 10 June.[31]

Lancastria dropped the evacuated troops in Glasgow and then transported other soldiers to Reykjavik, Iceland. She returned to Liverpool with a load of civilian detainees on 12 June, with the intention of paying off her crew and docking in the shipyard for a much-needed overhaul and refitting. Although the Dunkirk evacuation was over, thousands of British and Allied troops remained along the coast, hoping to be rescued before being overrun by German armor. All available ships were recruited to assist in the evacuations, and *Lancastria* recalled her crew and sailed for Plymouth on the afternoon of the fourteenth.[32]

As her captain, Rudolph Sharp, stated in his report of 26 June 1940: "We left Plymouth at midnight on the 15th June for Quiberon Bay where we arrived at 6:00 P.M. on the 16th. We left Quiberon Bay that night at midnight and anchored in the Charpentier Roads, St. Nazaire, at 4:00 A.M. on the 17th June. We lay at anchor in 12 fathoms of water, and from 8:00 A.M. on the 17th until noon we embarked 5,200 troops and a number of refugees including women and children."[33]

Troops were ferried out to *Lancastria* and other ships in small craft. Among those present in the harbor were *Glenaffaric, Oronsay, Fabian,* SS *John Holt* (convoy commander), and the escort destroyers HMS *Havelock* and HMS *Highlander. Lancastria* became so crowded that troops were accommodated on the open decks. She waited in the harbor until the other ships and her escorts were ready, although some accounts have her receiving passengers as late as 4 P.M. At 1:48 P.M., German Junker JU-88 and Dornier Do-17 bombers from the Luftwaffe's Kampfgeschwader 30 attacked, striking the nearby liner *Oronsay* in the bridge. Despite being struck, she sustained only minor damage and loss of life and sailed for England.[34]

At approximately 4 P.M., *Lancastria* was signaled to get under way, but without escort. She was preparing to haul in her anchor and swing about when a JU-88 dive bomber began a run on the ship. Most sources agree that the JU-88 went into a dive, dropping a string of four bombs, but in the confusion it is uncertain whether the liner was struck by two, three, or all four of the bombs. One bomb exploded close to the port side, rupturing her almost-full fuel tank and spilling a large quantity of oil into the sea. (The spill killed many and hampered rescue operations.) One bomb is said to have gone straight down the funnel of the ship, detonating in the engine room and blowing large holes in the ship's sides. Captain Sharp stated that besides the funnel, bombs struck the No. 2, No. 3, and No. 4 holds.

Lancastria survivors with Queen Elizabeth, 1972. *Imperial War Museum*

Wherever the bombs hit, all communication systems aboard ship were disabled, and fires started fore and aft. The damage was so extensive that the ship sank within ten to fifteen minutes, trapping many belowdecks.[35] Those who escaped the ship had to contend with the thick oil as well as machine-gun strafing by the bombers. At one point, the bombers dropped incendiary bombs, attempting to ignite the oil, but were unsuccessful.

There was an insufficient number of rafts, boats, and life belts to accommodate the number of men aboard, and many of the soldiers who couldn't swim remained on the ship. Other vessels, large and small, responded to assist in the rescue but were mired by the 1,407 tons of fuel oil on the water's surface and the bombing raid, still in progress. Approximately twenty minutes after being struck, *Lancastria* rolled to port, capsized, and sank bow first. Those in the water heard those remaining on board singing "Roll Out the Barrel" and "There'll Always be an England" as the ship slid under the waves. By most accounts, 2,477 men were rescued from the sea, including Captain Sharp. This meant that some three thousand were lost, including sixty-six of her crew.

Later in the war, Sharp would not be so lucky. In September 1942, while skipper of RMS *Laconia*, he was homeward bound from Suez with a crew of 692,

766 passengers, and 1,793 Italian prisoners when disaster struck. At 8:10 P.M. on the twelfth, while 130 miles north-northeast of Ascension Island, the ship was hit on the starboard side by a torpedo fired by *U156.* There was a great explosion, and hundreds of Italian prisoners were killed instantly. Though the vessel immediately took a list to starboard, Captain Sharp and his crew were bringing the vessel under control when a second torpedo hit the No. 2 hold. The ship was ordered abandoned, but this time Sharp went down with the ship, as well as an estimated twenty-two hundred others.[36] *U156* surfaced to rescue survivors, especially the Italian POWs. Besides *U156,* other U-boats and Vichy French surface craft were attacked by Allied bombers during the rescue operation, Admiral Dönitz subsequently issued orders that in the future U-boats were not to attempt to rescue survivors of stricken Allied vessels.

When news of the *Lancastria* sinking reached England, Prime Minister Winston Churchill placed a "D" notice on the story that banned publication of any information regarding the sinking, fearing its effect on morale. Survivors were forbidden under Kings Regulations from discussing the matter. After a report of the sinking appeared in the *New York Sun,* the news was cabled to England, where the story appeared in the *Times* and *The Daily Telegraph* the following day, 26 July, but without government sanction. The official report of the sinking remains suppressed under the Official Secrets Act until the year 2040.[37]

CONTE ROSSO, NEPTUNIA, AND OCEANIA

Lt. Comdr. Malcolm D. Wanklyn, RN, was the most successful British submarine skipper during World War II. As commander of the U-class submarine HMS *Upholder,* he became the nemesis of Axis convoys as they plied their way across Mediterranean waters to North Africa to supply General Rommel's Afrika Corps. Often referred to as Britain's "Undersea Ace" and the "Ultimate Submariner," the Scotsman and his crew of tough, experienced submariners played havoc with Italian naval vessels and the heavily laden transports that carried critical supplies and thousands of troops from Italian ports.[38]

Wanklyn took command of the newly commissioned *Upholder* in August 1940 and sailed for the Mediterranean, arriving at Valletta Harbor, Malta, home base of the 10th Submarine Flotilla, in January 1941. The flotilla consisted of ten U-class boats. U-class boats were short-hulled and simply designed. They were particularly effective when operating in restricted waters.

Wanklyn's first patrol netted the destruction of the eight-thousand-ton German merchant ship *Duisburg*. It wasn't until his fifth patrol that he again made contact with the enemy, sending the merchant ship *Antonietta Laura* to the bottom and sinking *Leverkusen,* a stranded German cargo ship. However, it was on 24 May that he scored his greatest victory when he sank the fully loaded Italian troopship *Conte Rosso*. A few days prior to his encounter with *Conte Rosso* he had sunk two enemy tankers, and it was during these attacks that the boat suffered damage to its ASDIC equipment and hydrophones; thus Wanklyn was unable to track attacking enemy destroyers. Though running low on fuel and with only two torpedoes left, he continued on patrol. Three days later, while running on the surface at dusk, he sighted three large transports. Charging through a screen of five destroyers, he fired his remaining torpedoes at one of the transports hitting it point-blank amidships. He dove under the bow of an oncoming destroyer and survived thirty-seven depth charge attacks before heading back to Malta. For his display of skill and valor under extremely hazardous conditions he was awarded Britain's highest military honor, the Victoria Cross medal.[39]

The 17,856-ton *Conte Rosso* had served as a commercial passenger ship for seventeen years before being converted into a troopship when Italy entered the war. Working for various shipping lines she made regular runs between Genoa and New York or Buenos Aires, and Trieste and Shanghai, and until 24 May 1941 she was used mainly to transport troops between Italy and North Africa. When torpedoed she was approximately fifteen miles east of Syracuse bound for Tripoli carrying twenty-five hundred soldiers. Convoy escorts rescued all but eight hundred of the ship's survivors.[40]

Neptunia and *Oceania* were sister ships built for the Italian Cosulich Line and launched in 1932. The nineteen-thousand-ton motor ships operated initially from Trieste and Naples to Brazil, Uruguay, and Argentina. In 1935 their travel schedules were changed to service routes between Genoa and Bombay and Shanghai via the Suez Canal. In 1940 they were converted to navy troopships and operated between Italian and North African ports until they were both sunk in the same convoy about sixty miles from Tripoli on 18 September 1941. Records indicate that seven thousand soldiers and crewmen were on board the two ships; however, historical sources differ as to how many men survived the

Conte Rosso. Steamship Historical Society of America

sinkings. Italian records indicate that only 384 men lost their lives due to the rescue efforts of other ships in the convoy.[41]

Lieutenant Commander Wanklyn, in command of *Upholder,* sank both Italian ships—each loaded with materials and reinforcements for North Africa—while on his twelfth patrol. Wanklyn scored two hits on *Neptunia* and the ship immediately foundered and sank.[42] Later that day Wanklyn hit *Oceania,* disabling her. Two destroyers took the ship in tow; however, she was subsequently struck by two more torpedoes and sank. On her twenty-fifth and last patrol, *Upholder* left Malta on 6 April 1942 to patrol the Gulf of Tripoli. She rendezvoused with HMS *Unbeaten* on the eleventh and was never heard from again. On 18 April Italian radio announced that the Italian torpedo boat *Pegaso* had sunk an enemy submarine on 16 April in the central Mediterranean. The British Admiralty accepted the grim truth that the submarine was most likely *Upholder.* No debris was ever found by any naval vessel and all hands were considered lost.[43]

Upholder was the top-scoring British navy submarine during World War II, sinking 119,000 tons of Axis shipping and claiming the lives of thousands of German and Italian soldiers and navy men. While commanding *Upholder,*

Neptunia. National Maritime Museum

Lt. Comdr. Malcolm D. Wanklyn, RN, (*second from left*) commanding officer of HMS *Upholder* shown with officers of his crew on Malta, 1941. Wanklyn was a recipient of Britain's highest military award, the Victoria Cross, and was often referred to as "Britain's Undersea Ace" and the "Ultimate Submariner." *Imperial War Museum*

Wanklyn, recipient of the Victoria Cross, also was awarded the Distinguished Service Order with two bars.[44]

STRATHALLAN

The fifth-largest ship to be sunk by a German U-boat during World War II, SS *Strathallan* had a relatively brief career as a troopship. The name troopship is, in itself, misleading, in that frequently troopships were converted liners, carrying passengers other than troops. Diplomats, wounded soldiers, enemy prisoners, civilians, and nurses also needed transport to and from combat zones. When *Strathallan* was torpedoed off the coast of Oran on 21 December 1942, among the 4,656 British and U.S. troops on board were 296 officers, 4,112 warrant and enlisted ranks, and 248 nurses, among the first to be sent into a combat zone. She also carried a crew of 466, for a total of 5,122 on board.[45]

Strathallan, and her sister ship, *Stratheden,* were built by Vickers-Armstrong at Barrow-in-Furness, England, the last prewar liners built for the Peninsular & Oriental Steam Navigation Company (P&O) line. At 23,732 gross tons, with a length of 664 feet and a beam of 82 feet, the ship was built to accommodate 530 first class and 450 tourist class passengers. With one funnel, two masts, and twin screws, *Strathallan* was capable of making speeds of up to twenty knots.[46]

Launched on 23 September 1937, *Strathallan* was scheduled for passenger service to Australia, and she made her maiden voyage on 18 March 1938. As tensions moved the world closer to war, it became inevitable that liners would be requisitioned as troopships. Shortly after the start of hostilities in September 1939, *Strathallan* was inducted for military service on 4 February 1940.[47]

Strathallan spent the early years of the war transporting troops in the Pacific. She was en route to Malaya, but was diverted to Java when Singapore and Jakarta fell to the Japanese in February 1942. She returned to Australia, and then to England. She made a total of eleven wartime voyages, her last to Algiers in late 1942.[48]

On 12 December 1942, British and U.S. troops boarded *Strathallan* at Greenock-on-the-Clyde, Scotland, for transportation to North Africa. Among the 4,656 troops embarking was a contingent of 248 nurses, including nurses of the U.S. 11th field hospital, as well as several American WACs and two notable celebrities: photography pioneer Margaret Bourke-White and Lt. Kay Summersby

Strathallan, the fifth-largest Allied ship to be sunk by a German U-boat during World War II. *Steamship Historical Society of America*

(Morgan), aide to General Eisenhower. It was by all accounts a cold, rainy morning as *Strathallan* weighed anchor and departed.

Bourke-White began her career in July 1929 when she went to work as photographer and associate editor of *Fortune* magazine in New York City. She was the first western photographer allowed into the Soviet Union when she was assigned to photograph a story on Soviet industry.   Recognized for her innate talent at photojournalism, Bourke-White discovered a second love, flying, after being assigned to photograph airliners from the air for an advertisement. She was among the inaugural staff of *Life* magazine, which debuted on 23 November 1936. It was Bourke-White's photo of Fort Peck Dam that graced the first cover.

She was in Moscow with her husband when Germany invaded the Soviet Union on 22 June 1941. The couple remained in their hotel room rather than seek the safety of a shelter during an air raid, and her photograph of a blacked-out Kremlin silhouetted by exploding bombs became famous. The couple returned to the United States, and Bourke-White published *Shooting the Russian War* (1942).

After the United States was attacked by the Japanese at Pearl Harbor, Bourke-White became the first accredited female war correspondent, designing her own uniform since none existed. She flew to London to record the arrival of the first thirteen U.S. B-17 bombers and their crews in England. She alternated her time between documenting the 8th Air Force and creating photographic portraits of noted world figures, such as Churchill, King George, and Emperor Haile Selassie; but despite repeated requests, she was denied permission to accompany bombers on a mission, it having been deemed too hazardous.[49]

Bourke-White was granted permission to cover the invasion of North Africa but had to be transported by sea aboard *Strathallan* rather than by air as she had hoped. *Strathallan* was the only ship in convoy KMF5 that carried females.

The other famous passenger, Kathleen Helen McCarthy-Morrogh (later Summersby), was born in Skibbereen, County Cork, Ireland, sometime in 1909, the daughter of a lieutenant colonel of the Royal Munster Fusiliers, an Irish Regiment. She worked as a fashion model before the war.

When war broke out in 1939, Summersby enlisted in the Women's Auxiliary and was assigned to the British Motor Transport Corps at Post #1 in London. Her early assignment was driving an ambulance under blacked-out conditions through the blitz-torn and rubble-filled streets in London's east end. She picked up corpses and transported them to hospital morgues, often dodging enemy bombs. She drove throughout the Battle of Britain and was considered an outstanding driver by her superiors, which no doubt had a part in her selection to drive visiting U.S. Army officers, one of whom was Dwight D. Eisenhower.

When Eisenhower returned to London, it was as newly promoted lieutenant general and commander of the European Theater, and he requested Summersby as his driver. Ike came to rely on her, and she soon assumed additional duties: she sat in on top secret meetings, lunched with Churchill, and dined with President Roosevelt and Secretary of State Cordell Hull. She was aboard *Strathallan* en route to North Africa to rejoin SHAEF Headquarters, which was already involved in Operation Torch.[50]

As *Strathallan* steamed east toward North Africa, German U-boats prowled the Mediterranean and its approaches seeking targets. Among those boats was *U562*, a type VIIC boat built by Blohm & Voss of Hamburg in 1940 and commissioned on 20 March 1941. Attached to the 29th U-boat Flotilla (29 Unterseebootsflottille) stationed at Marseilles, she was under the command of Kapitänleutnant Horst Hamm.[51]

Both Bourke-White and Summersby recalled numerous lifeboat drills aboard *Strathallan* as the convoy made its way to Oran, as many as "three times a day," Bourke-White wrote in her memoirs. She described the convoy as "an aircraft carrier, several troopships, and a body of destroyers." The weather was "rough" for a majority of the voyage, but the bad weather was welcome as it decreased the likelihood of a U-boat attack.

Despite apprehensions, the eight-day voyage was uneventful except for the boat drills, and spirits were high as the ship approached its destination. There was relief throughout the ship as everyone looked forward to disembarking at Oran and getting off the old, crowded liner. There were, by Summersby's account, "last night" parties late into the night as the ship neared its port. *Strathallan* was due to dock at Oran on the morning of 22 December.

At 2:25 A.M. on 21 December, the ship was approximately seventy miles off Oran when it was struck on her port side by a torpedo fired from *U562*. The resulting explosion flooded and disabled the ship's engine room and killed six crewmen (Third Engineer Morley, Asst. Engineer Knox, three Indian engineering crewmen, and an Indian seaman).[52] Captain Biggs ordered two white rockets fired into the dark morning sky to alert the convoy escorts. Summersby recalled that the explosion knocked her off her bunk. In the aftermath, she wrote, "The ship was shivering as if it had a monstrous chill and then began rocking ominously back and forth." The lights went out, and "boat stations" were sounded on the alarm gongs. The troops and crew responded in good order, and the boat stations were quickly manned. The emergency dynamo was started immediately and emergency lighting was restored throughout the ship. The captain, fearing that a second or third torpedo was probable, made the decision to lower boats onto the smooth seas, and all females, as well as one thousand troops, were disembarked into the boats.[53]

At 4 A.M. the destroyer HMS *Laforey* came alongside. After an inspection of the damage, the decision was made to attempt to tow the ship to Oran, and towing commenced at 6 A.M. The bilge pumps began to fail at about 1 P.M., and at 1:15 flames shot out of the funnel of the ship. As Captain Biggs stated in his report, "It appears now that oil had reached the still very hot brick work in the boilers and heated and ignited the fuel oil from settling tanks or bunkers."[54]

With fires flaring on the port side and concerns that they could spread into the ammunition storage areas, the decision was made to evacuate the remaining troops. They were loaded onto escorting destroyers HMS *Panther* and HMS

Kapitänleutnant Horst Hamm (in white cap) with members of his crew in the conning tower of *U562*. *U-Boot-Archiv*

Pathfinder, while attempts were made to try to contain the fires and save the ship. All but eleven of the personnel on board were rescued.

Summersby and Bourke-White found themselves assigned to the same lifeboat. One or two of the boats capsized as they were lowered, resulting in an undetermined number of deaths, possibly including several nurses. Bourke-White had the foresight to bring one of her cameras with her into the lifeboat and was able to take pictures of her rescue and the floundering *Strathallan.* The photos were published in *Life* magazine, and the incident later served as inspiration for filmmaker Alfred Hitchcock's *Lifeboat,* which starred actress Tallulah Bankhead. The destroyer HMS *Verity* recovered the females and other troops later, and carried them to shore. *Strathallan* was still being towed at 4 P.M. on 22 December when she rolled onto her port side and sank.[55]

Upon landing in Oran, Bourke-White learned that she had finally been granted permission to fly aboard a B-17 on a bombing mission over Tunis. Her pilot, Maj. Paul Tibbets, would later fly the *Enola Gay* over the Japanese city of Hiroshima and drop the world's first atomic bomb. Bourke-White was among the first photographers to enter a concentration camp as she accompanied

General Patton into Germany. Following the war, both Bourke-White and *Life* magazine became popular media institutions.

Kay Summersby arrived in Oran with only the uniform on her back. Ike later arranged for her to be commissioned a second lieutenant in the Women's Army Corps (WAC), even though she remained a British subject. She served as part of Ike's "official family" and was present when Germany surrendered in a little French schoolhouse in Reims, France, on 7 May 1945. She was also the first British female to enter Berlin after the war.

Strathallan was *U562*'s last victory. Six weeks later, on 19 February 1943, *U562* was attacked northeast of Bengazi in the Mediterranean. Accounts differ as to whether HMS *Iris,* a British destroyer, HMS *Hursley,* a destroyer escort, or an RAF Wellington bomber deserves the credit for the sinking. What is indisputable is that *U562* went to the bottom with all forty-nine crewmen.[56] For most of the troops, their experiences were not much different from those of Pvt. Harry Ball of the Royal Engineers: "They re-embarked us on the SS *Duchess of Richmond* within hours, and we sailed unescorted to Alger." Many went on to fight in North Africa, Sicily, and later Europe.[57]

World War II, 1943–1945

CERAMIC

The passenger liner *Ceramic* was built by Shaw, Savill & Albion in Belfast in the early 1900s. In 1913 she entered service for the White Star Line and for many years sailed between England and Australia, carrying passengers and cargo. During World War I she remained on this route carrying Australian troops to join Allied forces fighting in Europe and the Eastern Mediterranean. In 1934 the ship was sold to the Blue Funnel & Shaw Savill Line following the merger of the White Star and Cunard lines and continued her service between England and Australia. When World War II broke out she was requisitioned by the Ministry of Transport and converted into a troopship.[1]

In November 1942 *Ceramic* left Liverpool, England, with convoy ON149. She carried a crew of 264 and fourteen British seamen or D.E.M.S., who manned two deck guns for a total crew of 278. Her military passengers numbered 226, which consisted of forty-three British Army officers, eleven Royal Navy officers, nine Merchant Navy officers, thirty nurses, fifty Royal Engineers and some eighty-three military personnel of mixed rank and a few merchant seamen en route to new assignments. Additionally, the ship carried 152 civilian passengers (90 men, 50 women, and 12 children). Her total number of souls on board was 656. *Ceramic* carried 12,362 tons of general and government stores,

Ceramic carried 656 men when she was sunk in December 1942 west of the Azores by *U515*. One royal engineer survived the sinking, Sapper Eric Munday, who was captured and spent the rest of the war as a POW at Stalag 8B in upper Silesia. *Steamship Historical Society of America*

including aircraft spare parts. Among her passengers was Sapper Eric Munday, Royal Engineers. He was to be the sole survivor on *Ceramic*'s ill-fated journey.[2]

Ceramic was to sail with the fifty-ship convoy to a point off Greenland and then proceed independently to St. Helena, Durban, and Sydney. Although the threat of U-boat attack was ever present on such a long journey, the ship had been lucky. It had safely made the round trip up to now without incident, thanks perhaps to its seventeen-knot cruising speed. She could give an attacking U-boat a run for its money and under the right circumstances could outrun her adversary.[3]

On 5 December seven ships were detached from the convoy to take up specified routes to African ports. They sailed individually on a southeasterly course unaware that a "wolfpack" of U-boats (code named "Westwall") awaited them. *Ceramic* sailed in company with the Dutch freighter *Serooskerk* until she pulled away that evening. Sapper Munday remembered their detachment from the convoy amid a bright sunny day and calm seas; however, when the ship left *Serooskerk* the seas had become moderate and a light rain fell causing poor visibility. By 8 P.M. the ship's position was approximately six hundred miles northwest of the Azore Islands.[4]

However, off to the west, a lone, surfaced German U-boat had sighted the masts of the liner approximately sixteen miles to the east and proceeded to stalk the ship. *U515*, under the command of Kapitänleutnant Werner Henke, had only recently been ordered away from the Gibraltar area to intercept convoys further out to sea. Admiral Dönitz, Supreme Commander, U-boats, had suffered too many losses in the close-in sea routes leading to the coast of North Africa and the Mediterranean. He thus directed the Westwall boats to patrol west of the Azores.[5]

Henke's logbook described the U-boat's intercept of the liner and the attack on his unsuspecting enemy.

6.12

2 smoke clouds in sight, true 220 degrees, 7,000 ton freighter, true 70 degrees a large four masted passenger vessel. I am drawing ahead of four-master. At dawn vessel increases speed now to 17 knots. Only after hours-long full speed I am finally getting ahead.

Double shot tubes I and IV, depth 5, speed 15.5, bow right bearing 80, distance 1200, running time 30 seconds. Hitting mid-engine room. 2nd shot, hearing impact, apparently pistol failure. Vessel using radio. It is the *Ceramic*, 18,800 tons.[6]

Sapper Munday recalled that a torpedo hit the ship forward on the starboard side. Although the weather was fairly calm, it was very dark with poor visibility. The vessel took a list, but her speed did not lessen, as the engines were not damaged. Twenty minutes later Henke attacked again.[7]

7.12

0018 Catch shot tube V, depth 3, hitting forward 20, illuminating vessel, which is setting out lifeboats. I can see at close range several boats with soldiers in them.

0038 Catch shot tube VI, depth 4, hitting aft 40, vessel does not sink, many floats and boats are being set out.[8]

Almost immediately after the first torpedo crashed into the ship, "action stations" was sounded. After the first explosion, two torpedoes struck *Ceramic* amidships and the order was given to abandon ship. Munday recalled that all three explosions were dull, no columns of water were thrown up, and he estimated that the torpedo

Kapitänleutnant Warner Henke, commanding officer of *U515*, was captured later in the war when his boat was sunk and he was taken to an interrogation center near Washington, D.C., where he committed suicide in June 1944.
U-Boot-Archiv

hits were deep because there was no visible damage on deck. At the time of the attack he was in the lounge and quickly made his way to his boat station on the port side. He remembered some panic, probably owing to having women and children on board, but he considered it nothing serious and quite understandable, as it was so very dark that some confusion was inevitable. "I do not know what happened on the starboard side, but probably the starboard side was damaged, as there were many more people in my boat than were allocated to it, probably many people came over to the first boat they could find. The boat was lowered successfully, however, and we managed to get away from the ship's side after a struggle."[9]

Soon Henke sent another torpedo into the doomed ship.

> 0100   Catch shot tube II, depth 6 hitting forward 20, vessel is breaking up, sinking after 10 seconds. Suddenly there is a very strong detonation near to me, I am distancing myself fearing defense.[10]

Six or eight boats were able to get away from the sinking vessel along with numerous rafts. Munday later recalled:

> We lay to for the rest of the night, keeping the boat head to sea, as it was too crowded to move about in the darkness, also as there were mostly military personnel in the boat nobody knew very much about handling it. By daylight a northerly gale had sprung up,

with storms of rain and sleet, with high confused seas. Huge waves were breaking over the boat, we bailed furiously, but it was impossible to free the boat of water before another wave crashed over, swamping it so that it capsized and we were all thrown into the water. After a struggle the boat was righted, but it was three-quarters full of water; two or three men climbed in and tried to bail it out, but again it was capsized by the huge waves. It was then about 8 A.M. on the 7th, and I decided to swim off. I found some wreckage and clung to that for a little while, but the seas were too strong and it was washed away.[11]

In the meantime Henke had been ordered back into the area by Dönitz to gather intelligence about the ship. Headquarters wanted to know whether the ship was loaded with troops and whether there was any indication of its port of destination. Henke responded that *Ceramic* was full of troops and that he was going to the site of the sinking in order to capture the captain. His next message to headquarters relayed the following:

1200 Position 41.17 N/41.06 W, wind SSW 7, increasing westerly swell, overcast, cloudy 10 vis. 3-4 sm, hail showers. Approaching again location of vessel sunk in order to take the Captain prisoner. At the location where the ship sank there were many dead army and naval soldiers, about 60 floats and many boats and parts of planes. According to reports from survivors in water there had been on board 45 officers, about 100 ratings. Nothing can be found out about destination and cargo. I suspect that the cargo consisted exclusively of war materials. Submerged account weather condition.[12]

What Henke failed to mention in his official log was the retrieval of Sapper Eric Munday. "About four hours after swimming away from where the ship sank, at noon on the 7th December, I was picked up by the submarine. She had surfaced to look for the Captain, but being unsuccessful, and seeing me nearby in the water, I was hauled on board," he later recalled. Munday was interrogated shortly after his rescue, and according to *U515*'s war diary he told his captors that his ship carried forty-five officers and approximately one thousand men. Munday further stated in his postwar debriefing,

I do not know the number of the U-boat but I believe the Captain was a Lieutenant Commander named Henke . . . I was treated well on the whole; several of the crew could speak English fairly well, in particular a young Midshipman, who told me that a number of boats and rafts were seen to leave the ship and that the vessel took about 3 hours to sink. I am of the opinion that the weather was so bad when the storm blew up during the early hours of the 7th December, that no boat could have survived, and this accounts for the great loss in life.

The German midshipman told me that about a fortnight before the *Ceramic* was sunk, the U-boat had torpedoed a British cruiser [ship actually sunk was the destroyer tender HMS *Hecla*). A destroyer had come to the rescue of the crew, and whilst survivors were being picked up the submarine torpedoed her also. [Destroyer was HMS *Marne.*] I heard no other reports on this cruise, which had lasted about a month when the *Ceramic* was sunk.[13]

As *U515* continued on patrol, headquarters signaled the boat on 19 December that Henke had been awarded the Knight's Cross of the Iron Cross. Dönitz congratulated Henke's "brave crew and their demonstrated willingness to fight." Running low on fuel Henke returned to base on 2 January 1943.[14]

We arrived at Lorient on the 2 January 1943 in company with a Flotilla of U-boats. During the return voyage to that port we were attacked once by Sunderland flying-boats but no damage was sustained. On arrival at Lorient I met several Army and Air Force Officers and a Merchant Captain, from other ships, all of whom had been picked up by other U-boats. We were asked if we would like to give our names and addresses, together with the name of our respective ships, so that this information could be broadcast and our relatives thus learn that we were safe.

We all agreed to do this, I did not actually broadcast myself, and the German Ministry of Information report to this effect, is not true. I was sent to Stalag 8B in Upper Silesia, remaining there until liberated. The treatment was quite good at this camp.[15]

The Portuguese destroyer *DAO* and HMS *Enterprise* were ordered to *Ceramic's* last known position to search for survivors. *DAO* sailed at 9 A.M. on the ninth of December, but later reported that she was unable to make headway because of fierce weather conditions. The ship was obliged to return to Horta, Azores, having suffered considerable damage. *Enterprise* upon arriving on scene sent the following message:

Your 0805A/9. Arrived 090 degrees position of sinking 250 miles at daylight 11th December. Searched towards position of sinking at 18 knots zig-zag number 8 until

1255Z/11 when forced to heave to head north. Wind veered from south west force 7 to north force 12 within 15 minutes and in my opinion the resulting heavy confused seas, of typhoon character rendered it virtually impossible for any boat to survive this area. At 1700Z/11 I decided search must be abandoned and to proceed to Clyde when weather permitted. Northerly gale continued until 0600Z/12. After proceeding, a capsized white boat with red color bottom was passed in position 45 degrees 19 minutes north 33 degrees 33 minutes west at 1600Z/12. Nothing else was seen.[16]

Werner Henke

Little is known of Sapper Munday's life following his repatriation after the war; however, there is much more to tell about Werner Henke.

Henke was certainly a nonconformist when it came to following the rule of the code of military service. Although he was a brilliant commander at sea he often found himself in trouble with naval officials. As a cadet he was lax in his attitude and was often called to task for lacking self-discipline. He possessed an impetuous nature, and on one occasion struck an SS officer, although no charges were filed. He preferred the company of women even when it meant disobeying orders: In one circumstance he went AWOL and was found guilty of desertion and sentenced to three months at a remote post in disgrace. After serving out his term he was assigned—on probation—to the First U-boat Flotilla. Still, his past followed him, and the German navy decided to release him because of his numerous indiscretions. However, Dönitz needed a few maverick U-boat commanders—those who would go beyond the norm in risk-taking. Provided there was no more trouble with his activities ashore and that he could prove himself in action, there would be a place for him in the U-boat fleet. Working up through various positions of responsibility on different U-boats under the command of experienced commanders, Henke finally took command of the newly commissioned type IXC U-boat *U515* on 21 February 1942.[17]

Following his sinking of *Ceramic* and being awarded the Knight's Cross of the Iron Cross it would appear that Henke had overcome his past and become a well-respected ace in the U-boat arm. On 21 February 1943, the day Henke departed Lorient on his next patrol, Radio Berlin reported his successful sinking of *Ceramic*. The program boasted that several thousand soldiers had gone down with the ship, referencing comments made by Henke dockside when he returned from the patrol. At that time Henke mentioned that it was a large boat and that many soldiers were on board but gave no numbers. Radio Berlin's broadcast disputed Allied claims that troop transports suffered few casualties during the North African invasion. The German broadcast not only exaggerated the number of soldiers lost on the *Ceramic* but also mistakenly claimed that the ship had been part of the North African invasion force.[18]

Less than ten days after *Ceramic* went down, Allied propagandists began an attack on the U-boat service, citing it as a ruthless weapon of war, inhumane, and led by corrupt and reckless boat commanders. The chief villain was unsurprisingly Dönitz, and the propagandists, using the incident of the *Ceramic* disaster, labeled Henke as "War Criminal Number 1." Allied propagandists went so far as to accuse Henke of machine-gunning survivors in the water. This information was continuously broadcast by Allied radio outlets and though the Allied propagandists soon turned to other matters, Henke was now forever tainted as a criminal who must be dealt with harshly if captured.[19]

U515 was to become the most active U-boat of the 10th Flotilla, which operated out of Lorient. Under Henke's command, the boat sank or permanently disabled twenty-eight ships for a total of 177,000 tons.[20] This ended one evening in early April 1944, when he and his crew were caught by surprise by aircraft from the USS *Guadalcanal* (CVE-60) escort carrier group. After suffering unrelenting attacks by air and destroyer units, the U-boat was forced to the surface amidst withering fire at point-blank range by destroyer escorts *Flaherty* and *Chatelain* and aerial rocket and strafing attacks. *U515* went to the bottom 175 miles northwest of the Madeira Islands. Forty-four members of *U515* were rescued; among them was Werner Henke.[21]

When the captured crew was brought on board *Guadalcanal,* Henke and his officers were put in the ship's brig. Within a few days the ship's chief master at arms had become acquainted with Henke, and during one of their conversations the prisoner told him that the British had put out a propaganda broadcast concerning the sinking of *Ceramic.* They said that they had learned that the ship had been sunk by *U515,* and that *Ceramic* survivors had been machine-gunned in their lifeboats. The British added that, if anyone from *U515* fell into their hands, they would try them for murder and hang them if convicted.[22]

The chief brought this conversation to the attention of Capt. Daniel V. Gallery Jr., skipper of *Guadalcanal,* who used a ruse to get Henke and his crew to talk. He called Henke to his cabin and showed him a fake message that ordered him to hand Henke over to the British when the ship refueled at Gibraltar. To avoid British imprisonment and perhaps a worse fate, Henke signed a document agreeing to give information under the condition that he would be sent to the United States. Gallery had photostats made of the signed document and they were passed among the U-boat crew members. Convinced that their skipper had agreed to talk, information began to flow. Henke heard that his crew was cooperating and became recalcitrant.[23]

The U-boat crew was landed at Norfolk, Virginia, on 26 April 1944. Henke ended up at Fort Hunt, a special interrogation center located seventeen miles south of Washington, D.C., near Mount Vernon. The center housed POWs of particular interest, especially captured U-boat personnel. Naval intelligence interrogators continued to threaten him with a transfer to British authorities if he didn't talk. In fact, in June he was informed that he was to be turned over to the Canadians. Henke most likely thought that he would subsequently be given over to the British and perhaps tried as a war criminal.

Shortly after receiving this information, the former U-boat "ace" was killed by a compound guard as he tried to climb over a high wire fence surrounding the base. Rather than face a British tribunal he chose death in a suicidal escape attempt.[24]

DORCHESTER

The sinking of the U.S. Army transport *Dorchester* early in February of 1943 is remembered primarily for the extraordinary heroism and devotion displayed by four army chaplains, who selflessly gave of themselves at the cost of their own lives, and inspired a nation at war.

Built in 1926 by the Newport News Shipbuilding & Drydock Company in Virginia, the 5,649-ton luxury liner was operated by the Merchants and Miners Transportation Company along the eastern seaboard.[25] Shortly after Pearl Harbor, on 24 January 1942, *Dorchester* came under the direction of the Maritime Commission for service as a troopship for the War Department. Designated USAT *Dorchester,* the liner was converted to a warship by Agwilnes, Inc., of New York in February. Gun positions and lookout posts were constructed, and dining rooms and salons converted to accommodate the large number of troops she was to carry to various theaters of war. Barely a month later, the ship was ready for her first mission, a voyage to Kungiait Bay, Greenland.[26]

The troopship *Dorchester* was sunk with a heavy loss of lives in early February 1943. *William Hultgen Collection*

After a port call at Boston, she sailed to Greenland with stops at Narasarssuak, Ivigut, and Sonderstromfjord, returning to Boston in June. Other voyages in 1942 were to Argentina and St. John's, Newfoundland. By early 1943 *Dorchester* was again in New York, preparing for what would be her last journey. Replacement troops bound for Greenland began arriving at Fort Myles Standish at Taunton, Massachusetts. Among the troops were four army chaplains whose subsequent actions would gain them immortality: First Lt. George L. Fox, a Methodist minister; First Lt. Alexander D. Goode, a Jewish rabbi; First Lt. John P. Washington, a Catholic priest; and First Lt. Clark V. Poling of the Dutch Reformed Church.

George L. Fox, the oldest of the four, was a veteran of the First World War. Born in Lewiston, Pennsylvania, on 15 March 1900, one of five children of a railroad worker, Fox quit school and lied about his age to enlist in the army shortly after the United States' entry into World War I.[27] After training at Camp D. Baker in Texas, Fox was placed in the ambulance corps, and shipped to Camp Merritt, New Jersey, where he departed for France aboard USS *Huron* on 3 December 1917.[28] After docking at Brest, France, he was assigned to the 2nd Infantry Division, and in April his unit moved to the front. He endured artillery and air attacks and lived in constant fear in mud huts and trenches while battling the enemy and disease. By September his unit was moved from St. Nicholas to Bois L' Eveque to Bois de Jure, and Fox was often forced to move wounded soldiers under enemy fire. He recalled being sickened by the slaughter. On 10 November 1918, he was at the advance dressing station at Giraucourt, a partially destroyed brick factory, when it was attacked and bombed from the air. He was severely wounded during the attack. When he awoke in the evacuation hospital at Le Havre the following day, the war was over.[29]

Fox recovered quickly, spending only a month in the hospital before returning to his unit. He served with the occupation forces along the Rhine until being mustered out of the army in late 1919 with a 10 percent disability. He was awarded the Silver Star medal for "gallantry in action against the enemy in the Champagne sector," as well as the Purple Heart and the French Croix de Guerre.[30] He returned to Altoona, Pennsylvania, to take a job with the Guarantee Trust Company and to finish school. It was around that time that Fox received the call to preach. After attending the Moody Institute in Indiana, he married, left school, and became an itinerant Methodist preacher. After graduation from the Boston University School of Theology, he was ordained a Methodist minister on 10 June 1934. He accepted a position in a church at Union Village, Vermont, and was later appointed state chaplain and historian to the American Legion.

Following Pearl Harbor, Fox enlisted in the U.S. Army Chaplain Corps and was appointed a chaplain and first lieutenant on 24 July 1942, the same day his son Wyatt enlisted in the Marine Corps.[31] Fox was called to active duty on 8 August and ordered to the Chaplains School at Harvard University, where he met classmates Goode, Poling, and Washington, then went on to Camp Davis, where he was assigned as chaplain to the 411th Coastal Artillery. Early in 1943 the unit was ordered to Camp Myles Standish, Taunton, Massachusetts, a major embarkation point.[32]

Like Fox, Alexander D. Goode had previous military experience, although his service consisted of seven years in the National Guard. The youngest of the four chaplains, Goode entered the University of Cincinnati, graduating in 1934, followed by a bachelor of Hebrew letters degree (BHL) from Hebrew Union College in 1937 and a Ph.D. from Johns Hopkins University in 1940. He married his childhood sweetheart, Theresa Flax, a niece of entertainer Al Jolson, on 7 October 1935, and began his work as a rabbi, first at a synagogue in Marion,

Indiana, and later in York, Pennsylvania. With his brother Joseph in the army and the declaration of war in Europe Goode began believing in the inevitability of the United States entering the war. As early as January 1941 he had applied for a chaplain's appointment in the navy, but there were no immediate vacancies. Following Pearl Harbor, Goode applied for an assignment as a chaplain in the Army and was frustrated by the delay, hounding officials for news of his status. Finally, on 21 July 1942 he was commissioned a first lieutenant, U.S. Army Chaplain Corps, and was called to active duty and ordered to the Chaplains School at Harvard University on 9 August.

At Harvard, he took courses in land navigation, military law, military customs and ceremonies, chemical warfare, and first aid. He also made the acquaintance of chaplains Fox, Poling, and Washington. Following the completion of his studies, Goode was sent to Goldsboro, North Carolina, assigned as chaplain to the 333rd Airbase Squadron. Goode strongly desired to see action, and persistently requested assignment overseas. In October 1942, he received orders to report to Camp Myles Standish, where he was reunited with the others. When he discovered his orders were to Greenland, he tried unsuccessfully to get them changed to a more active theater of war, but in late January 1943 he obeyed orders and bordered *Dorchester*.[33]

Clark V. Poling wanted to follow in his father's footsteps and become a minister. Born in Columbus, Ohio, on 7 August 1910, one of four children, he attended Whitney Public School, then Oakwood, a Quaker high school in Poughkeepsie, New York. A star athlete, honor student, and president of the student council, he entered Rutgers University in New Jersey, then attended the Yale Divinity School at New Haven, Connecticut, where he graduated in 1936. Shortly after being ordained, Poling accepted his first assignment as pastor of the First Reformed Church in Schenectady, New York.

Following the entry of the United States into World War II, Poling was persuaded by his father, a World War I chaplain, to seek a commission with the Chaplain Corps rather than the infantry. He was commissioned as a first lieutenant and chaplain on 10 June 1942 and was called to active duty on 25 June. Assigned as chaplain to the 131st Quartermasters Truck Regiment at Camp Shelby, Mississippi, he was later sent to Camp Myles Standish in Massachusetts, where he attended Harvard Chaplains School, before receiving orders for Greenland.[34]

Kapitänleutnant Karl Jurgen Wachter (*shown on left*), commander of *U223*, which sank *Dorchester. U-Boot-Archiv*

John P. Washington was one of seven children, born on 18 July 1908 to a poor immigrant family in Newark, New Jersey. In his youth he was an altar boy and while still a teenager he resolved to become a priest. After graduating from Seton Hall in 1931, he attended Immaculate Conception Seminary in Darlington, New Jersey, and was ordained a priest on 15 June 1935. His first parish was St. Genevieve's in Elizabeth, New Jersey, followed by postings to St. Venantius and St. Stephen's parishes. After Pearl Harbor Washington tried to enlist as a navy chaplain but was turned down because of poor eyesight. He next tried the army and was appointed to the Army Chaplain Corps on 9 May 1942. He took his orientation at Fort Benjamin Harrison, Indiana, then was transferred to Fort George Meade, Maryland, where he was assigned as chaplain to the 76th Infantry

Division, a training unit, in June 1942. In November, he was ordered to Camp Myles Standish, where he met the others at the Chaplains School at Harvard University.[35]

By late January 1943, *Dorchester* was ready to sail, and departed Staten Island on 22 January filled to capacity with 751 passengers and troops, 130 crew, and twenty-three Armed Guard personnel. *Dorchester* joined convoy SG19 at St. John's Newfoundland. The convoy comprised two other merchant ships, SS *Lutz* and SS *Biscaya,* and three Coast Guard cutters as escorts, USCGC *Tampa* (WPG-48), USCGC *Comanche* (WPG-75), and USCGC *Escanaba* (WPG-77). The convoy then sailed for its ultimate destination, Narasarssuak, Greenland.[36]

The North Atlantic winter weather was frigid and dark, with icy seas and strong winds rolling across towering waves. Heavy icing decreased the speed of the convoy by half and resulted in delays as the cutters de-iced their frozen guns and depth charges with steam. The convoy proceeded with the cutter *Tampa* in the lead, screening, followed by *Dorchester, Biscaya,* and *Lutz* in line abreast formation, with *Escanaba* and *Comanche* flanking the ships, one to port, the other to starboard. Progress was slow.

On 2 February *Tampa* detected the presence of an enemy submarine but was unable to locate it and after a period resumed her position.[37] This was during the period known as the "happy time" by the Kriegsmarine U-boat arm, when the amount of Allied tonnage sunk still exceeded the tonnage of U-boats lost. The captain of *Dorchester,* Hans J. Danielsen, ordered the troops to sleep in their clothing and life jackets as a precaution, orders that were, to a large degree, ignored.[38] Danielsen requested antisubmarine patrol planes from Greenland but was advised that none were available.

Waiting in the darkness that February night was *U223,* a German type VIIC U-boat under the command of Kapitänleutnant Karl Jurgen Wachter. Built by the F. Krupp Germaniawerft in Keil, Germany, and commissioned on 6 June 1942, the boat began its second combat patrol on 1 February 1943.[39]

Sometime around 12:55 A.M. on the morning of 3 February (some sources say 3:55 A.M.), about 150 miles west of Cape Farewell (59°22'N/48°42'W), *Dorchester* sailed into the periscope hairs of *U223*. The ship had slowed to ten knots because of the ice floes, making it an easy target. A torpedo fired from *U223* struck *Dorchester* on the starboard side, amidships, and below the water-line. It was an easy shot for the U-boat since the escort *Escanaba* protecting the starboard flank of the convoy had no radar. Approximately one hundred people were killed in the initial blast, which knocked out all power, including the radios, so no distress signal could be sent out. Informed that his ship was rapidly taking on water and sinking by the bow, Captain Danielsen gave the order to "abandon ship."[40] In the confusion, no one thought to fire off a rocket or flare, and in the pitch darkness of the night the escorts weren't aware of *Dorchester's* plight until the transport had sunk.

Troops caught belowdecks struggled in the darkness to reach topside, many emerging into the frigid night air without life jackets or, in some cases, clothing. On deck, there was pandemonium, and nobody seemed in command. Only two of the fourteen lifeboats on board were successfully launched, and many of the life rafts tossed over the side of the floundering ship drifted away before anyone could board them.[41] Some rafts were dropped so hastily that they hit men swimming in the icy water , and several soldiers refused to leave the ship. Many of the passengers didn't hear the "abandon ship" signal since there was only enough steam for one blast, not the required six.

In the midst of the disorder, Chaplains Fox, Goode, Poling, and Washington circulated among the men, calming them and giving them encouragement. They tended to the wounded, guided disoriented soldiers to boats and rafts, and prayed with scared young men. When the order to "abandon ship" was given, they began distributing life jackets, but it soon became obvious that there were not enough vests for all the soldiers.

What happened next was reported by numerous survivors who witnessed it. When the jackets ran out, one of the four chaplains, it is not known which, took off his own jacket and gave it to a soldier who couldn't swim, saying, "Here, take mine. I won't need it. I'm staying." The other three removed theirs and gave them to three other soldiers. John Ladd, one of the survivors who witnessed the chaplains' selfless act, recalled, "It was the finest thing I have seen or hope to see this side of heaven."[42]

Twenty-seven minutes after the order to abandon ship, survivors in lifeboats and on rafts watched as the four chaplains, arms linked and heads bowed, prayed aloud as the ship sank into the sea. Immediately after the explosion, the Coast Guard cutters fired off a fusillade of star shells, illuminating the area. *Tampa* escorted the other two freighters to Skobfjord, while *Comanche* screened the area hunting for the sub and *Escanaba* slowed to search for survivors. The valor of the four chaplains was matched that night by Coast Guard crewmen who jumped into the deadly thirty-four-degree water (the ambient night air was thirty-six degrees Fahrenheit) in rubber suits to rescue individuals and tow life rafts to the cutter. Others hung on nets over the side, in rough seas, to assist survivors from lifeboats and rafts who were severely weakened by the freezing wind and water.

Escanaba is credited with rescuing 133 survivors, but one died aboard the ship. Many bodies were also recovered from the sea. A boatswain's mate aboard the returning *Tampa*, John Pearse, remembered, "There were acres of floating bodies, and in the dark, those red lights dotted the water everywhere you looked." The red lights were small, battery-powered beacons attached to the life jackets, but survival in the frigid water rarely exceeded several minutes, and many of those recovered were already dead.[43]

Comanche's captain, against orders, abandoned his screening duties several times to rescue survivors, pulling an additional ninety-seven men from the sea.[44] When it became unlikely that there were others alive, *Comanche* and *Escanaba* followed *Tampa* to Narasarssuak, Greenland, where the 229 survivors were transported to hospitals. Tragically, four officers, ninety-eight crewmen, fifteen Armed Guard personnel, and 558 troops and passengers died, mostly from hypothermia; in total, 675 men were lost.[44]

The following morning the U.S. seaplane tender *Sandpiper* was ordered to proceed to the area of the sinking to recover *Dorchester* survivors. Unable to reach the scene until the morning of the fourth because of frozen ice in the Arsuk fjord, she arrived on scene where three ships of the Greenland patrol were already searching the area. Hundreds of dead bodies were seen floating in life jackets on the water.

The nation both mourned the loss of *Dorchester* and celebrated the heroism of the four chaplains. The event was commemorated on a postage stamp, and on 14 December 1944 the chaplains were posthumously awarded the Distinguished Service Cross and Purple Heart in a ceremony at Fort Myer, Virginia.

Several of the crew of *Escanaba* were put in for medals, but never lived to receive them. She was torpedoed in the Belle Isle Straits, off Ivigtut, Greenland, on 13 June 1943 while escorting convoy GS24 to St. John's, Newfoundland. Only two of *Escanaba*'s crew of 130 survived the sinking.

By early 1944 Oberleutnant Zur See Peter Gerlach had assumed command of *U223* and operated with other U-boats in the Tyrrhenian Sea. In March of that year the British trawler *Mull* sank *U343* off Sardinia; *U450* was lost after an attack by a U.S. and three British destroyers. On 30 March *U223* was detected by sonar while operating in the area, and three British destroyers, *Laforey, Tumult,* and *Ulster,* began a relentless pursuit that lasted some twenty hours. Other British and U.S. destroyers and sub chasers joined in the hunt; however, Gerlach eluded his pursuers by going deep (772 feet) and surviving dozens of depth-charge attacks.

Gerlach finally surfaced in darkness to recharge his batteries after being submerged for twenty-five hours. He was detected by British destroyers *Blencartha, Hambleton, Laforey,* and *Tumult,* which took the boat under fire. Gerlach fired a T-5 acoustic self-steering torpedo at *Laforey* and sunk the craft with heavy loss of life. The commander of the 14th Flotilla, Capt. H. T. Armstrong, one of the Royal Navy's most distinguished destroyer captains, went down with the ship. Taking heavy fire, Gerlach ordered *U223* abandoned, and while his crew leaped over the side the crippled U-boat circled, and her propellers combined with British gunfire killed almost half of the German crew in the water. Gerlach's last words to his engineer were that he was "no good without my boat" and elected to go down with her. Only twenty-seven of the fifty German crew members survived.[46]

HENRY R. MALLORY

Few would argue that a critical factor in determining the outcome of the Second World War would be the ability of the United States to ship troops and war material overseas to combat zones as opposed to the Axis powers' ability to prevent those troops and supplies from reaching their destination. Thus, the mastery of the North Atlantic was essential to an Allied victory, so vital that the North Atlantic routes were referred to as a lifeline to the western Allies.

Initially, the advantage lay with the Axis powers, as U-boats sank Allied tonnage at a staggering rate. Slowly, with the development of improved convoy tactics, better technology (such as the HF/DF-High Frequency Detection Finder, "Huff-Duff"), and long-range air escorts,[47] the tide began to shift toward the Allies in what became known as the "Battle of the Atlantic."

This battle, which would last six years, would climax during a six-month period (November 1942 through May 1943) that came to be called the "Bloody Winter," because of the heavy losses suffered on both sides. After a loss of thirty-

Kapitänleutnant Siegfried Freiheer
von Forstner, commanding officer of
U402. U-Boot-Archiv

one boats in the first three weeks of May alone, Admiral Dönitz recalled all boats
from the North Atlantic on 22 May 1943.[48]

During the Bloody Winter, there were several crucial battles, such as with
convoys SC107, SC121 and SC122, but the battle that Dönitz himself called
the "hardest convoy battle of the war" was that of convoy SC118.[49]

In that four-day encounter (5–8 February 1943) the German U-boat Group
Pfeil (arrow) chased SC118, a slow convoy comprising sixty-three ships, escorted
by British Escort Group B-2 (originally eight, then later eleven, Allied destroyers and corvettes), as it steamed toward Iceland. Group *Pfeil* sank twelve merchantmen, at a cost of three U-boats lost and three other boats so heavily damaged that they had to return to base—a rate of payment the Kriegsmarine would
be unwilling and unable to sustain.

Of the twelve ships sent to the bottom, only one carried troops, SS *Henry
Mallory,* incredibly a veteran of World War I.[50] *Mallory* began life in the yards of

the Newport News Shipbuilding and Drydock Company, Newport News, Virginia, in 1916. She sailed briefly for the Mallory Lines before being acquired by the U.S. Navy on 13 April 1918.[51] Built with a length exceeding 440 feet and a gross tonnage of 6,063, *Mallory*'s reciprocating engines gave her a speed of sixteen knots. This, and her capacity to carry 404 passengers,[52] made her desirable for utilization as a troopship, and she was commissioned into the navy on 17 April 1918.[53]

Braving the dangers of the frigid, rough, and submarine-infested waters of the North Atlantic, *Mallory* made several crossings, carrying twenty-two hundred troops of the American Expeditionary Force (AEF) on each trip. Following the armistice, she brought many of the same troops home before being discharged from the navy and transferred to the War Department on 23 October 1919.[54]

Acquired by Agwilines Inc. after her release from government service, she spent the "long armistice" of 1919–39 as a passenger liner, but even before the entry of the United States in the Second World War plans were under way for the degaussing, arming, conversion, and manning of eighteen transports, including *Mallory*. In a secret memorandum from the Office of the Chief of Naval Operations dated 30 April 1941, the conversions were necessary to "give early support to United States Forces beyond the Continental Limits."[55]

Chartered by the navy as a troop transport, *Mallory* began sailing for the War Department in July 1942, making several voyages to Iceland, Newfoundland, Ireland, and the United Kingdom.[56] Her crew consisted of seventy-six Americans, one Canadian, two Puerto Ricans, one Russian, and one Filipino, many of them inexperienced, which was not unusual in a rapidly expanding merchant fleet. The inadequate training of the crew would be a contributing factor in the ship's forthcoming disaster.[57]

On 24 January 1943, *Mallory* departed New York as a part of a forty-four-ship convoy, SC118. On New Year's Eve, the convoy was off the coast of Newfoundland when it was joined by nineteen additional merchant ships from Halifax and St. John's. In addition, the local escort was replaced by British Escort Group B-2, consisting of three British destroyers (HMS *Vimy*, HMS *Beverly*, and HMS *Vanessa*), three British corvettes (HMS *Campanula*, HMS *Mignonette*, and HMS *Abelia*), the Free French destroyer *Lobelia*, and the American coast guard cutter *Bibb* (WPG-31).

The regular group commander, Comdr. Donald MacIntyre, RN, an experienced U-boat hunter, was absent because his ship, HMS *Hesperus,* was under repair, leaving the group under the acting command of Comdr. F. B. Proudfoot, who was unfamiliar to the group, only recently having assumed command of *Vanessa.* This also had an impact on later events, as poorly coordinated station keeping created gaps in the protective screen astern of the convoy.[58]

Elsewhere in the North Atlantic, a German U-boat group patrolled westward hoping to intercept the convoy as it headed toward Iceland. German intelligence services had intercepted and deciphered an Allied routing order for convoy SC118, data that was confirmed by a captured seaman from a tanker sunk in an earlier convoy, HX224. Dönitz ordered all available boats into a group designated *Pfeil.* The "wolfpack" consisted of thirteen boats (*U89, U135, U187, U262, U266, U267, U402, U413, U454, U465, U594, U608,* and *U609*). *Pfeil* was later reinforced by five boats from Wolfpack *Haudegen* (*U438, U613, U624, U704,* and *U752*) as well as two boats returning from the encounter with HX-224 (*U456* and *U614*).[59]

Allied HF/DF stations, picking up increased radio traffic between the subs, ordered additional escorts from Iceland to join the convoy. Two World War I destroyers, USS *Babbitt* (DD-128) and USS *Schenck* (DD-159), and USCGC *Ingham* (WPG-35) departed port to join the escort group.

Meanwhile, the two forces passed each other unnoticed the night of 3–4 February, and it might have ended there but for the accidental discharge of a snowflake rocket by a careless merchant seaman aboard SS *Annik.* The flare was observed by the watch of *U187* twenty miles away, and the incident was radioed to the *Pfeil* boats. Five boats were immediately ordered to the scene. Unfortunately for *U187* the signal was detected by the HF/DF aboard the convoy rescue ship *Toward,* which dispatched the destroyers *Vimy* and *Beverly.* After locating the sub by ASDIC, they made three depth-charge attacks, which forced the U-boat to the surface only long enough for the crew to abandon the submarine before she went under.

As the other U-boats swarmed into the area, the escorts were kept busy, charging from contact to contact, effectively driving off attempts to penetrate the screen during a winter storm that was moving through the area. It was only at 1 P.M. on 5 February that Group *Pfeil* was able to draw first blood, when *U413* sank *West Portal,* a 5,376-ton U.S. steamer that had fallen behind during the storm. Unable to mount a rescue, as no escorts could be spared, the ship was lost with all hands.

The U-boats continued to probe the convoy throughout the evening of the fifth and early morning hours of the sixth without success. During that time the additional escorts arrived from Iceland.[60] The weather cleared on 6 February and RAF Liberators flew over the convoy to provide air cover for the besieged ships. One of the Liberators soon made contact with *U465* and severely damaged the boat during an attack, forcing the U-boat to break off and sail for home. However, another straggler, the Greek freighter *Polktor*, was overtaken and sunk by *U266* at 6:20 P.M.,[61] and near midnight *U262* penetrated the screen and sank the 2,864-ton Polish ship *Zagloba*.[62] *U262* was subsequently detected and damaged by depth charges from the *Lobelia*, and the submarine had to return to port.

Up to this point, Group B-2 was holding its own in protecting the convoy, losing only one ship within its screen and two stragglers while sinking one and damaging two U-boats. The situation changed with the arrival of *U402* at 2:15 A.M. on the morning of 7 February. A type VIIC U-boat commissioned in Danzig on 21 May 1941, *U402* was on her sixth patrol and had been hunting the convoy for two days. Her captain, Siegfried Freiheer von Forstner, was a fourth-generation Prussian aristocrat and the son of a regular army general who commanded a regiment in World War I, winning the Pour le Merite. Von Forstner and his three brothers all served the fatherland, his two younger brothers in the army, while he and his brother, Wolfgang, went to sea.[63]

Within an hour of his arrival von Forstner sank the first of what would be seven kills during the battle.[64] When he sent the 1,571-ton rescue ship *Toward* to the bottom, the convoy lost one of its two ships that was equipped with HF/DF and left *Mignonette* responsible for rescuing survivors. Twenty minutes after sinking *Toward*, *U402* severely damaged the Norwegian tanker *Daghild*. Though it was finished off later by *U614* and *U608*, von Forstner was credited with two ships since the tanker carried the British LCT 2335 on board. These were considered his second and third successes. Von Forstner next sank the U.S. tanker SS *Robert E. Hopkins*.[65] *U614* registered the next kill sinking the British freighter *Harmala*, when it fell out of formation and trailed the convoy. The convoy's defensive screen unraveled as *Mignonette* was dispatched to pick up survivors, with *Lobelia* to provide cover, leaving only *Campanula* and *Schenck* to protect the rear area of the convoy. While searching for survivors, *Lobelia* caught *U609* on the surface and attacked with her guns as the boat dived. Following up with depth charges, the French destroyer sank the U-boat with the loss of all hands.

After reloading all of *U402*'s tubes, von Forstner returned to the battle and engaged and sank the British freighter *Afrika.* While attempting to catch up with the convoy, von Forstner came across another straggler, SS *Henry R. Mallory.* Closing to nine hundred yards he fired one torpedo at the ship.[66] Besides her crew of eighty-one, *Mallory* carried thirty-four Naval Armed Guards and 383 passengers consisting of 136 army, 173 navy, seventy-two marines and two civilians.[67] In addition she carried clothing, food, and trucks. Her captain, Horace R. Weaver, was on his first voyage as master having previously served as chief mate, which may explain why *Mallory* failed to keep her place in formation, frequently straggling to the rear.

No one on board the *Mallory* sighted the U-boat, or the torpedo track, and there was no warning when an explosion tore open the starboard side of the ship adjacent to the No. 3 hold, destroying sick bay and one lifeboat, and blowing the cover from the No. 4 hatch. Although the crew and Armed Guard were at battle stations, the passengers, jarred awake from the explosion, rushed on deck, many barely dressed. There was some confusion, and undoubtedly a degree of panic that might have been prevented by a display of leadership from those in charge. It never came.

No commands came from the bridge. No general alarm was sounded. No flares were ignited. No radio distress call went out. No order to "abandon ship" was given (accounts differ on whether this command was given).[68] In fact convoy *SC118* steamed on unaware that *Mallory* had been hit. On board, the lack of anyone in command led to individual initiative in launching the boats and rafts, but some of the boats capsized on launching. Only five of the nine undamaged boats got away from the ship, carrying just 175 men.

Others who launched and crowded into box and balsa doughnut-type rafts suffered terribly in the rough, icy waters. Thirty minutes to an hour after the torpedo hit (accounts differ), *Mallory* listed to port and then went steeply down stern first, leaving a litter of wreckage, rafts, swimmers, and corpses in its wake. Many of the rafts went down with the ship. None of the swimmers survived in the frigid waters, those fully dressed lasting (and suffering) longer.

Ironically, *Schenck* was sweeping the stern area, looking for survivors of *Toward,* but was ordered to rejoin the convoy. As she turned, her captain saw lights in the distance, and thinking they might be *Toward* survivors, he requested permission to investigate. Commander Proudfoot, aboard *Vanessa,* denied permission, explaining that the survivors would be picked up by *Lobelia.* Unknown to Proudfoot, *Lobelia* was thirty miles astern and fully occupied. Thus, an opportunity for an early rescue was missed, resulting in certain death for many who remained in the water.

It was not until 10 A.M., still an hour before dawn that far north, that the first survivors were picked up by *Bibb,* which was in the area hunting for U-boats. When *Bibb's* captain, Comdr. Roy Raney, radioed *Vanessa* requesting permission to commence rescue operations, permission was denied as both Proudfoot and Raney understood the danger of a lone ship stopping in submarine-infested waters at night. *Bibb* was directed to rejoin at "best speed." Taking a liberal interpretation of "best speed," Raney began directing his crew in a race against time to retrieve as many survivors as possible, sending crewmen over the side on nets, and even into the water to assist those too weak to help themselves. *Bibb* is credited with rescuing 205 survivors (three of whom died after being rescued). *Ingham,* which was ordered to the scene to assist, accounted for another twenty-two rescued (two died after being taken aboard) for a total of 222 rescued from 494 on board, or a loss of 272 men.[69]

Thirty-five minutes after sinking *Mallory,* U402 sighted the 4,965-ton Greek freighter *Kalliopi,* which she torpedoed for her sixth kill. With the arrival of dawn, air patrol activity resumed, and there was little opportunity for the U-boats to attack. A B-17 from the 220th Squadron sank *U624,* and there were numerous close calls, yet *U402* and the other boats pursued the convoy throughout the seventh. It wasn't until around midnight of 7–8 February that von Forstner claimed his seventh victim, the 4,625-ton British ship *Newton Ash.* Elsewhere *U135* and *U614* were damaged in air attacks. Thus ended the battle of convoy SC118. On the evening of 9 February, *U402* received the news by radio that her captain had been awarded the Knight's Cross.[70]

During her eighth patrol, *U402* was sunk by a VC9 *Wildcat* from escort carrier USS *Card* (CVE-11), von Forster and his entire crew were lost in the encounter.[71]

By the end of May, Allied antisubmarine forces included additional warships, escort carrier groups, new weapons systems such as the "hedgehog" and air-dropped homing torpedoes, and a newly perfected "Huff-Duff" to more accurately pinpoint the source of U-boat communications. The Allies also benefited from the development of a microwave radar that the enemy could not detect, and renewed British success was experienced in decoding the Kriegsmarine submarine cipher.

Though U-boats continued to enjoy success in northern Atlantic waters, convoy losses gradually decreased because they could be escorted across their entire route. At the same time U-boat losses increased to the point that Dönitz transferred his boats south to the central Atlantic seeking better hunting grounds.

BENJAMIN CONTEE

On 3 October 1940, Cyril Thompson and Harry Hunter disembarked from the Cunard liner *Scythia* in New York harbor on a mission vital to the survival of Great Britain. The two men represented the British Shipbuilding Mission to the United States, the purpose of which was to convince a still-neutral United States to build sixty merchant ships for Great Britain, currently at war with Italy and Germany.[72]

Liberty Ships
The British shipping situation was critical as German U-boats were sinking Allied merchant ships faster than British and Commonwealth shipyards could replace them. In the first year of the war (September 1939–August 1940), England lost 385 ships totaling 1.7 million gross tons, nearly 10 percent of her prewar merchant tonnage. In addition to losses from submarines, a number of ships were lost to air attacks, mines, accidents, and storms.[73]

England, an island nation of shipyards, was unable to meet the demands of merchant shipping for a variety of reasons. To begin with, the majority of its shipyards were committed exclusively to the production of warships. British shipyards were old, and there was little land available for expanding or constructing new slipways. In addition, the process was restricted by a shortage of materials, like iron ore, as well as a shortage of trained manpower, many men having been absorbed into the military. To complicate matters further, the blackout in effect after dark limited the hours that work could proceed on ship production, as floodlights tended to invite unwanted Luftwaffe attention.[74]

As Thompson and Hunter arrived in October, there was also the question of whether a sympathetic President Roosevelt, up for re-election in November, would risk the political fallout from a still predominantly isolationist United States. Fortunately, the man who headed the United States Maritime Commission

The launching of *Patrick Henry*, Fairfield, Maryland, 27 September 1941.
Bethlehem Steel Corporation

was Rear Adm. Emory Scott Lane, an old friend of the president from his days as secretary of the navy, and a former naval attaché in London. Unlike many other senior naval officers, Lane was predisposed to cooperate with the British, and he gave the clearance for the mission to seek a U.S. firm to build the ships.[75]

Despite concerns that U.S. shipyards were already working to capacity producing new naval tonnage coupled with a reluctance by many American businesses to commit to what was perceived as the losing side and a nation on the edge of collapse (Great Britain at this point was alone in the war, Russia and the United States were not yet involved), an agreement was reached on 20 December.[76]

Roosevelt well understood that the best planned and executed strategy and tactics depended on logistics, the ability to transport military units and keep them supplied with fuel, ammunition, rations, weapons, vehicles, and spare parts. Recognizing the importance of the role that the merchant marine would play in the coming war, President Roosevelt announced a $350 million Emergency Ship Construction program on 3 January 1941.

The ships, designated EC-2 (EC for Emergency Construction and 2 for heavy) by the U.S. Maritime Commission, were constructed in a simple, standardized design suitable for mass production. Prefabricated sections were produced throughout the country and assembled in the yards by welding rather than by riveting, which shortened production time considerably. The first EC-2, *Patrick Henry*, was completed on 27 September 1941. Roosevelt commemorating the occasion referred to Patrick Henry's words spoken on 23 March 1775, when he said "Give me liberty or give me death." The president stated that these new ships would bring liberty to Europe, and the EC-2 was forevermore the "Liberty ship."[77]

The resulting Liberty ship, based on a British design, was 441 feet long and 56 feet wide and powered by a three-cylinder reciprocating steam engine. Its two oil-burning boilers were capable of speeds up to eleven knots, and it could carry almost one thousand pounds of cargo in its five holds plus additional war materials lashed to its deck. Built at a cost of under two million dollars, Liberty ships carried a crew of approximately forty-five and an Armed Guard complement of between ten to twenty to man a single 5-inch 127mm gun and ten antiaircraft guns on Liberties that carried them.[78]

In nineteen shipyards across the country, more than twenty-seven hundred Liberty ships were built during the war, an average of more than one a day. Of these, 2,580 were standard EC-2s, sixty were "Ocean"-class vessels built for Great Britain, twenty were aircraft transports, eight were tank carriers, and sixty-two were tankers.

The navy reconfigured 133 Liberty ships for use as cargo ships, repair ships, water carriers, and store issue ships, while the army reconfigured twenty-six as hospital ships and mule transports, and twenty-two were reconditioned for use as POW transports. One of those designated for POW transport was SS *Benjamin Contee*.[79]

Benjamin Contee transported German and Italian POWs from Europe to the United States. In August 1943 with eighteen hundred Italian POWs aboard, she was sunk by a German torpedo bomber off Bone, Algeria. *William Hultgen Collection*

Named for Benjamin Contee (1755–1815), a Maryland clergyman who served as an officer in the Revolutionary War and later as a member of both the Continental Congress (1787–88) and the first United States Congress,[80] SS *Benjamin Contee* began life as USMC (United States Marine Commission) hull #0125 at the Delta Shipyard in New Orleans on 2 February 1942 when her keel was laid. At 441 feet long and 56 feet wide with a gross tonnage of 10,920, her three-cylinder reciprocating steam engines, fed by two oil-burning boilers, were capable of speeds of approximately eleven knots. She was armed with one 5-inch 127mm gun, one 3-inch, and eight 20mm antiaircraft machine guns.

The conversion of a Liberty ship to carry troops required little modification, remaining essentially a cargo ship. Tiers of bunks, five high, were installed in the holds as well as additional facilities to provide food, water, and sanitation for approximately five hundred prisoners per hold. In addition, extra lifeboats, life rafts, and life vests were carried, and personnel were not as a rule confined below the waterline. Two additional emergency escapes were installed in each hold.[81] Thus, by November 1942, *Benjamin Contee* was the first Liberty ship converted to carry troops, albeit enemy troops.

Operated by the Mississippi Shipping Company, *Benjamin Contee* was launched on 15 June 1942 and chartered by the USAT (Army Transport Service), which took delivery on 7 August of that year. In November *Contee* was allocated to Britain, along with two freighters, *Agwimonte* and *Alcoa Prospector,* for service transporting German and Italian prisoners of war from behind British lines at El Alamein to POW camps in United States.[82]

The ships traveled south around Cape Town to arrive in Egypt in late November, and began a series of cruises transporting prisoners across the Atlantic. In May 1943 *Agwimonte* was sunk by *U177* in the Indian Ocean, and later that summer *Alcoa Prospector* was damaged by the Japanese submarine *I-27.*

On 16 August 1943, *Contee* loaded eighteen hundred Italian POWs and departed Bone, Algeria, under a full moon to meet a convoy bound for Oran. Besides the forty-four-man crew and the prisoners, she carried twenty-six British guards, seven U.S. Army security personnel, and an Armed Guard unit of twenty-seven.[83]

At 11:23 P.M. *Contee* was sixteen miles west of Bone when a German torpedo bomber attacked, gliding in with its engines off to avoid detection by an escorting British corvette. The aircraft released a torpedo that struck the ship between the No. 1 and No. 2 holds, blowing open a fifty-foot by twenty-one-foot hole in the hull and injuring hundreds of prisoners. As the sea rushed in, the ship began to settle by the head, and panicked prisoners rushed onto deck, working to release lifeboats and rafts.[84]

The citation for the Merchant Marine Distinguished Service Medal awarded to Capt. Even Evensen, master of *Contee,* best describes what followed: "Exercising forceful command, Captain Evensen herded the panic-stricken prisoners from the forward to the after decks. Then, releasing the remaining 900 prisoners from the after deck, he flooded those holds to bring his ship to an even keel. Supported by the fine discipline of a loyal crew, he was able to bring his ship into a safe port and deliver the surviving prisoners into proper military hands."[85]

Some accounts have *Contee* being towed to Gibraltar, others have her returning to Bone under her own power. What is agreed is that 264 POWs lost their lives and another 142 were injured, with no casualties among the crew or escorting guards. She returned to service following repairs at Gibraltar, and by 24 January 1944 she was back in New York.[86]

Like many a veteran, *Benjamin Contee* became involved in the preparations for the invasion of Europe, and like many a veteran, she found herself in a position where sacrifice would be necessary to accomplish her mission: *Contee* was among twenty-six freighters selected for use as "blockships."

Allied strategic planners understood that a successful invasion of Europe would depend on the ability to land sufficient ammunition, food, medicine, fuel, and equipment to support the invasion. The choice of Normandy as the invasion site, as opposed to the Pas de Calais, would require the rapid construction of artificial harbors, and plans were made to tow prefabricated piers, code-named "Mulberries," across the channel to create causeways for ships unloading supplies. These "ports" were augmented by "Gooseberries" (breakwaters of steel), concrete caissons, and blockships like *Contee* that were towed into position under fire and sunk in place to form protective shelters.[87] One crewman recalled army engineers coming aboard *Contee* to set charges of dynamite in the holds before they headed out to sea on 1 June to rendezvous at Portsmouth, England. On 8 June (D-Day +2), *Benjamin Contee* was among seventeen blockships scuttled that day.[88]

Her sacrifice would not be in vain. The seven thousand tons of vehicles and supplies unloaded each day substantially allowed the Allies to win the race to build up forces in the beachhead area. A week after the landing, the U.S. Mulberry at Omaha was destroyed by a storm, but the British Mulberry at Gold Beach survived and continued in use for many months.

ROHNA

On 26 November 1943, the day after Thanksgiving, German bombers attacked Allied convoy KMF26 in the Mediterranean, resulting in one of the earliest uses of air-to-surface missiles, and the greatest loss of U.S. troops at sea during World War II when the British transport HMT *Rohna* was struck by a German HS-293 glide bomb and sent to the bottom.[89]

Built by Hawthorn Leslie and Company at Newcastle upon Tyne for the British India Steam Navigation Company in 1926, *Rohna* initially carried mail along the Madras-Singapore route in the Far East, along with her sister ship, *Rajula*. However, prior to assuming her duties upon arrival in India, she was commandeered to carry British reinforcement troops to Shanghai and therefore didn't begin sailing the Madras route until June 1927.[90]

The next twelve years were spent carrying cargo and passengers between Madras, Nagapatam, Penang, and Singapore. Five oil-fired boilers carried the

The British troopship *Rohna,* which was sunk in November 1943 by German bombers using air-to-surface missiles in the Mediterranean. Her sinking resulted in the greatest loss of American soldiers at sea during World War II. *National Maritime Museum*

8,062-ton vessel at speeds up to thirteen knots. In July 1939, with war clouds gathering over Europe and Japanese aggression steadily increasing in the east, *Rohna* was requisitioned for short periods as a personnel ship, a status made permanent in May 1940.[91]

Early in the war, she was utilized in the east, searching for mines and transporting troops and supplies between Ceylon and Bombay, India. *Rohna* also assisted in the evacuation of Indian women and children from Singapore in 1941.[92] In 1942 *Rohna* was ordered west into the Mediterranean area of operations, where she participated in the invasion of Sicily and served briefly as a naval accommodation ship at Algiers before receiving orders to board troops in Oran and join convoy KMF26 which was bound for India.

Now painted a flat black, and armed with eight 50-caliber machine guns, six 20mm Oerlikon cannons, two Hotchkiss and two twin Lewis 30-caliber machine guns, *Rohna* carried an eighteen-man gunnery complement of sixteen naval and two army gunners.[93]

U.S. troops began loading as early as 24 November 1943. They included elements of the 853rd Engineer Aviation Battalion (793 men), 44th Portable Surgical Hospital (36), 31st Signal Construction Battalion (259), 322d Flight

Control Squadron (285), and the 705th Infantry Replacement Battalion, whose ultimate destination was Burma. Part of the difficulty in determining the precise number of troops eventually lost was the fact that units were loaded, then sometimes switched among *Rohna* and five other convoy ships: HMT *Rajula,* HMT *Egra,* HMT *Karoa,* HMT *Ranchi,* and the French-registered *Banfora.*[94]

Loading was completed early on the morning of the twenty-fifth, and the troops aboard *Rohna* enjoyed a Thanksgiving day meal consisting of a large greasy sausage (about one fourth meat and three fourths soybean), accompanied by a plate of slippery green onions, a slice of bread, and weak coffee. Shortly before midnight, *Rohna,* under Australian Capt. T. J. Murphy, departed Oran in company with the five other ships to join eastbound KMF26.

Rohna sailed from Algeria with 2,201 men aboard, although accounts differ as to exactly how many passengers and crew she carried. Most sources list the crew as numbering 195. Although numerous sources cite "almost 2,000" to describe the number of U.S. troops, several references list the number as 1,988 (1,889 enlisted, 92 officers and seven Red Cross workers which would put the total on board at 2,201).[95] This is consistent with sources that list 2,183 as the number, but possibly they didn't take into account the eighteen gunners.

Ten days earlier, on 15 November, KMF26, consisting of eighteen ships, had formed on the River Clyde, off Gourock, Scotland, under the command of Commo. H. D. Wakeman Colville aboard the flagship cruiser HMS *Birmingham.* (He later transferred his flag to the transport HMT *Ranchi*).[96]

At Gibraltar, most of the escorting warships turned back toward the Atlantic, but six remained with the convoy; HMS *Pelican* and *Woodpecker,* the frigates HMS *Evenlode* and *Rother,* and the destroyers HMS *Jed* and *Brilliant.* As the convoy proceeded eastward, it was joined by an additional nine British and three U.S. vessels. British vessels included HMS *Slazak, Catterick, Miaoules,* and *Atherstone;* the antiaircraft cruisers HMS *Cleveland* and *Coventry;* the corvette HMS *Holcombe;* the cargo/rescue ship *Clan Campbell;* and the tug *Mindful.* The U.S. ships were USS *Frederick C. Davis* (DE-136) and USS *Herbert C. Jones* (DE-137), both Edsall-class destroyer escorts, and the Raven-class minesweeper USS *Portent* (AM-106). They were later joined by another minesweeper, USS *Pioneer* (AM-105).[97]

On 26 November the convoy was picked up by German air reconnaissance unit I/F 33 out of Montpallier a little before 9 A.M., and their progress was monitored throughout the day. Near dusk, at about 4:30 P.M., German bombers attacked the convoy in two waves. There were approximately thirty aircraft involved, including Junker JU-88 and Heinkel He-111 bombers of Kampfgeschwader KG-26, He-177 bombers and Folke-Wulf FW-200K fighters from KG-40, and Dornier Do-217s from KG-100.[98]

Scrambled to protect the convoy from the air attack were six Beaufighters from RAF 153rd Squadron, four P-39s from the 347th Squadron of the USAAF, and twelve Spitfire fighters, flown by pilots of French 1/7 Squadron, twenty-two fighters in all. In the course of the air battle, nine German planes were destroyed (with another two probable) and five damaged.[99] The Allied force lost one Beaufighter.

The first wave (4:40–5:00 P.M.) resulted in little damage to ships in the convoy but the second wave (5:15–5:40 P.M.) was much more successful. At approximately 5:25, a He-177 piloted by Maj. Hans Dottermann approached from north-northeast, coming at the convoy from out of the sun. The six-man bomber (pilot, bombardier, wireless operator, mechanic, and two gunners) carried two HS-293 glider bombs under her wings, each with 1,100 pounds of explosives.

The HS-293 was essentially a radio-controlled guided missile. The pilot would circle the target at a high altitude while the bombardier activated the guidance system. The bomb would be released (port side first), and the pilot would fly a parallel course as the bombardier attempted to guide the missile onto the target. The procedure would be repeated to launch the starboard weapon. The extended time required to launch both weapons made the bombers highly vulnerable to increasingly improved Allied fighters, such as the P-38 Lightning. It was Dottermann's starboard missile that was launched against *Rohna*.

As Second Officer Willis recorded in his statement, "The bomb struck the engine room on the port side, just above the waterline. The No. 4 bulkhead collapsed." The bomb explosion caused extensive damage blowing holes in both sides of the ship so large that one survivor recalled, "you could drive a truck through them." Fires broke out, and power was lost, resulting in no lights, no communication, and no water pressure. An estimated three hundred men died in the initial explosion.[100] Powerless in the dark, and with no other options, Captain Murphy ordered the ship to be abandoned, though lack of power prevented his order from being broadcast throughout the ship.

Opinions differ as to the behavior of the Lascar crew, with one War Department adjutant general's report, (AG704DEAD), dated 5 May 1944, stating that "the Lascars had no thoughts in the emergency for anyone but themselves," a sentiment reinforced by reports from surviving U.S. troops. The fact that 115 crewmen and five ship's officers died in the sinking suggests otherwise.

Rohna sank just after dusk, about 6:30 P.M.[101] The rescue effort was hampered by failing light, high seas, and the loss of a significant number of lifeboats, both from the initial explosion and subsequent mishandling by troops and crewmen. Despite this, the crews of the rescue ships performed, by all accounts, magnificently. USS *Pioneer* alone picked up 606, the tug *Mindful* another 200, the *Glen Campbell* hindered by high decks was able to rescue 83, and the destroyer *Atherstone* and corvette *Holcombe* plucked an additional few survivors from the sea. Even so, the losses were staggering.

Sources are much more consistent in their figures regarding the numbers lost, which most place at 1,149. Almost all sources agree with 1,015 as the number of U.S. troops lost, and most note that 120 of the crew (five officers and 115 crewmen) perished. With three Red Cross workers and eleven gunners, the total comes to 1,149, a number consistent with David Williams's *Wartime Disasters at Sea,* Jackson's *Forgotten Tragedy,* and Waddington's *History of the HMT Rajula.*[102]

The survivors were transported to Bougie, Phillipville, and Djidjelli.[103] News of the disaster was suppressed during the war, and casualties were reported only as "missing in action" and later "killed in action."[104] Regrettably, the silence continued for almost a half century after the war.

The *Rhona* Survivors Association was formed in 1995, and the following year, on Memorial Day, a monument was dedicated at the Fort Mitchell National Cemetery in Seales, Alabama. Finally, in October 2000, Congress officially recognized the heroes of *Rohna,* ending years of frustration for the survivors and their families. As survivor Bob Brewer recalled, "A lot of people didn't believe it ever happened."[105]

PAUL HAMILTON

One of the greatest naval losses to occur in the Mediterranean during the Second World War was the sinking of the Liberty ship SS *Paul Hamilton* off the coast of North Africa on 20 April, 1944.

Paul Hamilton exploding after being hit. All hands were lost. *U.S. Naval Historical Center*

Hamilton was a veteran of four previous voyages since her launching on 20 October 1942. With a speed of eleven knots and a range of seventeen thousand miles, she was a typical Liberty ship, armed with one 5-inch gun, one 3-inch gun, and eight 20mm cannons.[106]

On 3 April 1944, *Hamilton* commenced her fifth voyage, departing Hampton Roads, Virginia, as part of convoy UGS38.[107] Besides her complement of eight officers, thirty-nine crewmen, and twenty-nine Naval Armed Guards, she carried 504 troops, including a U.S. demolition squad bound for Anzio and 154 men of the 831st Squadron, U.S. Army Air Corps. Previously two other Liberty ships, *Samuel Huntington* and *Elihu,* were attacked at Anzio by German aircraft using glider bombs while the ships were discharging munitions—and both blew up with spectacular explosions.[108]

It was unusual, and contrary to good sense, to carry volatile cargoes such as high-octane fuel or high explosives on ships that were transporting troops, and yet incredibly *Hamilton* was loaded with both troops and high-explosive ammunition.[109]

UGS38 comprised eighty-five ships and two tankers accompanied by Task Force 66, a twenty-one-warship escort under the command of Capt. W. H. Duvall, USN, aboard the coast guard cutter *Roger B. Taney* (WPG-37).[110] Among the escorts were twelve destroyer escorts (including *Laning, Menges,* and *Newell*), another coast guard cutter *Duane* (WPG-33), the destroyer USS *Lansdale* (DD-426), and the Netherlands flak cruiser HNMS *Heemskerck,* which joined the convoy at Gibraltar.[111]

The Atlantic crossing was accomplished without incident, and the convoy reached the Azores on 13 April and sailed along the North African coast.[112] Toward dusk on the evening of 20 April, the convoy was thirty miles off the coast of Cape Benegut, Algiers, and shortly after dark, at approximately 9:00 P.M., UGS38 was attacked by three flights of Junker JU-88 dive-bombers and Heinkel HE-111 medium bombers armed with between twenty-five and thirty torpedoes.[113]

The planes approached low from the east, with the shoreline at the rear, which assisted in evading the ship's radar and the attack caught the convoy by surprise.[114]

The leading JU-88s in the first wave attacked head on, dropping torpedoes, one of which struck *Hamilton,* resulting in a tremendous blast as the high explosives in the hold detonated sending flame and debris more than one thousand feet into the air.[115]

By all accounts, when the smoke cleared thirty seconds later, *Hamilton* had completely disappeared with the loss of all 580 onboard. Also struck and damaged in the first wave was SS *Samite.*[116]

A second wave split, dropping torpedoes that damaged SS *Stephen T. Austin* and sank SS *Royal Star.*[117] The third wave concentrated on the destroyer *Lansdale,* which was providing effective antiaircraft fire. Five HE-111s attacked *Lansdale* from two directions, ripping open her forward fire room to the sea on both sides and breaking her keel.[118]

With the *Lansdale* powerless and sinking, her captain, Lt. Comdr. D. M. Swift, ordered the crew to "abandon ship" at 9:30 P.M., and shortly thereafter the ship broke apart and slid under the waves; 235 crewmen were picked up by U.S. destroyer escorts *Menges* and *Newell,* but forty-seven men went down with the ship.[119]

In a matter of minutes, the attack was over, with three ships lost and another two damaged. The convoy reached Bizerte, Tunisia, on the twenty-first, although wartime conditions suppressed news of the sinking for many years.

OPERATION TIGER

Since the days of the Gallipoli amphibious disaster during World War I, military forces have ensured that adequate training and coordination be a part of any planned invasion by sea. Normandy, the greatest amphibious operation in history, required numerous rehearsals before D-Day and, as in many such exercises, men were lost to a variety of unforeseen circumstances. Operation Tiger was one such instance that cost the United States the lives of hundreds of young soldiers just days before they were to swarm ashore in France.

By late 1943 some eight hundred thousand British and Canadian troops and more than 1.3 million Americans were in the United Kingdom preparing to invade German-held Europe. Security became a major factor as more and more Allied officers and enlisted men had to be briefed on any or all aspects of the operation. Thus, a system called "Bigot" was established to ensure that documents of the greatest secrecy, dealing with specific operational matters, were afforded a degree of security over and above that accorded by the classification "Most Secret." The Germans knew an invasion was imminent but didn't know when, where, and how the attack would unfold. Allied personnel who were exposed to such critical documents were given Bigot clearances, and although there were breaches by some of the cleared personnel—who were dealt with harshly—the security of the Normandy invasion plans remained intact thanks to luck and the fact that the Germans had no espionage agents in Britain at the time.[120] The Bigot factor was to become a major problem during Operation Tiger, one of ten simulated landings that took place in Devon County, England, at Slapton Sands, a beach on the English Channel east of Plymouth in Lyme Bay. The exercises were each designed to test the readiness of plans for the forthcoming invasion and to measure the efficiency of the troops.[121]

Slapton was an unspoiled beach of coarse gravel, fronting a shallow lagoon backed by bluffs that resembled Omaha and Utah beaches. The British government took possession of thirty thousand acres of land in proximity to the oper-

USS LST-507 was the first boat to be attacked by German E-Boats (motor torpedo boats) during an invasion rehearsal off Slapton Sides, England, 28 April 1944.
Imperial War Museum.

ations area. This meant the closure of 180 farms and the relocation of three thousand people. The area was deserted by January 1944 and using maps and intelligence taken from current photo reconnaissance of the German Normandy defenses, Allied military men moved in with heavy equipment and constructed bunkers, blockhouses, and hardened gun sites to replicate what the Germans had in place. The first exercise, Operation Duck, took place in January 1944; next came "Beaver" at the end of March. Allied commanders considered the exercises less than successful due to lack of coordination between units. Navy, army, and airborne participants remember them mostly for the confusion experienced as the planned sequence of events fell apart during the operations. The problems encountered in these first two events were carefully critiqued and remedies were put in place for Operation Tiger.[122]

The flagship for the task force was the cruiser USS *Augusta* (CA-31). Rear Adm. Don P. Moon and his staff were on board the USS *Bayfield* (APA-33), the "Force U" (Utah) flagship. On 26 April 1944 the task force and observing forces left their respective ports for Slapton Sands. Moon was in charge of running the exercise and delivering the U.S. troops safely to the beach. The observers were looking for perfect timing, execution, and air support from

British "Typhoons," ground support aircraft that would cover the force with air-to-surface rockets.[123]

The initial exercises did not encounter any German opposition in the way of aerial, U-boat, or surface attacks. However, the Germans were aware of the constant activity of Allied maneuvers along the English coast, especially off Devon, and their naval forces were considered to be very active in *Der Kanal.* Germany's main offensive force in the channel was the *Schnellboote,* a fast motor torpedo boat that could reach speeds of up to forty-two knots. The boats were armed with two 21-inch torpedoes and light antiaircraft guns. In late May 1944 Marinegruppe West consisted of thirty-eight S-boats (called E-boats by the Allies) deployed in five flotillas under the command of Kapitän zur See Rudolf Petersen. Petersen's boats had been successful in attacking various Allied ships plying channel waters, especially against convoys PW300 and WP300 in February 1943. In 1944 up until D-Day they sank eleven merchant ships and accounted for one minesweeper.[124]

"Tiger" was to be the largest exercise to date, involving some three hundred ships and thirty thousand men. Naval and air support were to use live ammunition. Thirty of the ships were LSTs, which loaded at Plymouth, Brixham, Dartmouth, the same ports that the Allies would use during the actual Normandy invasion.[125] In addition to his role in Operation Tiger, Rear Admiral Moon was to provide naval support for the actual landings at Utah beach on 6 June 1944. The U.S. troops who participated in the operation were the 4th Infantry Division, the 101st Airborne and the 82nd Airborne Divisions, the 1st Engineer Special Brigade, and naval and air force units. Air drops were simulated. Airborne troops were brought to a staging area, briefed, and then taken by truck to drop zones. The paratroopers called these maneuvers "The GMC Jump."[126]

The main assault force landed on Slapton Sands the morning of 27 May. H-hour had been delayed one hour, which caused landings and naval bombardment to coincide since all ships had not received the delay message. However, amidst some confusion, the troops hit the beach without suffering casualties. The landing of additional soldiers and unloading of supplies and equipment on the beachhead continued during the day.[127]

Convoy T4 consisted of eight LSTs, four from Plymouth (515, 496, 511, and 531) and four from Brixham (58, 499, 289, and 507). T4 was one of the follow-up convoy groups that was to land at H +24 hours. The landing craft joined up with the sixteen-knot flower-class corvette HMS *Azalea* and proceeded at six knots in one column in the above order with *Azalea* in the lead. The force was under the command of Comdr. B. J. Skahill, who was aboard LST-515. Most of the troops carried by the ships were of the 1st Engineer Special Brigade. On board were amphibious trucks and combat engineers who would manage the traffic on the beach and ensure that the operation proceeded smoothly. T4 arrived in Lyme Bay in the early hours of 28 April and maneuvered to set course for the beach. The convoy was to be protected by a roving British destroyer, HMS *Scimitar*. The British felt that two warships would be sufficient to ward off potential enemy attacks since they had used the same number of ships before and experienced no enemy encounters. Unfortunately, *Scimitar* had been rammed by U.S. LCI(L)-324 earlier and suffered a sizable hole in its starboard side some twelve feet above the waterline. When the ship arrived at Plymouth to refuel, the skipper was told to tie up and remain in port until the damage could be repaired. He informed the authorities that he was to provide protection for convoy T4 and was seaworthy to perform that task. However, senior officials had never heard of T4 and destroyers were at a premium at the time. This decision made the T4 LSTs highly vulnerable to enemy attack. Admiral Moon and Commander Skahill were not informed of the loss of their escort. Since the Plymouth command was busy preparing for the next exercise, Operation Fabius, Vice Adm. R. Leatham, the Plymouth commander in chief, paid little attention to Operation Tiger. [128]

By the end of the day on the twenty-seventh all of the ships of the main force lay empty at Slapton Sands awaiting escort ships to cover the return to their home bases. They were informed by the commander in chief of the British base at Plymouth that there were no available escorts since they had been assigned to various convoys, patrols, and screens. [129]

Since Lyme Bay had often been the site of German E-boat raids the British did assign four special patrols to Operation Tiger, consisting of three motor torpedo boats, two motor gunboats, and four destroyers. They patrolled primarily along the line of movement of the main exercise force that landed during the daylight hours of the twenty-seventh. A fifth patrol of eight motor torpedo boats was positioned off Cherbourg to engage any E-boats that might venture out into the channel. However, while T4 was at sea, nine E-boats slipped through the British screen under the cover of darkness on a routine patrol. [130]

Close-up view of damage sustained by LST-289. *U.S. National Archives*

As T4 prepared to depart Lyme Bay for Slapton Sands, the Americans sighted white and yellow flares off in the distance shortly after midnight. Thought to be British, they paid little heed until more flares were fired; some were rocket flares others were parachute flares. The flares had been fired from closing E-boats traveling at thirty-six knots. With no destroyer escort protection the LSTs were sitting ducks.[131] By 1:30 A.M. the Plymouth Command realized that they had made a grievous mistake by holding HMS *Scimitar* in port and upon receiving information that three groups of E-boats were on the loose in the channel ordered HMS *Saladin* to join T4 as soon as possible. Unfortunately, the ship was thirty miles away and it would take an hour and a half to reach the convoy.[132]

At 2:04 A.M. the convoy was attacked by nine E-boats of the 5th and 9th S-Boote flotilla based at Cherbourg. No warning of the presence of enemy boats had been received until LST-507 was torpedoed and burst into flames as survivors abandoned ship. Several minutes later LST-531 was torpedoed and sank within six minutes. LST-289, which opened fire at the E-boats, was also torpedoed but was able to reach port. LST-507 carried 165 officers and men and 282 army troops of the 1st Engineer Special Brigade.[133]

A survivor, Lt. Eugene E. Eckstam, MC, USNR, (Ret.), a medical officer on LST-507, recalled the tragic affair.

I was a brand new Naval Reserve medical officer, fresh out of an abbreviated senior year and internship, totally unprepared for what was to follow. I knew only about the role of such physicians on LSTs and this training was short.

My first assignment in January 1944 was Great Lakes Naval Training Station in Illinois. I followed the other physicians on the North Shore electric train to the Great Lakes Naval Hospital and checked in. The next morning I found the difference between Hospital and Mainside! I was assured all the paperwork would be transferred. It wasn't, as I later discovered.

At the recruiting Center, Mainside, we examined an average of 1,700 recruits a day. In a week I became an expert in hemorrhoids, hernias, and right ears. Then I, and perhaps 50 other new physicians, reported to Lido Beach, Long Island. A few thousand hospital corpsmen of all ranks were there too. Thus, individual outfits of "Foxy 29," the code name for our medical unit, were formed by taking two physicians and an assortment of 40 corpsmen. We were supposed to drill and train our men. After the brass saw hilarious marching formations colliding, the Marines took over.

Our training at Lido Beach was the introduction to the LST and its uses as a medical evacuation ship. We had some exposure to gas warfare, and endured unpleasant contacts with several chemical agents. Units shipped out at regular intervals on LSTs. We left on 10 March 1944.

As LST-507 was dropping off cargo and loading supplies in various English ports, our medical unit was sent to Fowey for a week of intensive training on chemical warfare and general first aid. This all added up to very little preparation for an invasion with major casualties.

When our medical unit reported back to LST-507, it was in Brixham on the afternoon of 27 April scheduled to join five LSTs coming from Plymouth. Only recently I found out that our British escort had been warned about E-boats in the area, but the U.S. forces had not been given the correct radio channel to monitor. We sailed along in fatal ignorance.

General Quarters rudely aroused us about 0130. I remember hearing gunfire and saying they had better watch where they were shooting or someone would get hurt. At 0203 I was stupidly trying to go topside to see what was going on and suddenly "BOOM!" There was a horrendous noise accompanied by the sound of crunching metal and dust everywhere. The lights went out and I was thrust violently in the air to land on the steel deck on my knees, which became very sore immediately thereafter. Now I knew how getting torpedoed felt. But I was lucky.

The torpedo hit amidships starboard in the auxiliary engine room, knocking out all electric and water power. We sat and burned. A few casualties came into the wardroom for care and, since there was ample help, I checked below decks aft to be sure no one required medical attention there. All men in accessible areas had gone topside.

The tank deck was a different matter. As I opened the hatch, I found myself looking into a raging inferno which pushed me back. It was impossible to enter. The screams and cries of those many Army troops in there still haunt me. Navy regulations call for dogging the hatches to preserve the integrity of the ship and that's what I did.

Until the fire got so hot we were forced to leave the ship at 0230, we watched the most spectacular fireworks ever. Gas cans and ammunition exploding and the enormous fire blazing only a few yards away are sights forever etched in my memory.

Ship's company wore life jackets, but the medics and Army personnel had been issued inflatable belts. We were told only to release the snaps and squeeze the handle to inflate. Climbing down a cargo net, I settled into the 42 degree F. water gradually getting lower as the life belt rose up to my arm pits. The soldiers that jumped or dove in with full packs did not do well. Most were found with their heads in the water and their feet in the air, top heavy from not putting their belts around their chests before inflating them. Instructions in their correct use had never been given.

I recall only brief moments of hearing motors, of putting a knee on a small boat ramp, and then "awakening" half way up a Jacob's ladder. I was on the only American ship, LST-515, to rescue survivors. This was at dawn, about 0600. I had been in the water over 2 hours fully dressed and insulated. Those that had stripped to swim, only God knows where they died. Drowning and hypothermia were the two major causes of death. I often wonder if many "dead" victims were really in a state of hibernation, and what would have happened had we been able to immerse them in warm tubs. But whoever heard of a tub on an LST in wartime? We couldn't even do a reliable physical exam under the circumstances.

Both dead and alive were taken to Portland. The dead went on to Brookwood (actually Blackwood) Cemetery near London where they were buried individually . . . We got dry clothes, courtesy of the American Red Cross and then an exam at an Army field hospital in Sherborne.[134]

This brief action off Slapton Sands resulted in 551 dead and missing soldiers. Navy losses numbered 198. The disaster was kept secret until after the invasion for security reasons. However of immediate concern to Allied commanders was the accounting of any Bigots that were on the two lost LSTs. The fear that one or more might have been captured and reveal the Normandy plans raised the possibility of having to cancel the invasion and replan the operation. Interviews with several survivors indicated that there was ample opportunity for the E-boats to seize some of the struggling soldiers in the water. Others reported that the E-boats were driven off by British escorts. Intelligence analysts identified ten Bigots aboard the two ships; all were missing and presumed drowned. Divers were sent down to the sunken wrecks. Some bodies were found and dog tags recovered. However, not all could be accounted for because many bodies floated away from the wrecks and were never recovered. However, SHAEF (Supreme Headquarters, Allied Expeditionary Force) was satisfied that security had not been breached. Along with the bodies recovered, the Bletchley Park enigma analysts detected no indications of the incident in German military communications traffic and no repositioning of enemy forces, then concentrated in the Pas de Calais area, was reported by Allied reconnaissance overflights. A 28 April German broadcast of the attack noted the sinking of three Allied ships in a convoy totaling nineteen thousand tons.[135]

On 5 August 1944, SHAEF released statistics on the casualties associated with the Normandy invasion, which included information about the German E-boat attack on 28 April. This information was also published in the 7 August issue of *The Stars and Stripes*, the daily newspaper of the U.S. Armed Forces in the European Theater. The story of Slapton Sands has remained somewhat obscure even though over the years it has often been related in various history journals and periodicals.[136]

Aftermath: Commemorating the Dead
Operation Tiger surfaced again in 1968 when Kenneth Small, a former British

policeman, moved to a village just off Slapton Sands where he bought and operated a small guest house. As he walked along the beach he found relics of war, unexpended cartridges, buttons, and fragments from uniforms. Talking with longtime residents he learned of the heavy loss of life during Operation Tiger. Small wondered why there was no monument to those who had died, particularly since the U.S. Army had already erected a monument to the British citizens who had left their homes to make way for troops to train for the Normandy invasion. He learned from local fishermen that a U.S. Sherman tank lay beneath the waters a mile offshore, a tank lost not in Operation Tiger but in another rehearsal a year earlier. At considerable personal expense, Small managed to salvage the tank and place it on the plinth just behind the beach as a memorial to those Americans who had died. The memorial was dedicated in a ceremony on the fortieth anniversary of D-Day.[137]

The ceremony conducted on the fortieth anniversary of D-Day prompted the first spurt of accusations by the British and U.S. press of a cover-up, but they were soon silenced by publication of two detailed articles about the tragedy: one in an *American Heritage* magazine coauthored by a former medical officer, Dr. Ralph C. Greene, who had been stationed at one of the hospitals that treated the injured; the other in a respected British periodical, *After the Battle*. Both were carefully researched, authoritative, and comprehensive articles; if anybody had consulted them three years later, they would put to rest any charges of a cover-up and various other unfounded allegations.

Kenneth Small, meanwhile, wanted more. Although persuaded at last that there had been no cover-up, he nevertheless wanted an official commemoration by the U.S. government to those who had died. Receiving an invitation from an ex-army major who had commanded the tank battalion whose lost tank Small had salvaged, he went to the United States where the ex-major introduced him to his congresswoman, Beverly Byron (D-Md.), who as it turned out was the daughter of General Eisenhower's former naval aide, Capt. Harry Butcher.

With assistance from the Pentagon, Representative Byron arranged for a private organization, the Pike's Peak Chapter of the Association of the U.S. Army in Colorado, where the 4th Infantry Division was stationed, to provide a plaque honoring the American dead. She attached a rider to a congressional bill calling for official U.S. participation in a ceremony unveiling the plaque alongside Ken Small's tank at Slapton Sands.

Information about that pending ceremony scheduled for 15 November 1987 set the news media off. There were accusations not only of cover-up, but also of heavy casualties inflicted by U.S. soldiers, who presumably did not know that they had live ammunition in their weapons when they fired on other soldiers. Nobody questioned why soldiers would bother to open fire if they thought they had only blank ammunition, or why a soldier would not know the difference between live ammunition and blanks when one has bullets, the other not. Nor was there any evidence of anybody being killed by small arms fire.

There surfaced a new allegation made earlier by a local resident, Dorothy Seekings, who maintained that as a young woman she had witnessed the burial of "hundreds" of Americans in a mass grave (she subsequently changed the story to individual graves). Seekings also claimed that the bodies were still there.

At long last, somebody in the news media, a correspondent for BBC television, thought to query the farmer on whose land the dead were presumably buried. He had owned and lived on that land all his life, said the farmer, and nobody was ever buried there. This tallies with U.S. Army records, which show that in the first few days of May 1944, soon after the tragedy, hundreds of the dead were interred temporarily in a World War I U.S. military cemetery at nearby Blackwood. Following the war those bodies were either moved to a new World War II U.S. military cemetery at Cambridge or, at the request of next of kin, shipped to the United States.

Yet many like Ken Small continued to wonder why it took the U.S. government forty-three years to honor those who died off Slapton Sands. Those who wondered failed to understand U.S. policy for wartime memorials. Soon after World War I, Congress created an independent agency, the American Battle Monuments Commission, to construct overseas U.S. military cemeteries, to erect within them appropriate memorials, and to maintain them. Anyone who has seen any of these cemeteries, either those of World War I or World War II, recognizes that no nation honors its war dead more appropriately than the United States.

Only the American Battle Monuments Commission—not the U.S. Army, Air Force, or Navy—has authority to erect official memorials to American dead, and the American Battle Monuments Commission limits its memorials to the cemeteries, which avoids proliferation of monuments around the world. Private organizations, such as division veterans' associations, are nevertheless free to erect unofficial memorials but are responsible for all costs, including maintenance.

Soon after the end of the war, veterans of the 1st Engineer Special Brigade, which incurred the heaviest losses in Operation Tiger, did just that, erecting a monument on Omaha Beach to their dead, presumably to include those who died at Utah Beach and those who died in preparation for D-Day.

At Cambridge there stands an impressive official memorial erected by the American Battle Monuments Commission to all those Americans who died during World War II while stationed in the British Isles. That includes the 749 who died in the tragedy off Slapton Sands, and there one finds the engraved names of the missing. Long before 15 November 1987, the U.S. government had already honored those soldiers and sailors who died in Operation Tiger. [138]

HELLSHIPS

During World War II approximately 126,000 Allied prisoners were transported by Japanese vessels known as "hellships" because of the horrible conditions and brutality the prisoners had to endure as they were moved from island to island, to Japan and Manchuria. The prisoners were transported aboard Japanese ships on more than 150 occasions during the war. Allied submarine commanders operating in the Western Pacific were unaware that many of the enemy ships they sent to the bottom carried Allied POWs. As a result, more than twenty-one thousand of these men lost their lives. These tragic losses are told in the following profiles of several hellships that were sunk carrying thousands of Allied soldiers to their death.[139]

Montevideo Maru

Montevideo Maru, a 7,266-ton passenger-cargo ship built by Mitsubishi in 1926 was the first Japanese hellship to carry Allied POWs during World War II. It was sunk by USS *Sturgeon* (SS-187) on 1 July 1942.[140]

Early in the war the only Allied military presence in New Guinea, the Bismarcks, and the Solomon Islands was seven hundred Australian "coast-watchers" who kept tabs on the movement of Japanese troops and ships along the twenty-five hundred miles of island coastal areas. Information collected by these daring men was forwarded to a coordination center at Rabaul, New Guinea. Since these men were only "watchers" and not armed, the Australians sent troopers of the 23rd Brigade of the 8th Division to take up strategic posi-

Montevideo Maru was the first Japanese cargo-passenger ship to carry Allied POWs during World War II. Because many Allied submarine forces were unaware that the Japanese were transporting POWs in these ships, many such ships were sunk resulting in the loss of more than twenty-one thousand POWs. *National Maritime Museum*

tions along the undefended territory. The Sparrow Force (2/40 Battalion) was positioned at Timor, the Gull Force (2/21 Battalion) at Ambon, and the Lark Force (2/22 Battalion) at Rabaul.

When the Japanese invaded the islands, the coastwatchers and the defenders were overwhelmed by the sheer force of the enemy. After a brief skirmish the Australians surrendered and were taken as prisoners to Malaguna Road Camp in June 1942. On 22 June 1,050 men of the 2/22 Battalion and two hundred Australian civilians were taken on board *Montevideo Maru*. Because the ship could make eighteen knots and had the potential to outrun any lurking Allied submarine, she sailed unescorted from Rabaul for Samah, Hainan. Like conditions on hellships to follow, *Montevideo Maru* was vastly overcrowded and the POWs were given little food and water.[141]

Sturgeon, under the command of Lt. Comdr. L. "Bull" Wright, was on patrol northwest of Cape Bojeador, Luzon, Philippines. In the evening hours of 30 June, the boat's lookouts reported a darkened ship south of their position traveling on a westerly course. Because of *Montevideo*'s speed, Wright spent an hour and a half chasing the ship, trying to get in position to attack it, but could not close to less than eighteen thousand yards. Finally, when he was about to give up, the ship unexplainably slowed to twelve knots.

Wright changed course to position *Sturgeon* forward of the ship. At four thousand yards he fired four torpedoes from his stern tubes. At that distance Wright had a fifty-fifty chance of success, but he figured that perhaps one of the four fish would hit the ship. At 2:29 A.M. Wright observed an explosion abaft of the ship's stack. The ship began to list to starboard and started down by its stern. It took just eleven minutes for *Montevideo* to go down. Wright subsequently surfaced and recharged *Sturgeon's* batteries and departed the area, unaware of the human devastation his boat had caused.

Japanese survivors reported that two torpedoes struck the No. 4 and No. 5 holds, and although pumps were used to stop the flooding of the ship, the situation was hopeless. When the crew was ordered to "abandon ship," none of them were concerned about the human cargo the ship carried in its holds. Japanese survivors in lifeboats headed for the coast of Luzon where Philippine natives attacked them as they tried to land. By the time they found a Japanese army outpost, only eighteen crewmen had survived the ordeal.

No Australians survived. They were either lost in the initial explosions or left to drown. Relatives of those lost didn't learn the fate of their loved ones until after the war, when Japanese records revealed the details of the sinking of *Montevideo Maru.*[142]

Convoy HI72

In early September of 1944 *Rakuyo Maru,* a single-funneled, double-masted, 9,419-ton steamship was in convoy HI72, which consisted of thirteen merchantmen, tankers, and escorts. The merchantmen and tankers included *Asaka Maru* (cargo-passenger ship), *Shincho Maru* (tanker-passenger ship), *Nankai Maru* (heavy transport ship), *Zuiho Maru* (tanker), *Kimikawa Maru* (seaplane tender), and *Rakuyo Maru* and *Kachidoki Maru* (passenger-cargo vessels). The ships were en route from Singapore to Yokohama, Japan. *Rakuyo Maru* carried bauxite and 1,350 British, Australian, and U.S. prisoners of war. *Kachidoki Maru* was also loaded with bauxite and carried nine hundred British prisoners and the ashes of 582 Japanese soldiers. Convoy escorts consisted of the destroyer *Shikinami* and the frigates *Hirado, Mikura,* and *Kurahashi.* The POWs were loaded into the ships' holds, which were filthy with dirt and manure from mules and horses transported earlier by the ships. The men sweltered in the heat, and Japanese guards distributed inadequate supplies of food and water.

HI72 sailed on 6 September 1944, and when the convoy was a hundred miles

Rakuyo Maru in a Peruvian port, 1938. *U.S. Naval Historical Center*

northeast of the Paracel Islands it joined up with convoy MAMO03, which had sailed from Manila. Three more ships were added to the convoy, *Kagu Maru* (seaplane tender), *Kibitsu Maru,* and *Gokoku Maru* (passenger-cargo ships). The ships proceeded northward in three columns.[143]

By September 1944 U.S. submarines patrolling western Pacific waters were operating in wolfpacks and causing havoc with Japanese merchant shipping. The U.S. submarine *Sealion II* (Comdr. E. T. Reich) along with *Growler* (Comdr. T. B. Oakley) and *Pampanito* (Comdr. P. E. Summers) composed the attack group known as "Ben's Busters." By the war's end the three submarines would sink twenty-six enemy ships totaling eighty-nine thousand tons.[144]

The Japanese convoy was sighted on the night of 11 September by the wolfpack and they positioned themselves for an attack on the unsuspecting Japanese ships. During the early morning hours of the twelfth, *Growler* sank the leading escort frigate *Hirado* and destroyer *Shikinami*. At sunrise *Sealion II* sent the merchant ship *Nankai Maru* to the bottom and hit *Rakuyo Maru* with two torpedoes, critically damaging the steamship. The remaining ships changed course and headed for Hainan. As the sun began to set, those sailing for Hainan thought that they had eluded their attackers when suddenly *Zuiho Maru* exploded, and a torpedo struck the No. 7 hold of *Kachidoki Maru*. *Pampanito*

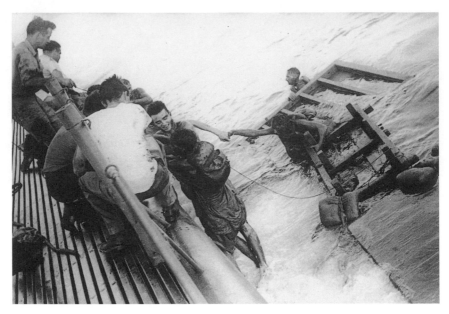

Allied POW survivors of *Rakuyo Maru* are shown being rescued by USS *Sealion II*.
U.S. National Archives

had followed the vessels and sent two more ships of HI72 to the bottom.[145] During the course of the day mayhem broke out on *Rakuyo Maru* and later on *Kachidoki Maru* as prisoners and Japanese crewmen and guards fought for their survival. The Japanese on both ships launched lifeboats and beat off POWs, who attempted to come aboard or clung to the sides of the boats. Before the ships sank, prisoners killed Japanese guards and in turn many were shot as they tried to avenge their mistreatment. As the surviving POWs of *Kachidoki Maru* grasped floating debris they watched as the remaining Japanese frigates picked up their fellow crewmen. By 7 P.M. of the twelfth, it appeared to the POWs that there would be no rescue for them. In fact, in an act of viciousness the frigates were maneuvered back through the POWs, chopping some up with their propellers and drowning others.

POWs that survived the sinking of *Kachidoki Maru* and the scourges of the sea were the first to be rescued. Japanese ships from Hainan found the POWs crowded into two lifeboats and on rafts, while others clung to pieces of flotsam. The POWs had managed to tie the boats and rafts together; however, many who remained in the water gave up hope and slipped silently into the depths below. All were badly sunburned and what food and water they brought with them when the ship went down was barely enough to keep them alive. The POWs were taken aboard several Japanese ships during the morning of the thirteenth. Those that were rescued by frigates were hosed down and given rice and water. Unfortunately some were beaten by *Kachidoki Maru*'s surviving crewmen.

On the fourteenth the escorts of MAMO03 were ordered back to where HI72 was attacked, and—much to the surprise of the many desperate POWs—began to rescue them. However, as they were taken on board the ships they were beaten with rifle butts and batons. Many who had survived were killed during the rescue. During the two days the POWs were in the water, hundreds died from the lack of water and despair over the hopelessness of their situation.[146]

After sinking *Zuiho Maru* and *Kachidoki Maru*, *Pampanito* returned to the area where *Rakuyo Maru* went down and patrolled the area with *Sealion II*. On 15 September lookouts on *Pampanito* sighted wreckage ahead and soon the sub was sailing through a sea of bodies and debris. However, among the devastation were living men clinging to rafts and the broken remains of the hellship. Summers immediately radioed Reich for help, and soon *Pampanito* and *Sealion II* rescued 127 POWs. Later that day thirty-two more survivors were picked up by *Barb* and *Queenfish*.

Out of 1,318 POWs on the *Rakuyo Maru*, 1,159 died. Of the 900 British prisoners on the *Kachidoki Maru*, 400 lost their lives.[147]

Junyo Maru

Junyo Maru was a single stack merchant ship built in Liverpool in 1908, and after serving with various British shipping lines, the 5,056-ton ship was sold to the Japanese. The freighter was four hundred feet in length and had a beam of fifty-three feet. In September 1944 the ship was loaded with seventeen hundred Dutch prisoners, fourteen Americans, 506 Ambonese and Menadonese prisoners, and 4,320 Javanese native conscripts. The ship was heavily rusted and in a state of general disrepair. The Javanese were loaded into the forward hold and the prisoners crammed into the after hold. There was so little space in the after hold that the POWs had to stand, which led them to believe that the journey would be short.

Junyo Maru, showing a painted *652* on its funnel, departed Batavia (Jakarta) for Padang, Sumatra, on 16 September 1944, escorted by two small gunboats. Unbeknownst to the human cargo on board, they were destined to work on the

The British submarine HMS *Tradewind* sank *Junyo Maru* in September 1944. Of 2,200 Allied and Indonesian POWs, 1,520 lost their lives; only 200 of the 4,320 native Javanese conscripts were saved. *Imperial War Museum*

Sumatran railroad that would transport coal across the island for shipment to Singapore. With its hatches open and a few hundred prisoners on deck because of overcrowding in the after hold, the air became unbearably hot, and the sun blistered the men as the ship came to a full stop shortly after leaving port and didn't resume its journey for more than an hour. Those that survived the forthcoming ordeal remembered that the ship carried only two lifeboats, and several life rafts, which were lost under the prisoners' baggage. Upon leaving port the Japanese guards donned life jackets; none were given to the passengers. As the ship turned northwest and sailed off the Sumatran coast, two aircraft appeared briefly overhead. By now the men had figured that they were headed for Padang. Shortly after the aircraft departed late in the afternoon of the eighteenth, the ship was jolted, then blasted again. Many thought the boiler had burst, and as smoke billowed out of the after hold prisoners scrambled up rope ladders to the main deck. The ship's sirens were sounded and general confusion reigned on the ship.

Junyo Maru had been torpedoed by the British submarine *Tradewind*, which was on its third Far East patrol. Skippered by Lt. Comdr. H. L. C. Maydon, the thirteen-hundred-ton T-Class submarine had departed Trincomalee, Sri

Lanka, on 8 September and sighted *Junyo Maru* on the eighteenth. At eighteen hundred yards, Maydon fired four torpedoes at the unsuspecting merchant ship. After hearing two explosions, Maydon took his boat deep and departed the area. Several minutes later he heard the sounds of depth charges exploding in the distance as the gunboats attempted to find their attacker.

Passengers, guards, and large sections of the ship's superstructure were blown high above the doomed ship. Pandemonium broke out as the prisoners and Javanese conscripts clawed their way out of the ship's hold trying to reach topside and abandon the ship. Japanese guards jumped into the water carrying their guns and personal equipment; others manned the two lifeboats and battered anyone who attempted to grab onto the boats. The sea was filled with struggling men and dead bodies. As *Junyo Maru* began to go down by its stern, hundreds of men could be seen clinging to the ship's sides and deck. Finally the ship stood up vertically against a sunset sky and slipped from sight amidst foaming water and rising smoke.

Later that day Maydon returned to the area to witness a gunboat taking aboard survivors. The thought crossed his mind to wait until the boat was full and then surface and sink the escort with torpedoes and his 4-inch deck gun. However, he decided that such action wouldn't be profitable and sailed for home, reaching Ceylon on 4 October.

The gunboats initially picked up Japanese soldiers who waved small Japanese flags so they could be sighted and saved. Of the twenty-two hundred Allied and Indonesian POWs, 1,520 lost their lives. Only 200 of the 4,320 conscripts were saved. The loss of 5,640 POWs and conscripts was the highest of any ship sinking in the Pacific during the war. The 680 survivors were taken to Sumatra to work on the railroad. At war's end ninety-six POWs remained alive. None of the conscripts survived.[148]

Arisan Maru

As MacArthur's Southwest Pacific forces supported by the U.S. Navy's Third Fleet prepared to invade the Philippines in October 1944, the Japanese began moving POWs out of the country. Some were destined for Japan, others for the Kwantung army in Manchuria. On 11 October 1944, 1,782 U.S. Army, Navy, and Marine POWs and one hundred civilians were loaded on board the 6,688-

Transport *Eiko Maru* was in convoy MATA-30 with *Arisan Maru* when sunk by USS *Seadragon* (SS-194) on 24 October 1944. *U.S. Naval Institute*

ton cargo ship *Arisan Maru,* which departed Manila for the west coast of Palawan. There the ship waited for a week to avoid expected Allied air raids on Manila that occurred between 15 and 18 October. The ship returned to Manila where it joined convoy MATA30, which consisted of eleven transports, a fleet supply ship, a sub chaser, and three escorts. The convoy put to sea on 21 October.

Three hours out of port the escorts began to pick up multiple underwater contacts. MATA30 officers were unaware that they had entered an area that, at the time, contained the largest concentration of Allied submarines in the Pacific. The Allies called the area between Formosa and Luzon "Convoy College" because of the abundance of good Japanese shipping targets. The Japanese quickly split the convoy, sending the fastest ships out in an endeavor to make it to Takao. However, nine Allied subs awaited them.

Beginning in the late afternoon of 23 October the massacre of MATA30 began when eight ships were torpedoed and sunk in quick succession. What ships were left scattered, all except *Arisan Maru,* one of the slowest ships in the convoy. The following day the ship was in company with two escorts when *Snook* (SS-279) hit the ship with two torpedoes. One hit the No. 3 hold and the other the stern.

As *Arisan Maru* slowly sank, POWs were cast into frigid waters with waves fifteen feet high. Those that didn't die when the ship was hit or drown when the ship went under clung to debris from the ship. However, emaciated from their captivity in Philippine camps, hundreds died during the night hours, too weak to fight the roiling sea. Some tried to climb aboard Japanese ships only to be beaten back into the water.

Nine POWs survived the sinking of *Arisan Maru*. It was the largest at-sea loss of American lives (1,773) during World War II.[149]

LEOPOLDVILLE

On 24 December 1944, Christmas Eve, U.S. forces were involved in operations that could never have been confused with anything having to do with peace on earth or goodwill toward men.

In the Pacific, planes of the 7th Air Force and guns of USS *Salt Lake City* (CA-25) bombarded the island of Iwo Jima in preparation for the coming invasion. In Belgium, the surrounded defenders at Bastogne continued to hold out, waiting for relief, as German forces pushed toward Antwerp with the hope of seizing the port and cutting Allied forces in two. And at Pier 38 in Southampton, England, troops of the 66th Infantry Division (Black Panthers) began loading aboard the Belgian liner SS *Leopoldville* for a nine-hour voyage to Cherbourg, France.[150]

The troops, elements of the 262nd and 264th Infantry Regiments, consisted of failed air cadets and soldiers from the canceled Army Specialized Training Program (ASTP, a college-university program that the army canceled on April Fool's Day, 1944). Mostly they were engineers. They believed themselves to be on the way as reinforcements for the Battle of the Bulge in the Ardennes, but in fact they were scheduled to relieve the 94th Infantry Division in the Lorient–St. Nazaire sector of Brittany, so that the veteran division could be sent to the Bulge.

The troops had been on alert since the previous day, waiting endlessly on the pier for embarkation in the early morning hours of 24 December. Finally, at 2 A.M., the troops began to board *Leopoldville* and another Belgian liner, SS *Cheshire* (which carried the 263rd Infantry Regiment). In the confusion on the pier, troops arriving in company strength were boarded piecemeal, resulting in missing or incomplete rosters, disorganization, impaired communication, and a fragmented command structure. All of this would contribute to the impending disaster.[151]

Unlike the 66th Division, *Leopoldville* was a seasoned veteran by Christmas Eve, 1944. Built in Hoboken, New Jersey, in 1929, the 11,500-ton, 501-foot ship spent

The Belgian liner *Leopoldville.* Loaded with more than two thousand U.S. troops, the ship was torpedoed by *U486. Steamship Historical Society of America*

eleven prewar years sailing between Antwerp and the port of Matadi in the Belgian Congo. *Leopoldville* was at sea on 10 May 1940 when Germany invaded Belgium, Luxembourg, and the Netherlands. After a brief stop at the French port of La Pallice, she returned to the Congo and then to New York, before being chartered by the British Ministry of Transport in September 1940.

Under British control, the Belgian officers and crew were to continue to serve aboard for the duration of the war, traveling to the North Africa–Middle East area and ferrying Allied soldiers (primarily British, U.S., and Canadian troops) between England, South Africa, and the Suez Canal. *Leopoldville* took part in the invasions of Algeria, Sicily, and Italy, as well as landing more than two thousand British troops at Normandy on D-Day +2. Following Normandy, she made an additional twenty-three channel crossings between June and December, carrying 53,217 Allied soldiers to the European Theater of operations. In all, prior to 24 December *Leopoldville* had traveled more than a quarter of a million miles without one enemy-inflicted casualty.[152]

The wartime ship had a crew of 193 (one hundred Belgians and ninety-three Africans from the Congo) as well as thirty-five British naval and military personnel permanently assigned on board, which included a Royal Army antiaircraft complement under the command of Sgt. John Razey; a Royal Navy antisubmarine unit under the command of Lt. John Williamson, RN; a medical detachment under the command of Maj. (Doctor) Donald Brook Mumby; Lt. Col. D. F. L. Campbell, the officer in command of troops, and his adjutant, Capt. William G. Bowles, a Royal Artillery officer. Also aboard was Alvin Penrice, a merchant marine captain who functioned as a liaison with the Belgian captain, Charles Limbor, and his officers.

Leopoldville was fitted with antiaircraft and antisubmarine weaponry, including ten Bofors guns (four by the bridge, four on the boat deck, one forward, and one aft), one 3-inch gun at the bow, one 4-inch antisubmarine rifle, and a 3-pound antiaircraft gun also at the stern. In addition, she carried a smoke-making capacity.[153] *Leopoldville* and *Cheshire* would be escorted across the channel by three Royal Navy destroyers (*Brilliant, Anthony,* and *Hotham*) and the Free French frigate *Croix de Lorraine*. This was because of increased submarine activity in the channel.[154]

As *Leopoldville* loaded her troops, the German *U486* lay submerged five and a half miles off Cherbourg, waiting for a target. This type VIIC submarine had been launched at the Kiel Shipyard on 12 February 1944 and commissioned on 22 March. Under the command of Oberleutnant Gerhard Meyer, the boat had recently sunk her first ship before beginning patrol of the channel in mid-November.[155]

Meanwhile, the confused loading continued in Southampton, as the two regiments were split between the two liners and units were separated from their officers and equipment. Complicating an already muddled situation, the two officers most responsible for liaison with the Belgian crew, Colonel Campbell and Captain Penrice, were absent from this voyage, leaving Captain Bowles as the senior British officer. The ranking American, Lt. Col. J. Ralph Martindale, was commanding officer of the 3rd Battalion, 262nd Infantry Regiment, and, as senior officer, was designated commander of troops. As such, he was responsible for coordinating with the ship's master on the safety and conduct of the troops at sea. However, it appears he never had any contact with Captain Limbor, and depended instead on Captain Bowles to communicate with the Belgian crew.[156]

Conditions aboard *Leopoldville* were typical of a troopship—overcrowded, uncomfortable, and unequipped with sufficient lifeboats (just fourteen, with a capacity of 797, mostly assigned to the crew). As well, there were insufficient life preservers for the number of troops on board: 2,235. The men made themselves

The crew of *U486* is shown with commanding officer, Oberleutnant Gerhard Meyer (*fourth from left, lower deck*). *U-Boot-Archiv*

as comfortable as they could, and by 9:15 A.M. the convoy departed from Southampton, dropping their pilots at 11:05 and passing St. Catherine's Point at 1 P.M.[157]

The convoy commander and captain of *Brilliant,* Lt. Comdr. John Pringle, RN, ordered the convoy into a diamond formation with *Brilliant* leading, followed by *Leopoldville* and then *Cheshire,* trailed by *Croix de Lorraine,* and flanked by *Anthony* and *Hotham.* He also ordered the convoy to commence zigzagging.

Shortly after putting to sea, *Leopoldville* held a boat drill. By all accounts, the Belgian crew and British gun crews responded well, but few American troops knew where their stations were, and many remained belowdecks asleep, or indifferent to the drill. This was due in part to the fragmented command structure, which resulted in poor—often no—communication between the Belgian ship command, the British liaison, and the U.S. commanders.

Those troops that did go on deck found little direction. There did not appear to be enough preservers to go around, and there was no instruction as to how to lower the boats or unlash the rafts. Nor was critical information provided on proper ways to enter the water in the event it became necessary to abandon ship, how to secure the life vests to prevent injury, and the necessity of removing wool overcoats, helmets, and gear before going over the side. The drill soon ended, and the men wandered back belowdecks to seek escape from the bitter cold and the strong winds. Only the seasick remained on deck, where the fresh air helped their condition.

Below, some of the more ambitious troopers scrounged hammocks or places where they could stretch out on duffle bags, but most were required to sit on long wooden benches and tables. The food was barely edible and the latrines were filthy and filled to capacity. The stench was overpowering, the conditions crowded, and the crossing filled with tension and the dread of sub attacks.[158]

At 2:30 P.M., *Leopoldville* had her first submarine alert, and many troops came topside to watch as the destroyers broke formation and went into a sub-hunting pattern, dropping depth charges into the rough, icy North Atlantic waters. The ships secured after about fifteen minutes, but a second alert sounded at 3 P.M.— again, without results.

Whether *U486* was the submarine involved, or whether there really was a submarine involved at all, remains unknown. Nervous crews often accounted for false alarms. What is known is that at 5:54 P.M., *U486* was approximately five and a half miles off Cherbourg Harbor (49°45'N, 1°34'W) when she found *Leopoldville* in her sights and fired a torpedo that struck the troopship on the starboard side aft.

The torpedo hit in the No. 4 hold (the ship had four holds, with No. 1 at the fore and No. 4 in the stern), exploding into compartments E-4, F-4, and G-4, and destroying stairwells. Between three hundred and five hundred men were trapped in the flooding compartments. The precise number of troops killed in the explosion versus those who died when the ship went down will never be known, due in part to incomplete rosters. Belgian and British authorities tend to estimate a higher number of those killed outright (as many as seven hundred), as it decreases those who perished because of confusion and the lack of lifeboats and preservers. They also tend to describe rougher sea conditions than American sources. For more than half a century, neither the Belgian, the British, nor the U.S. governments were very forthcoming on details.[159]

Survivors in the No. 1 and No. 2 holds recalled hardly feeling the impact, unlike those in No. 3. But most casualties were in the No. 4 hold. Troops began moving to the upper decks, but nobody appeared to know what was going on, the officers as uninformed as the men.[160]

On the bridge, Captain Limbor and another officer who was scheduled to take over as master of the ship on her next voyage, Captain Verworst, surveyed the situation. Both knew she had been torpedoed, but rather than investigate her condition personally Limbor sent his officers to report. Not until Captain Bowles came to the bridge were the Belgians reminded to sound the alarm.[161] By all accounts, the disciplined behavior of the American troops was exemplary, with no disorder or panic. They filed topside in an orderly fashion and waited for instructions, which, when they came over the loudspeakers, were confusing and contradictory, variously stating that a tug was on the way to tow them to Cherbourg, that the men would be transferred to other ships, and that there was no danger of the ship sinking. This last seemed to create an unwarranted sense of complacency among the men.

The seriousness of the attack dawned on some, though, as wounded were brought to the infirmary, where Dr. Mumby was assisted by the ship's doctor, Belgian Nestor Herrent, and the American doctors. Still the loudspeaker announced that there was no danger.[162]

Lt. Comdr. John Pringle, commanding the convoy from *Brilliant,* was advised by the destroyer *Anthony* that *Leopoldville* had taken a torpedo astern on her starboard side. Pringle immediately radioed a report, but the British escort radios were tuned to the British frequency at Portsmouth, England, which was eight hours away. The U.S. radios at Cherbourg were on a different frequency with different codes, and were therefore unable even to monitor British radio traffic. There was a direct telephone line from Portsmouth to Cherbourg, but for some unaccountable reason, the call was delayed from one hour to the next morning. Official memories differ as to when the message was sent and received.[163]

Meanwhile, U.S. officials at Fort L'Ouest, on the breakwater of Cherbourg Harbor, noticed the convoy stopped offshore at about 5:55 P.M. Darkness was falling by 6 P.M., but they could still tell from radar that the convoy was stopped when they lost the light.

The fort was the entrance control point for the harbor, and it was not unusual for ships to stop outside it. They watched the warships break off into a hunting pattern, but this also was not unusual, with submarine scares common. They sent a blinker message to the convoy inquiring what the matter was, and if assistance was needed. No answer came from any of the ships. Since shore messages to ships at sea were often disregarded, no great significance was attached to this lack of response.[164]

The army officer-in-charge (the fort was a joint U.S. Army-Navy operation), Lt. Col. Richard H. Lee, was relieved at 6 P.M., anxious to attend the Christmas party downstairs, where there was a rumor that forty WACs would be attending. Still, he returned to the tower at 6:10, even though off duty, to find no response from the stalled convoy. At 6:15 he observed one of the vessels drifting from the cleared channel into a minefield, and ordered the ship signaled and advised of the danger. Still no response from any ship. They continued to signal, but not until 6:25, almost a half-hour after the explosion, did any response come.

Lee knew that there were sufficient boats available to go out and assist the convoy, including U.S. PT (motor torpedo) and PC (submarine chaser) boats, French and U.S. destroyers, a cruiser, tugboats, French fishing vessels, and Coast Guard cutters, all capable of reaching the convoy within an hour. He also knew that any effort would be complicated by the absence of any rescue boat on alert; most of the others had cold engines that would delay their getting under way, and were undercrewed due to the Christmas holiday. Command centers staffed by junior officers would be unwilling to disturb senior commanders at Christmas parties. Lee was also aware that as of yet, there was no official notification that there was even a problem.[165]

Shortly after receiving the warning from shore, Pringle ordered *Leopoldville* to drop anchor to arrest her drift into the minefield (6:16 P.M.). This would present a problem later on, when Captain Limbor ordered all but essential crew to abandon ship at 6:25 P.M. When tugs arrived later, there was nobody left on board who knew how to raise the anchor, making a tow to shore impossible.[166]

There was still no panic among the Americans, and with a lack of a command structure, many took it upon themselves to initiate rescue operations on their own. Stories abound of individual heroism. Many of the troops were still unaware that the ship had been torpedoed, and there was no official announcement. But a sense of unease must have swept through the troops as they watched the Belgian crews boarding and lowering the lifeboats.

The wounded were evacuated in the hospital lifeboat, but many of the boats left in such a hurry that they were half-filled, and no crew members remained to instruct the troops in how to lower the remaining boats or how to unlash the rafts. In any event there was still no official word directing the actions of the troops, and the situation turned to "rats leaving a sinking ship," as one survivor remembered the scene.[167]

Finally, at 6:25 P.M. *Brilliant* signaled the shore, "Taking off survivors. Need assistance." The fort signaled back, "Survivors of what?" *Brilliant* now clarified: "*Leopoldville* hit. Need assistance," and the fort returned, "What kind of assistance?" Despite repeated requests, there was no further response.

Lieutenant Colonel Lee and his naval counterpart, Ensign Matt Devoll, now attempted to raise the alarm but were unsuccessful in conveying a sense of urgency to higher command. First they requested permission to radio the ships; permission denied. Then they requested permission to send out a patrol boat; again, denied. The situation was "not grave enough" to justify that measure. Finally, at 6:45 a call went through to General Aurrand, who ordered out the army rescue boats. Lt. Comdr. Richard "Shakey" Davis, the port defense officer, ordered out the navy boats despite having no authority over port vessels. His "sulfuric" vocabulary apparently expedited cooperation.[168]

By this time, in what has been described as an extraordinary feat of seamanship, *Brilliant* came alongside in rough seas. High waves washed over the sides of the ships bashing the two vessels into each other and crushing two lifeboats that had not yet been lowered. By 7:20 P.M. *Brilliant* pulled away with about five hundred troops aboard. Later criticized for his departure, Pringle explained that his concern was to get the wounded to hospitals in Cherbourg, and that there were now a number of craft responding to the scene. In any event, he may not have been fully aware of the condition of *Leopoldville.*

The first three PT boats arrived from Cherbourg at about 7 P.M. and began radioing from the scene, ignoring orders and ending radio silence. The boats were ideal for rescue work, their eighty-foot decks mostly clear and free from obstructions. The first radio reports finally aroused the port and alerted PC boats, navy tugs, and a variety of small craft, both military and civilian.

The smaller craft responding from the port had a more difficult time coming—and staying—alongside in the rough waters. The troops had to carefully time their jumps across to the small boats, a slow and hazardous procedure. By 8 P.M. there were still about twelve hundred troops on board (a figure based on estimates of three hundred killed, five hundred removed by *Brilliant,* and another two hundred taken off on rafts or lifeboats).

Many of the rescue boats could have taken more troops, but large numbers were unwilling to make the jump; and, in some cases, officers prohibited them, still waiting for official orders. Many remained unaware and uninformed about the danger of the ship sinking. Their sense of security may have been enhanced by the lights of Cherbourg, clearly visible less than six miles away.

There may have been as many as twenty boats in the area, but only a few came alongside in the rough seas, including a large rescue tugboat with a capacity of five hundred—but the men were unwilling to risk the jump. The tug was then ordered to tow *Leopoldville,* but could not because of the anchor and no crew aboard to raise it. At some point, the remaining twenty-four Belgians and ten Britons boarded the last lifeboat and lowered it into the water, Captain Limbor announced from the bridge, "Gentlemen, we have done all we can." The launch of the last lifeboat delayed navy rescue tug ATR-3 from coming alongside.[169]

Like many of the issues surrounding *Leopoldville,* the time of her sinking is a matter of dispute. The Belgian Line places it at about 8:05 P.M. The 66th Division records estimate the time as between 8:20 and 8:25, and the U.S. Navy as 8:30. The British Admiralty states that she went down between 8:20 and 8:40.

Fort L'Ouest was too busy to keep records. Survivors agree that *Leopoldville* gave a "series of lurches, followed by two quick explosions." Within minutes, the ship slid under the waves, men clinging to her highest point. The remaining troops went into the icy, forty-eight-degree water. Following tradition, Captain Limbor went down with his ship, the only Belgian officer to give his life.[170]

Many of the troops died when they entered the water, never having been advised to unfasten their helmets or tie their life jackets tightly. Many wore their heavy woolen overcoats under their vests, making them impossible to remove. The sodden material dragged them under. The dark night filled with screams and prayers of the troopers as rescue ships moved among them, recovering bodies as often as numb and freezing live soldiers.

Estimates of American casualties range around 764 (the official U.S. figure), which would represent about 33 percent of the 2,235 troops boarded. Five Belgian crewmen (including the captain), or approximately 2 percent of the 230-member crew, were lost. The British have never disclosed their losses, but they were certainly fewer than ten.

The survivors were transported to Cherbourg, and slowly the division was reformed, with replacements arriving in early January. Within a week elements of the division went into the line near the Lorient–St. Nazaire sector of Brittany, where they kept fifty thousand German troops contained until the end of the war. Casualties in both regiments numbered an additional thirty-eight men in the next five months. The 94th Division, which they relieved, went on to fight at the Battle of the Bulge, at a heavy cost.[171]

The British crew was reassigned to the Belgian liner SS *Persier,* and most survived the war. The crew of *U486* was not as fortunate. After sinking two British frigates, the boat returned to Norwegian waters. On 12 April 1945, HMS *Tapir* torpedoed the sub in the North Sea west of Bergen, Norway (60°44'N, 4°39'E). Her crew of forty-eight all perished when she was forced to surface, due to a snorkel malfunction.

The investigation into *Leopoldville's* sinking was immediate, and criticism was spread among the several parties involved. Lieutenant Commander Pringle was reprimanded for not communicating the seriousness of the ship's condition, for his simultaneous ordering of a tug, and the dropping of *Leopoldville's* anchor. He was also taken to task for not ordering one of the other destroyers from the hunt to assist in the evacuation, and for casting off from the stricken ship prematurely. He received an official reprimand, but continued his naval career for another ten years.

The deceased Captain Limbor and the Belgian crew were also criticized. By allowing the crew to depart before the passengers, there was no one left aboard to launch lifeboats or rafts, raise the anchor, or fasten towlines. More damning, Limbor was chastised for failing to appraise the damage to his vessel, for not working more aggressively to save his ship, and for failing to provide training to the troops in how to use life jackets and launch lifeboats and rafts. Additionally, Limbor was castigated for never issuing an official "abandon ship" order.

The Port of Southampton was censured for failing to provide proper boarding documents and for the piecemeal manner in which the regiments were loaded aboard the two troopships. No official criticism was offered toward the actions of the Americans: all parties agreed that the troops' behavior had been exemplary and that acts of personal heroism had occurred despite a fractured command structure.

In short, the investigation revealed the incident as a series of tragic errors. Gen. George C. Marshall, in a memo dated 6 January 1945, wrote: "Had this disaster occurred in peacetime, it would have been regarded as a shocking scandal." The decision was made to keep silent about the loss, and survivors were instructed not to talk about it—even in letters home. Official letters to families of the deceased explained that "the ship sank swiftly" and that 517 soldiers were "missing," even though both statements were known to be false.[172]

The Navy and War Departments used security as an excuse for not making the sinking public, fearing that the loss of Allied troops on such a scale could raise German morale. There was no enthusiasm after the war to raise issues better left undisturbed. U.S. documents were declassified in 1958–59, but the British did not allow access to their papers until 1996.[173]

Despite efforts by the governments of the three nations, the story refused to stay submerged. In 1960 Jacquin Sanders, a former 66th Division Infantry man who had witnessed the torpedoing of *Leopoldville* from *Cheshire*'s deck, began collecting information for a book on the disaster. Accessing recently declassified government documents and interviewing survivors of the sinking, Sanders began piecing together events which had long been shrouded in "incredible rumors" and "wartime secrecy." His book, *A Night Before Christmas,* was published in 1963.[174]

In June 1968 a group of 66th Division veterans got together and started the Panther Veterans Organization (PVO), the 66th Division Association.

Numbering approximately 1,800, they have held reunions every two years since 1969.

Following Clive Cussler's discovery of the wreckage in the summer of 1984, interest in the fate of *Leopoldville* was rekindled. The discovery also allowed forty-four Panther veterans to visit the site of the sinking on 29 September 1989 aboard the French minesweeper *Phenix* as guests of the French government. With a French admiral in attendance, taps was blown and a memorial performed by eight survivors of the Christmas Eve sinking. Also in attendance was Raymond Roberts, a 66th veteran of the 760th Ordnance Co., who crossed the channel five days after the sinking, on 29 December, aboard an LST.[175]

Roberts interviewed seven of the survivors, and between 1990 and 1997 he continued to contact and interview survivors, ultimately resulting in three books: *Survivors of the Leopoldville Disaster* (1997), *Sequel to Survivors of the Leopoldville* (1999), and *More Tales of the Leopoldville Disaster* (2001). Also in 1997, Allen Andrade published *SS Leopoldville Disaster: December 24, 1944.*[176]

On 7 November 1997, a monument was dedicated at Sacrifice Field, across from the Infantry Museum at Ft. Benning, Georgia. Listing 802 names, the inscription reads:

> Dedicated to the memory of the brave American soldiers of the 66th Infantry Division (Panthers) named hereon who were lost on Christmas Eve, December 24, 1944, when their transport ship, the *Leopoldville,* was torpedoed in the English Channel. The division was en route to reinforce Allied forces fighting in the Battle of the Bulge.
>
> This monument also honors the memory of the members of the 66th Infantry Division who survived the tragedy of the *Leopoldville,* but were later killed in action.[177]

In the near sixty years since the disaster, numerous accounts have surfaced, not always in agreement. Official records differ. Some remember announcements in English, some in Flemish, some recall no announcements at all. Some recall panic. Most recall the troops as orderly and disciplined. Perhaps the most accurate description of the disaster can be found in the words of author Jacquin

Sanders: "A small body of experienced men behaved on the whole badly, and a large body of inexperienced men behaved very well."[178]

Hank Andersen and Leopoldville

Hank Andersen was a sergeant in the Heavy Weapons Platoon of Company E, 262nd Infantry Regiment, when he crossed the English Channel aboard *Leopoldville* that Christmas Eve, 1944.

After boarding at Southampton, Andersen and several of his buddies became disenchanted with the accommodations belowdecks, conditions that worsened with the nausea and diarrhea that followed a barely edible dinner served in rough seas. "I had made up my mind that I was going to be up on that deck all night rather than stay in that hold."

Shortly after dinner at 5 P.M., Andersen was on deck and viewed the lights of Cherbourg in the distance. "How wonderful it was to see the land, the Christmas lights sprinkled around the hills of Cherbourg. At that point, we decided to go down through the holds of the ship and serenade everyone below deck with Christmas Carols." Although he recalls that reaction was mixed to their impromptu concert, approximately two hundred men accepted their invitation to come up on deck and greet Christmas of 1944.

It was an invitation that saved countless lives, as Andersen believes that the overwhelming majority of those killed in the sinking died belowdecks as a result of the torpedoing. The men who accepted Andersen's call might otherwise have been belowdecks.

Andersen and his fellow carolers were among those able to make the treacherous jump to HMS *Brilliant,* which had pulled alongside and subsequently removed close to five hundred soldiers. He recalled being transported to Cherbourg, where a black quartermaster unit would give up their Christmas dinner and serenade the survivors with the same Christmas carols they'd been singing earlier.

After a week's rest, the remnants of the 66th Division, reinforced with replacements, entered the line at Lorient–St. Nazaire where they would remain until the end of the war. For Andersen, that Christmas Eve was an epiphany. Following the end of the war he entered the ministry of the Presbyterian Church, retiring in 1989.

KYLE V. JOHNSON

When the Japanese invaded the Philippine Islands on 22 December 1941, two weeks after Pearl Harbor, they landed the main body of their troops at Lingayen Gulf, approximately 120 miles north of Manila. It was not surprising, therefore, that when General MacArthur fulfilled his promise to return to the Philippines, he would select the same beachhead from which to begin the liberation of Luzon.[179] There were, however, differences.

In 1941 the Japanese had the advantage of surprise on the defending forces, comprised of a small cadre of trained troops supporting a larger body of largely untrained Filipino reserves. By early 1945 General Krueger's 6th U.S. Army, supported by Admiral Kincaid's 7th Fleet, faced General Yamashita's 260,000-plus veterans behind three years' worth of improved fortifications.[180] In addition, Allied forces had to contend with the first large-scale use of suicide planes, or *kamikazes,* by the Japanese.[181]

The kamikazes or "divine wind" (named for the legendary typhoon that saved Japan from a Mongol invasion in the thirteenth century) were units of Zero fighters equipped with 550-lb. bombs designed to be crashed into enemy ships. Although several pilots had intentionally crashed their planes previously, the Kamikaze Air Corps was officially formed on 19 October 1944 at the direction of Vice Adm. Takijiro Onishi, commander of Japan's First Air Fleet, and suicide planes became an accepted tactical weapon.[182] Because experienced pilots were in short supply, most kamikaze pilots were young and inexperienced with only enough skill to take off and crash. In total, 1,228 kamikaze pilots sank thirty-four U.S. ships during the war.[183] The majority of kamikaze aircraft used during the period—October 1944–March 1945—were the A6M5 variant of the Zero, although toward the end of the war they were replaced by the Ki-115, an aircraft designed solely as a suicide attack plane. The Ki-115 had no instruments, no weapons, no protective armament, and used whatever engine was available.

Kamikazes flew 424 missions in the Philippines, destroying sixteen ships and damaging an additional eighty. Early in January 1945, an 850-ship invasion fleet departed Leyte, en route to Lingayen Gulf. It was attacked by kamikazes at the entrance to Lingayen Gulf on 6 January, resulting in eleven vessels damaged, including the battleship USS *New Mexico* (BB-40) and cruiser USS *Louisville* (CA-28).[184]

As the Liberty ship *Kyle V. Johnson* approached Lingayen Gulf in convoy, during the invasion of Luzon on 9 January 1945, a Japanese kamikaze plane crashed into the ship. The
ensuing explosion killed 129 American soldiers and set the ship on fire.
William Hultgen Collection

A second convoy of one hundred ships departed Hollandia, New Guinea, for
the Philippines on 3 January 1945. The convoy comprised forty merchant ships,
forty LSTs, and twenty PTs, escorted by nine destroyers and destroyer escorts.[185]
Twenty-five merchant ships were subsequently sunk or damaged. Seven were
Liberty ships, five of which were damaged on the same day, 12 January. Among
those five, only one would sustain casualties, *Kyle V. Johnson*.

Of the more than twenty-seven hundred Liberty ships produced during the war,
120 were named for heroes of the U.S. Merchant Marine; not only those who had
lost their lives by enemy action but in other disasters at sea. Kyle Vaughn Johnson
(1904–44) was an ordinary seaman serving aboard SS *Lafayette* between
7 September and 21 September 1942, when he won the Merchant Marine
Distinguished Service Medal for action against the enemy. As a gunner on a 20mm

antiaircraft gun, he was credited with downing three enemy aircraft and assisting in the destruction of two others. His citation credited him with coolness under attack, which contributed immeasurably to the safety of the ship.

Johnson was among the eight crewmen (one officer, two armed guards, and five merchant seamen) killed aboard SS *Maiden Creek,* when, as part of convoy SNF17 (Naples, Italy, to Oran, Algeria), it was torpedoed by the German U-boat *U371* at 9:20 A.M. on 17 March 1944, thirty miles north northeast of Bougie, Algeria. The first torpedo struck *Maiden Creek* forward of the No. 4 hold, breaking the shaft and flooding the engine room. The eight officers, forty crewmen, twenty-nine armed guards, and sole passenger successfully abandoned ship in two lifeboats and a raft, but were ordered back aboard by the escort commander after two hours to await a tow. The deaths occurred when the freighter was torpedoed a second time under the stern, port side.[186] In August 1944 a Liberty ship built by Waterman Steamship Company in Mobile, Alabama, for the War Shipping Administration (WSA) was christened *Kyle V. Johnson* in his honor.

Identical to the majority of the Liberty ships produced, the 7,176-ton *Kyle V. Johnson* was armed with one 5-inch gun, one 3-inch gun, and eight 20mm anti-aircraft guns, crewed by eight officers, thirty-five crewmen and twenty-nine armed guards under the command of Capt. Carl W. Moline.[187]

In late December, *Johnson* tied up at Hollandia, New Guinea, and began loading elements of the 1896th Aviation Engineering Battalion in preparation for transport to the Philippines. Members of the battalion and headquarters company spent both Christmas and New Year's stuffed belowdecks. Along with 506 American troops, *Johnson* carried twenty-five hundred tons of vehicles and fuel.[188]

On 9 January 1945, U.S. and Filipino forces began the invasion of Luzon, and three days later, on 12 January, the convoy which included *Johnson* approached Lingayen Gulf. Shortly after dusk at around 6:30 P.M. the convoy was attacked by a number of enemy suicide planes.[189] As is often the case in the confusion of combat, there is no agreement as to the exact number of planes that attacked. What cannot be argued is that one of the kamikazes penetrated the convoy's antiaircraft defenses and dove straight in, striking *Johnson*'s starboard hull in the area of the No. 3 hold. The impact penetrated the hull through the 'tween deck area into the No. 3 hold. Survivors reported an explosion that blew the steel hatch beams higher than the bridge.[190]

The cargo in the hold caught fire, and *Johnson* slowed and dropped from the convoy with a single destroyer escort for protection. The fear was that the smoke and flames from the burning freighter would attract other kamikazes. The crew battled the fire by flooding the hold with fire hoses, bringing the fire under control in fifteen minutes and completely extinguishing it within an hour.[191] *Johnson* rejoined the convoy and arrived in Lingayen Gulf on 13 January.

Although four other merchant ships were damaged that day (*David Dudley Field, Edward N. Westcott, Elmira Victory,* and *Otis Skinner*), *Kyle V. Johnson* was the only one to suffer loss of life. Along with one member of the crew, Steward Francis Miller, 129 American soldiers, mostly members of Company B who were quartered in the 'tween deck section, were killed in the explosion.[192]

Additionally, kamikazes damaged two destroyer escorts, USS *Richard W. Suesens* (DE-342) and USS *Gilligan* (DE-508), as well as an attack transport, USS *Zeilin* (APA-3) and a tank landing ship, LST-700.[193]

The sixty-eight thousand men of the 6th Army that landed on 9 January at Lingayen Gulf began what was to be the largest land campaign in the Pacific war.[194] By 4 March Manila was liberated, but more than fifty thousand of Gen. Tomoyuki Yamashita's troops withdrew into the mountains, where they held out until the Japanese surrender.[195]

Kyle V. Johnson survived the war, continuing to work as a cargo ship until being scrapped in Panama City, Panama, in 1975.

OPERATION HANNIBAL: THE GERMAN EVACUATION OF THE EASTERN PROVINCES

In January 1945 it became obvious to even the most optimistic German that the war was lost. On 12 January 1945, Stalin launched Operation Vistula-Oder, pitting six million Soviet soldiers against a force of roughly two million German troops, with the goal of advancing to the Oder River.[196] The German units were a mixture of well-equipped veteran soldiers, old men comprising the *Volksstrum,* and the young boys of the Hitler Youth. Through a series of staggered attacks, they put the Germans to flight, reaching the Oder in late January.[197]

As the land paths westward were closed by the Red Army, hordes of refugees fled toward the Baltic ports of Danzig (Gdansk) and Gotenhafen (Gdynia)in East Prussia, hoping to escape westward across the water. Panicked by the tales

During Operation Hannibal, *Wilhelm Gustloff* was torpedoed by the Russian submarine *S-13*. This was the largest ever loss of life at sea. *Steamship Historical Society of America*

of brutality of the advancing Russians, the ports were clogged with a variety of women and children, the elderly, and escaping officials and wounded soldiers.

In Berlin, where even the word "defeat" could land one in front of a firing squad, Grand Adm. Karl Dönitz began plans for an evacuation under fire that would dwarf many times over the evacuation of Dunkirk in 1940. Dubbed Operation Hannibal, the plan involved utilizing all remaining Kriegsmarine and German merchant vessels to remove German civilians and troops across the Baltic Sea to ports in western Germany. Additionally, the order permitted local commanders to "take precautionary evacuation measures according to the local tactical situation." This far exceeded Dönitz's authority as commander in chief of the German navy.[198]

Nonetheless, despite resistance from Nazi Party authorities, the Naval High Command went ahead with the determination that by no means should it be allowed for any German, civilian or military, to fall into the hands of the marauding Red Army. On 21 January 1945, the order was given and Operation Hannibal was put into action. In the five months that "Hannibal" was in effect, a series of German ships were sunk, resulting in some of the worst losses of life in maritime history, including the largest ever loss of life at sea, *Wilhelm Gustloff.*

Wilhelm Gustloff

Wilhelm Gustloff was already in Gotenhafen when she received orders assigning her to the planned naval evacuation, together with other large passenger ships stationed at Danzig, Pillau, and Gotenhafen, along the Baltic. These ships included *Cap Arcona, Robert Ley, Hamburg, Hansa, Deutschland, Potsdam, Pretoria, Berlin, Steuben,* and *Goya*—127 passenger ships in all.[199] *Gustloff* had served for the past four years as a *Wohnschiff* (barracks ship) of the Kriegsmarine, housing the 1st, and later the 2nd Unterseeboots-Lehrdivision.[200]

Built by Blohm & Voss of Hamburg for Deutsche Arbeitsfront (DAF) or the German Labor Front, *Wilhelm Gustloff* was one of two ships built especially for the *Kraft Durch Freude* (Strength Through Joy) program, a propaganda ploy by the National Socialists to gain the support of German labor while presenting a benign image of the Third Reich to the world. The program provided low-cost cruises to German workers in the mid-1930s and was popular with the average German worker. *Gustloff* and her sister ship, *Robert Ley,* were built as single-class cruise ships, the first of Germany's "classless" cruise ships.

Named after the National Socialist party leader in Switzerland who was felled by an assassin's bullet in 1936, the 25,484-ton, 648-foot *Wilhelm Gustloff* was christened by her namesake's widow and launched on 5 May 1937 as the flagship of the entire KdF fleet.[201]

For almost the next two years, *Gustloff* carried happy National Socialist workers on pleasure cruises on the Atlantic, and Mediterranean and North seas. Then in May 1939, *Gustloff* was among six ships sent to Spain to return the victorious German Condor Legion to Germany following the defeat of Republican forces by the Nationalists under Franco. *Gustloff* and the other ships (*Robert Ley, Deutsche, Stuttgart, Sierra Cordoba,* and *Oceana*) arrived in Vigo, Spain, on 24 May 1939 and unloaded large quantities of medical supplies. They departed two days later, with *Gustloff* carrying 1,405 men who disembarked in Hamburg on 30 May to massive celebrations.[202]

On 22 September 1939, only weeks after the start of the Second World War, *Gustloff* was officially commissioned into the Kriegsmarine as Lazaretschiff-D (Hospital Ship D), serving as a floating hospital for sick and wounded troops.[203]

Painted all white, with a green stripe along both sides and red crosses on the deck, stacks, and sides (as required by international law), she was first utilized in the Danzig-Neufahrwasser region, taking aboard 685 wounded soldiers of the defeated Polish Army.[204]

For the next several weeks, *Gustloff* helped carry thousands of Baltic Germans westward from the territories of Poland now occupied by Soviet forces. In May 1940 she was sent to Norway to support operations there as a floating hospital, and she departed for Stettin on 2 July 1940 carrying 563 wounded.[205] She returned to Oslo, Norway, on 20 October transporting an additional 414 wounded soldiers to Swinemunde.

In November 1940 *Gustloff*'s services as a hospital ship came to an end. She was ordered to Gotenhafen for duty as a static accommodation ship,[206] and there she remained until being reactivated for Operation Hannibal in early January 1945.

On 22 January 1945, the crew and personnel aboard *Gustloff* worked to prepare her to take on thousands of exhausted refugees and wounded soldiers.[207] Karl Hoffman, a German sailor, recalled that "in the midst of military collapse, and the impending arrival of the Russians, there prevailed an atmosphere of indescribable chaos" and that "people stormed forward onto the ship" once the gangplank was lowered, resulting in confusion with "children separated from parents."[208]

The port of Gotenhafen had more than sixty thousand refugees desperate to escape the advancing Soviet Army, and they streamed aboard filling every available space. In the confusion, many people escaped being listed on the manifest. According to the ship's official records, the list of passengers of the 30 January rescue mission included "918 naval officers and men, 173 crew, 373 members of the Women's Naval Auxiliary, 162 wounded and 4,424 refugees" for a total of 6,050.[209] Sources are not in agreement regarding the exact number of passengers.[210] The ship's purser, after years of amassing data, placed the number at sixty-six hundred passengers, while crewman Hoffman estimated the number to be between seven thousand and eight thousand. A newly published book by Heinz Schon states that the number on board was 8,956 refugees,[211] 918 officers and men of the 2nd Unterseeboot-Lehrdivision, 373 female Naval Auxiliaries, 173 Naval Armed Forces Auxiliaries, and 162 severely wounded soldiers for a total of 10,582 persons on board,[212] but the exact numbers will never be known.

On the morning of 29 January, a hospital train arrived, more wounded were embarked, and a couple of antiaircraft guns were mounted on the stern. Anxious

Goya was sunk by the Russian submarine *L-3*. Out of 7,000 aboard only 183 were pulled from the sea. *Steamship Historical Society of America*

to leave, Capt. Frederich Petersen was refused permission to depart and ordered to continue embarking refugees.

Finally, at 10 A.M. on 30 January, orders were received permitting *Gustloff* to depart, but the crew was advised that their escort would be delayed.[213] Fearing additional disorder on the ship should the departure be delayed, Captain Petersen opted to depart without an escort.

At 12:30 P.M. four tugboats towed *Gustloff* from her berth in temperatures of ten degrees below zero into swelling seas and ice floes drifting on the surface of the harbor. The crew was kept busy removing ice from the deck and guns as *Gustloff* steamed westward toward Stettin. At approximately 9:10 P.M. *Gustloff* was sailing north of the Stople Bank when she was struck by a pattern of three torpedoes fired from the Russian submarine *S13*, commanded by Capt. Alexander I. Marinseko. The first torpedo struck the bow below the waterline. The second exploded amidships under the swimming pool on E-Deck, killing almost all of the female auxiliaries quartered there. The third and last torpedo hit just forward of the engine room, knocking out all power as the sea rushed in.[214]

Despite the best efforts of the captain and crew, there were insufficient lifeboats for the number of passengers, most having been removed while the ship

Cap Arcona was loaded with five thousand prisoners and 280 SS guards when she was attacked by British Hawker Typhoon fighter-bombers and set afire. The ship capsized and most of those on board were trapped belowdecks. *Steamship Historical Society of America*

was being used as a barracks for U-boat crews. Pregnant women, wounded soldiers, and children were stampeded as the panicked crowds rushed the lifeboats. Hoffman recalled that of the few lifeboats aboard most were frozen in place, and many passengers chose suicide over drowning. "I saw families shoot themselves rather than suffer the slow and terrifying death through drowning that awaited them."[215] Others remained on the sinking and listing ship, hoping for a last-minute salvation.

The stern began to rise as the forecastle sank below the waves, and within forty-five to fifty minutes *Gustloff* disappeared into the depths below. The screams of the passengers in the frigid waters subsided as hypothermia took its toll.

As with the original tally of passengers on board, the number rescued from the sea differs from source to source, with most agreeing on the figure of 964. The Jason Pipes article, "A Memorial to the *Wilhelm Gustloff*" gives the figure saved as 1,239.[216] Hoffman was taken aboard *Torpedoboot T-36*, along with 563 others. *Torpedoboot Lowe* rescued another 472, with smaller boats accounting for the rest. The survivors were transferred to the Danish military hospital ship *Prinz Olaf*.[217] Hoffman puts the number of survivors at 996.

A Polish diving team's report, dated 12 September 1979, states that *Gustloff* lies on her port side on the bottom at 55°07'N 17°42'E. It has been officially designated a gravesite by the Polish government. *Wilhelm Gustloff* remains the largest loss of life at sea in history.

Despite the sinking of *Gustloff*, evacuation efforts continued as every available ship worked to carry fleeing refugees and soldiers west, away from the advancing enemy. The next major loss of Operation Hannibal occurred ten days after *Gustloff* went down when the liner *Steuben* was sent to the bottom by Soviet torpedoes.

Steuben

Built by AG Vulkan Werke in Stettin, Germany, in 1922, the 14,690-ton liner was constructed for Norddeutscher Lloyd (NDL). The ship was 551 feet in length with a sixty-five-foot beam.[218] Christened *München III,* she sailed on her maiden voyage from Bremen to New York on 21 June 1923.[219] Her triple expansion SR engines with LP turbines gave her a speed of sixteen to seventeen knots, and she could accommodate 1,079 passengers.[220]

Refitted and refloated in New York following a major fire that sent her to the bottom of the Hudson River on 11 February 1930, *Munchen* was renamed *General von Steuben,* in honor of the Prussian who served as inspector general of the Continental Army during the American Revolution. She spent the 1930s as a passenger cruise liner, shortening her name to *Steuben* in 1938.[221]

Inducted into the Kriegsmarine following the start of World War II, she was assigned as a navy accommodation ship for German sailors in Kiel, where she remained for the next four years. In the summer of 1944, she returned to sea duty, transporting troops east across the Baltic and returning with wounded to Kiel.[222]

With the collapse of the German army in the east early in 1945, the *Steuben* was put to work as part of Operation Hannibal, evacuating German troops and civilians westward. She began her last voyage on 9 February 1945 departing Pillau (Baltiyski) on the Baltic, bound for Kiel. The number of persons on board is in question, but most sources place the number at approximately 3,450 (2,000 wounded, 1,000 refugees, 320 nurses, 30 doctors, and her crew of almost 100).[223]

Shortly after midnight on 10 February, *Steuben* took two torpedo hits just below the bridge, fired by the same submarine, *S13*, in the same area as the *Gustloff* sinking eleven days earlier. She sank within seven minutes. Most who went into the freezing water died before they could be rescued, and escorting ships were only able to save about three hundred.[224] The survivors were taken to Kohlberg. In less than two weeks, Capt. A. I. Marinseko's *S13* had sunk two ships, with a loss of lives exceeding ten thousand.

Goya

Another German ship that suffered the same fate as the *Gustloff* and *Steuben* was *Goya*. Named for the Spanish painter who produced a series of satirical etchings on the theme, ironically enough, "Disasters of War,"[225] the 5,320-ton *Goya* was constructed by the J. Ludwig Mowinckels Rederei shipbuilding company in Oslo, Norway, and launched in 1940. When Germany invaded Norway and captured all the major ports in that country, the Norwegian High Command ordered a cease fire on 9 June 1940 and surrendered to the Germans.

Goya and other Norwegian ships were converted for use by the German navy as transports. Some accounts have her serving as a U-boat target ship in the early years of the war,[226] but by late 1944 she was engaged in transporting refugees west across the Baltic from ports in Prussia and Poland, carrying some twenty thousand passengers in four voyages.[227]

By April Russian troops were penetrating into Berlin itself, and the Soviets controlled the majority of the Baltic, except for a small section of the Hela Peninsula. Despite almost constant fire from Russian artillery, planes, and a sea force that included twenty submarines, the evacuation continued, rescuing 264,887 in the month of April alone.[228]

On 16 April 1945, *Goya,* painted in typical camouflage, joined a convoy bound for the Danish capital of Copenhagen from Hela, under the command of Captain Plunneke. Like the other ships, there was no accurate count taken as refugees stormed aboard, but most estimates put the number at about seven thousand, both civilian and military, including survivors of the 35th Tank Regiment.[229]

The ships were about fifty miles north of Rixholt on the Stolpe Bank when, at precisely four minutes before midnight, *Goya* was struck by two torpedoes fired by Soviet submarine *L3*, commanded by Capt. Vladimir Knonvalov. One struck amidships, the other in the stern. Almost immediately, the ship broke in

Before soldiers, their dependents, and civilian passengers could be unloaded from *Robert Ley,* the ship was hit, set afire, and burned to a shell. Most of the passengers were killed in the attack. *Imperial War Museum*

two, the rushing water trapping many of the passengers. Within four to seven minutes (accounts differ), *Goya* slid under the waves. Of the almost 7,000 aboard, only 183 were pulled from the sea, resulting in at least sixty-eight hundred casualties. For this victory, Knonvalov was promoted to rear admiral.[230]

The War's End

By the end of April, the Third Reich was in its final days. Mussolini and Hitler both died days apart, Mussolini shot by partisans on 28 April and Hitler by his own hand on the thirtieth. In between, all German forces in Italy surrendered on 29 April.

In Berlin, while the remains of the German army fought Soviet troops for control of the capital, the new Führer, Grand Admiral Dönitz, continued to supervise the evacuation of Germans west, away from the advancing Russian juggernaut. At the same time, fanatic Nazis, under orders from Reichsführer Heinrich Himmler, planned to ensure that not all of those evacuated from the east would arrive safely in the west.[231]

Meanwhile, at the headquarters of the 83rd Group, 2nd Tactical Air Force, Royal Air Force, in Suchtein, commanders alerted by rumors of ships assembling at Lubeck Bay and Kiel Bay to transport the Nazi leadership to Norway issued Operation Order #73, which directed "the destruction of the concentration of enemy ships in Lübeck Bay, west of Poel Island . . ."

In obedience to orders that "no prisoner was to fall into the hands of the enemy alive,"[232] the evacuation of the eastern concentration camps began, leading to death marches, starvation, and executions, as Nazis scrambled to obliterate evidence of their crimes. Prisoners from the Neuengamme concentration camp, as well as prisoners from Stutthof and Mittelbau-Dora were marched or transported in cattle wagons to Lübeck harbor, the first arriving on 19 April 1945. Between the nineteenth and the twenty-sixth, thousands of prisoners were transported, with about half dying en route.[233]

The plan was to load the prisoners aboard ships, sail out into the Baltic Sea, and scuttle the ships, killing all the prisoners on board. For this purpose, several ships were commandeered, most notably *Cap Arcona, Thielbek,* and *Athen.*[234]

Built for the Hamburg–Süd Amerika Line by Blohm & Voss of Hamburg, the 27,561-ton *Cap Arcona* was launched on 14 May 1927 and sailed on her maiden voyage to La Plata on 19 November. She spent twelve years sailing between Hamburg and Rio de Janeiro before being conscripted into the Kriegsmarine for wartime service on 25 August 1939.[235] *Cap Arcona* spent the war years as a navy accommodation ship from 29 November 1939, while docked at Gotenhafen, until 31 January 1945, when she was called up for service in Operation Hannibal.

During the war, *Cap Arcona* was used as the set for the German movie *Titanic,* a propaganda film that had the corrupt British crew failing to heed the warnings of the ship's only (fictional) German officer. Although the director, Herbert Selpin, was experienced at making films with a nautical flavor, he was not very experienced politically. Annoyed by some German naval officers' attentions toward his actresses, and angered by delays, he made some unflattering remarks about the German navy. He was subsequently arrested by the Gestapo, and "committed suicide" while in custody. He was replaced by Werner Klinger. The film fared little better than its director. Banned by the Nazis, it was not shown in Germany until 1955.[236]

As the Russians advanced in early 1945, *Cap Arcona* made three voyages between Gotenhafen and Copenhagen, transporting twenty-six thousand

German civilians, troops, and party officials to the relative safety of German con-trolled Denmark.[237] On her last voyage, worn turbines required an overhaul, and even after the overhaul she was barely maneuverable upon her return to Lübeck Bay on 14 April. No longer of use to the navy, she was discharged and returned to the Hamburg-Süd line.[238]

Thielbek, a 2,815-ton freighter, was also in port, having damage repaired from an air raid during the summer of 1944. Requisitioned by the Gauleiter of Hamburg, she was ordered to Lübeck before the repairs were completed. Another damaged freighter, *Athen,* was to be used to ferry prisoners to other ships.

On 18 April 1945, a meeting was held aboard the *Thielbek.* Present were John Jacobsen, captain of *Thielbek,* Capt. Heinrich Bertram of *Cap Arcona,* and rep-resentatives of the SS. Ordered to prepare to embark soon-to-be-arriving con-centration camp prisoners, both captains refused. The following day Captain Jacobsen was removed from command of *Thielbek,* and the first of an estimated eleven thousand prisoners arrived in Lübeck aboard cattle wagons from Neugammen.[239]

New groups of prisoners arrived daily until the twenty-sixth, with the first seg-ment being embarked onto the *Thielbek* on 20 April.[240] That same day, twenty-three hundred prisoners and 280 SS guards boarded *Athen* to be ferried out to *Cap Arcona,* anchored off Neustadt. Although Captain Nobmann of *Athen* initially refused to take the prisoners on board, the threat of being summarily tried and shot persuaded him to reconsider, and he carried the prisoners out to *Cap Arcona.* Once again, Captain Bertram refused to take the prisoners on board, and the *Athen* returned to Lübeck fully loaded on the twenty-first.[241]

Communications between the Nazi hierarchy, the Kriegsmarine, and the chairman of the Hamburg-Süd line continued for the next few days, but on 26 April a motorboat carrying an SS Sturmbahnführer, an advisory merchant marine captain, and a party of armed SS troops pulled alongside *Cap Arcona.* They presented written orders to Bertram advising him that he would be shot without trial if he refused to allow prisoners to board. At this point, Bertram ceased his protests and renounced all responsibility.[242]

While waiting for *Athen* to pull alongside, a second launch arrived with addi-tional SS troops who removed all life vests and life belts, locking them in stor-age.[243] All lifeboats and rafts had previously been removed for use in the evacuations in the east.

Accounts differ as to how many prisoners were boarded on each of the ships. Most sources agree that *Cap Arcona* carried about five thousand. Captain Bertram, in a report to Hamburg-Süd dated 31 January 1947, stated that on 28 April, he had sixty-five hundred prisoners on board.[244]

On 30 April two thousand prisoners were transferred from the vastly over-crowded *Cap Arcona* back to *Athen*. With forty-five hundred prisoners on board, as well as four hundred (some accounts say five hundred) SS guards, five hundred naval gunners and a crew of seventy-six, the total on board was 5,476. *Thielbek* had approximately 2,800 and *Athen* 1,998 on board. It is impossible to know for sure how many prisoners were on board each ship as the lack of sufficient food, water, medicine, and sanitary facilities, as well as confinement in overcrowded, damp, and airless holds, resulted in thirty to fifty deaths daily.

The ships were loaded to such an extent that there was no room to load the approximately one thousand prisoners that arrived by barges on 2 May. That evening, SS and naval troops began shooting the prisoners, murdering four hundred.[245]

On 3 May, in obedience to Operation Order #73, Hawker Typhoon fighter-bombers of the 83rd Group launched the last major air raid on enemy shipping in the Baltic. The Typhoon, first produced in 1941, had a range of six hundred miles fully loaded. The aircraft had four wing-mounted 20mm cannons and could carry nineteen hundred pounds of bombs or eight 127mm rockets. With a maximum speed of 420 miles per hour and no German opposition in the air, the ships sailing the Baltic were easy targets.

The first squadron to attack was the 184th commanded by Flight Lt. Derek Stephanson,[246] which departed its base at Hustedt at 12:05 P.M. The eight Typhoons fired their rockets at *Cap Arcona*, *Thielbek*, and *Deutschland*, which was also anchored off Neustadt. (*Athen* had rammed a quay at Neustadt and hoisted a white flag, saving the ship and its passengers.)

Next in were nine planes of Group Captain Johnny Baldwin's 198th Squadron out of Plantlunne. Five Typhoons fired forty rockets at *Cap Arcona*, setting it on fire. The other four attacked *Thielbek* and *Deutschland*. Baldwin had already garnered fame for leading the attack on Rommel's staff car on 17 July 1944.[247]

At approximately 2:30 P.M., the 263rd Squadron led by Group Captain Martin Rumbold, followed by the 197th Squadron commanded by Flight Lt. J. Harding, both from Ahlhorn,[248] attacked. *Thielbek* sank within twenty to forty-five minutes, with only fifty survivors, and *Deutschland* burned furiously for four hours before keeling over. *Cap Arcona,* also on fire, capsized after only an hour trapping many belowdecks.[249]

Another "Strength Through Joy" (KDF) ship that participated in Operation Hannibal was *Robert Ley.* Her construction was ordered a year after the keel was laid for *Wilhelm Gustloff.* The ship was named in honor of Robert Ley (1890–1945), the Nazi Labor leader and head of the Deutsches Arbeitsfront (DAF). The son of a farmer before joining the Nazi Party in the early days of 1924, he became Gaultier of Cologne in 1928. A close friend of Hitler, he supervised the mobilization of "foreign" as well as German manpower during the war, leading to charges of using forced slave labor. He was arrested and tried as a war criminal at Nuremberg following the end of the war. Captured by the 101st American Airborne on 16 May 1945 near Berchtesgaden, he committed suicide by hanging himself in his cell on 25 October 1945.[250]

Adolf Hitler personally attended the launching of *Ley* on 29 March 1938 and was aboard her during her maiden voyage. Following her service as a KDF luxury liner and service as a troopship, hospital, and accommodation ship she was among those ordered to the eastern shores of the Baltic to evacuate German civilian and military personnel. *Ley* carried passengers westward, until ordered to Hamburg in early March 1945. Shortly after arriving, the city and port were attacked by RAF bombers. The ship was hit, set afire, and burned to a shell. With soldiers, their dependents, and refugees still on board waiting to disembark when the bombing occurred, many were killed and injured.[251]

Operation Hannibal came to an end with the surrender of all German forces on 8 May 1945. Despite the horrendous losses suffered, including three of the worst maritime disasters in history, Operation Hannibal must be considered a success of a magnitude far exceeding that of the better known Dunkirk evacuation. In all, 509 ships, including 127 passenger liners,[252] were able to move 2,116,500 German soldiers and civilians from the eastern territories in a little over four months with losses of approximately twenty thousand or roughly 1 percent.[253] Thus, the largest evacuation in history was also one of the most successful.

ASHIGARA

Launched in August 1929 the Japanese A-class heavy cruiser *Ashigara* seemed to live a charmed life during World War II. Though the ten-thousand-ton warship

Both Axis and Allied troops used all types of transports in the Asian battle theater. Shown here are Allied soliders on a barge, powered by outboard motors, crossing the Irrawaddy River near Tigyiang, Burma, December 1944. *U.S. National Archives*

participated in numerous operations only two incidents damaged the ship before it was sunk. The first happened during summer maneuvers in 1935, when she suffered a flareback explosion which wrecked her No. 2 turret during a gunnery exercise off Muroran, Japan. Forty-four of her crewmen were killed. Late in the war she was hit by a bomb from a U.S. B-25 medium bomber, but survived the attack to continue on with her raid on invading American forces, who were storming the beaches at San José in the Philippines.[254]

Following the 7 December 1941 attack on Pearl Harbor, Japanese naval and ground forces were already on their way to the Philippines. *Ashigara* was assigned to the Northern Covering Force, which was to provide support for the Japanese landings at Lingayen Gulf. Sixty-six transports began landing troops ashore while being harassed by U.S. Navy PBYs and army planes from Clark Field. One army B-17C *Flying Fortress* of the 19th Bombing Group managed to reach the Japanese fleet standing offshore. The pilot, Capt. Colin P. Kelly Jr., reported that he had bombed and severely damaged a Knogo-class battleship setting it afire. He identified the enemy ship as *Haruna*. On his way back to Clark he was attacked by more than twenty Japanese fighters, including one piloted by air ace

Saburo Sakai. Kelly managed to hold the plane level as his crew bailed out but was himself unable to abandon the aircraft and was killed when the plane crashed as he approached Clark. Sakai was credited with the kill. It was the first combat loss of a B-17 in World War II. The news of Kelly's exploit quickly spread back home and America had its first hero of the war. It was rumored that he had been awarded the Congressional Medal of Honor; however, after the war it was ascertained that he achieved no hits but came closest to hitting *Ashigara,* which he had mistaken for *Haruna.* He was awarded a posthumous Distinguished Service Cross for his heroic action and President Roosevelt addressed a letter to General Eisenhower requesting that he appoint Colin Kelly's nineteen-month-old son to West Point when he came of age. Kelly's son graduated from the Point in 1963 and served as a chaplain.[255]

In 1937 *Ashigara* was selected to represent Japan at a Coronation Review held at Spithead, England, in honor of King George VI. Major Japanese warships were rarely seen in those days and when the ship was sighted off Hong Kong by the surprised crew of the submarine HMS *Regulus,* one young British officer who watched did not know that several years later he would destroy the cruiser in the southwest Pacific. *Ashigara* operated in the China Sea in 1939 and served as the flagship of the Second China Expeditionary Fleet in 1941.[256]

After the fall of the Philippines, Japanese forces moved quickly into southern Asia capturing the Malay Peninsula and Singapore, Rabaul in New Britain, Borneo, Java, Sumatra, the Dutch West Indies, and other islands that could provide bases from which to attack Australia. The Japanese fleet also moved into the Indian Ocean to support the advance of Japanese ground forces in the East Indies. Playing for time, American, British, Dutch, and Australian (ABDA) naval units tried to stem the advance of the Japanese, but were soundly defeated at the Battle of the Java Sea. Acting as a flagship during the encounter, *Ashigara* did not engage the enemy until she and other cruisers fired on the heavy cruiser HMS *Exeter,* and destroyers HMS *Encounter* and USS *Pope* (DD-225). Overwhelmed by the firepower of the enemy, the Allied warships were sunk after a brief battle. *Pope* was the last ship of the Allied Java Sea Fleet to go down.[257]

Following the defeat of Allied naval forces in the South Pacific, *Ashigara* operated around the Dutch West Indies and in northern waters. When the Allies went on the offensive in 1942 with the invasion of Guadalcanal, *Ashigara* was ordered south to carry reinforcements between islands. Since the sinking of Japanese troop transports by U.S. and British submarines had become critical, troops were carried in all types of vessels, including warships. In fact, the transport of Japanese troops between occupied islands became a major task for Japanese naval forces. *Ashigara* transported elements of the 2nd Infantry Division in September 1942 from Java to the Shortland Islands in the Solomon Sea to reinforce Guadalcanal. After a refit in Sasebo in 1943, she once again operated in southern waters, transporting troops from Singapore to Merqiui in January 1944.[258]

As the war progressed and Allied forces closed in on the Japanese home islands, the Japanese activated their "SHO GO" naval operations. Imperial naval groups were formed to defend the following critical areas: "SHO 1 GO" (Philippines), "SHO 2 GO" (Formosa, Nasei Shoto, and the southern Kyushu area), "SHO 3 GO" (Kyushu, Shikoku, the Homshu area, and the Bonin Islands), and "SHO 4 GO" (Hokkaido area). All of the nine surviving A-class cruisers participated in SHO 1 GO, which was initiated on 17 October 1944 and led to a series of complex naval engagements. During these actions all nine of the cruisers fought American invading forces and suffered heavy losses. *Atago, Maya, Chokai,* and *Nachi* were sunk and *Takao, Myoko,* and *Aoba* were heavily damaged. Only *Haguro* and *Ashigara* remained in fighting condition.[259]

In December 1944 *Ashigara* and the light cruiser *Oyodo* with six destroyers participated in a raid against the U.S. San José beachhead in the Philippines. *Ashigara* was hit by a 500-lb. bomb on the port side by a B-25 of the 71st Reconnaissance Squadron of the 5th Air Force. The bomb killed ten crewmen and started heavy fires. However, the crew was able to control the damage and *Ashigara* was able to fire fifty-eight high explosive shells and sixty-eight illuminating shells at the San José landing area. Between February and May 1945, *Ashigara* made short cruises to Sumatra and the eastern part of the Gulf of Bengal to transport troops and war materiel.[260]

In early June 1945, *Ashigara* and escort destroyer *Kamikaze* sortied out of Singapore bound for Batavia (Djakarta) via the Banka Strait. The cruiser was to load up some sixteen hundred army troops and 480 tons of supplies and return to Singapore. The trip was not without danger because U.S. and British submarines patrolled the shipping lanes in the Java and South China seas. Among the Allied undersea force was HMS *Trenchant,* commanded by the young officer who had witnessed the underway sailing of *Ashigara* off Hong Kong many years ago, Comdr. A. R. Hezlet, RN, DSO, DSC. During the inter-

The Japanese A-class heavy cruiser *Ashigara* was struck by five torpedoes and set afire by HMS *Trenchant* as she passed through the Banka Strait. *National Maritime Museum*

vening years Hezlet had commanded six different boats and sunk numerous enemy ships. As the first and only skipper of the first British submarine named *Trenchant,* he was to experience the highlight of his career during the sixth patrol of the boat in Southeast Asian waters.[261]

Trenchant was a Triton-class submarine that was built at the Chatham Dockyard. She was launched in March 1943 and completed in February 1944. The 1,571-ton sub (with ballast tanks flooded) was fitted with six internal bow tubes twenty-five feet long and twenty-one inches in diameter and five external torpedo tubes (two fore, three aft), for which she carried seventeen torpedoes. Other armament included one 4-inch MK X11 deck gun and one 20mm anti-aircraft gun. After trials and work up she was sent to the Far East via the Suez Canal and based at Trincomalee, Ceylon, where she joined the 4th Submarine Flotilla. During her first five patrols she sank many enemy coasters, motor launches, junks, trawlers, landing craft, lighters, and a German U-boat as it approached her operating base at Penang, Malaya. *U859,* a "Monsoon boat," was a large type IXD2 sub commanded by Kapitänleutnant Johann Jebsen. Seventeen German crewmen survived the attack and were picked up by *Trenchant.* They were taken into custody as POWs by the British army when the boat returned to Trincomalee.[262] The 4th Submarine Flotilla moved from Trincomalee to Fremantle, Australia, and *Trenchant* became part of U.S. Task Force 71 (TF-71), which was located at Perth, a few miles inland. In addition to the 4th Submarine Flotilla, two U.S. submarine squadrons were based at Fremantle. Visiting TF-71 Headquarters, Hezlet obtained critical intelligence regarding enemy naval operations in the Java and China Seas. More important, he learned that the Japanese were frequently using their cruisers to support and move their troops between bases in Java and Sumatra, and Batavia and Singapore. On 13 May *Trenchant* left Fremantle, in company with HMS *Taciturn* and HMS *Thorough* for operations in the Java and China Seas. They were ordered to wage unrestricted submarine warfare against the enemy in order to destroy its combatant ships and shipping and to deny the enemy use of vital traffic lanes.

It had been decided that the three British submarines would operate as a wolfpack; however, after a few days out they were ordered to make a reconnaissance of the area south of Lombok and Sape Straits. Hezlet coordinated the new mission and detached *Thorough* to patrol an area south of Sape Strait and sent *Taciturn* westward toward the Lombok Strait. The three boats joined up again a few days later; none had sighted any enemy shipping. *Thorough* was detached on orders from Fremantle and *Trenchant* and *Taciturn* continued on with their patrol. On 25 May an enemy minesweeper and a coaster were sighted off Mandalika. *Trenchant* surfaced and took the minesweeper under fire. The craft was soon out of control and ablaze; it went down as survivors jumped into the sea. In the meantime the enemy coaster had beached itself.

On 29 May *Trenchant* received a message from the task force commander that a convoy was transiting the Sunda Strait. Before *Trenchant* could make contact the convoy was attacked by either USS *Boarfish* (SS-327), which was known to be in the area, or Allied aircraft that Hezlet could see some distance away. After passing through Karimata Strait, Hezlet received a report that a heavy Japanese cruiser was making a trooping trip between Singapore and Batavia. Hezlet asked for permission to patrol the northern entrance to Banka Strait with the hope of intercepting the warship. On 6–7 June Hezlet received a report that a Japanese cruiser and a destroyer had arrived at Batavia. Hezlet positioned his boat in the Banka Strait submerged and patrolled the area during the seventh. At 4 A.M. on the eighth, he received a message from USS *Blueback* (SS-326) that two enemy ships had left Batavia and were heading north, apparently returning to

Singapore. Cruising on the surface later that morning the officer of the watch called Hezlet to the bridge; he had sighted a ship entering the strait. They identified it as the Japanese destroyer *Kamikaze,* probably reconnoitering for a troop-carrying warship that was no doubt following the ship at a distance. As the ships closed, the destroyer sighted *Trenchant* and fired her forward gun followed by a fusillade from her antiaircraft guns, none of which hit the sub. As they opened the distance between them, *Trenchant* fired one of her stern tubes. The destroyer saw the splash of the torpedo being launched, increased her speed, and continued through the strait until out of sight in the open sea.

Trenchant had little room to maneuver in the strait because the waters were so shallow. Hezlet contacted HMS *Stygian,* which was positioned in the open sea northwest of the strait, and communicated that they had encountered the destroyer and that she was heading his way. Hezlet moved his boat further down the channel reaching a minefield laid the previous April by *0.19,* a Dutch submarine, at 6:16 A.M. Here he stopped to wait for daybreak, hoping to sight the second enemy warship coming through the straits. At mid-morning explosions were heard seaward, and Hezlet assumed that HMS *Stygian* and *Kamikaze* were engaged. At 11:48 A.M. the officer of the watch sighted an enemy cruiser moving briskly along the Sumatra shoreline. Hezlet took the boat under and studying the ship through his periscope could see that the upper deck was crowded with khaki-clad soldiers. He identified the ship as the Japanese cruiser *Ashigara.* Estimating her speed at seventeen knots, Hezlet fired a salvo of eight torpedoes as the cruiser passed within four thousand yards. Five torpedoes hit the warship, one abreast the after turret, another right forward, and then another amidships. Two more hit the ship, which was now engulfed in heavy smoke. *Ashigara* stopped dead in the water and began to list to starboard. Her bow had been blown off and her forecastle deck destroyed. Though severely damaged, the crippled ship sighted *Trenchant*'s periscope and directed antiaircraft fire at her attacker. Hezlet was going to send two more torpedoes at the doomed warship but by then uncontrollable fire had swept over the ship gradually taking on a greater list. Men were abandoning ship, and as *Kamikaze* suddenly reappeared the warship slowly capsized and sank. Hezlet had two tubes loaded and had decided to fire them at the destroyer if she stopped to pick up survivors; however, the escort continued under way and within a short time enemy aircraft appeared and Hezlet thought it best to leave the area.

Trenchant was ordered to continue with her patrol even though she had only five torpedoes left. Hezlet was then directed to join USS *Puffer* (SS-268) off Pulau Tenggol, an island off Malaya. The submarines arrived at their designated patrol area on 11 June, and the ship was dispatched to cover Allied landings in North Borneo. On 15 June Hezlet was ordered to Subic Bay in the Philippines. Upon his arrival, the U.S. Navy awarded him the Legion of Merit Medal, Degree of Commander. On 26 June *Trenchant* sailed for Fremantle. En route she sunk an enemy schooner in the Gulf of Bonin in the Celebes and destroyed an enemy sub chaser, tug, and barge in the Lombok Strait. *Trenchant* arrived in Fremantle to a rousing welcome. The Admiralty had approved a bar to Hezlet's Distinguished Service Order (2nd award) and delivered orders for Hezlet to report for duty at the Admiralty. The entire *Trenchant* crew was awarded medals or Mentioned in Despatches. HMS *Trenchant* was awarded the Battle Honor, Malaya, 1944–45.[263]

THREE

THE END
OF AN ERA

1950–2003

KOREA

During the Korean War (1950–53) there were no combat-incurred troopship casualties because the North Koreans and Chinese posed no surface ship or submarine threat to such ships. Most of the casualties suffered by United Nations (UN) naval forces (especially destroyers) were due to mines and shore battery engagements. A few British vessels were damaged by air attacks. Fortunately, none of the UN transports encountered mines as they delivered thousands of soldiers to beleaguered South Korea at the beginning of the war and supported subsequent amphibious assaults as the conflict progressed. A number of U.S. World War II troopships saw Korean service; however, U.S. Navy transports (APs) and assault transports (APAs) played a significant role carrying troops from home ports to the battlefields of Korea. U.S. troopships *Ainsworth* and *Shanks* participated in the landings in support of Pusan perimeter combat engagements in July 1950.[1] In September of that year several troop transports took part in various aspects of amphibious landings, including the attack force and the second and third echelon movements. In October 1950 *Marine Phoenix* supported the landing of twenty-two thousand Marines at Wonson.[2] A few months later some two hundred U.S. ships (six APAs, six AKAs, thirteen APs, seventy-six MSTS time charters, eight LSTs, and eleven LSDs), many making multiple runs, evacuated the U.S. troops who had

In 1952 the troopship *General Nelson M. Walker* traveled thirty-five thousand miles in three months transporting Turkish, Dutch, Greek, and Colombian soldiers to Korea.
Naval Historical Center

escaped from the Chosin Reservoir. In just seventeen days 105,000 Marines, U.S. Army, and allied soldiers, 91,000 civilians, 350,000 measurement tons of cargo, and 17,500 vehicles were taken aboard these ships at Hungnam.[3] In 1952 the U.S. troopship *General Nelson M. Walker* traveled thirty-five thousand miles in three months transporting Turkish, Dutch, Greek, and Colombian soldiers to Korea. A year later *Walker* made eight transpac round trips and brought the first POWs home from Korea.[4] Among the many British "Empire" troop carriers, the *Empire Fowey* (ex-German vessel *Potsdam*) and *Empire Orwell* distinguished themselves during the war transporting British and Australian troops to join the forces of sixteen allied nations fighting in Korea.[5]

Six of every seven people who went to Korea went by sea.[6]

VIETNAM

The U.S. Navy's Military Sealift Command (MSC)(formerly known as the

Among the many British "Empire" troop carriers, *Empire Orwell* (shown here) and *Empire Fowey* distinguished themselves by transporting many British and Australian troops to Korea. *Imperial War Museum*

Military Sea Transport Service[MSTS]) was the lifeline for U.S. forces in Vietnam. By the mid-1960s, 527 reactivated World War II Reserve Fleet ships, charter ships under U.S. and foreign registry, and new roll-on/roll-off ships were under the control of the MSC. These included sixteen troopships that transported more than forty thousand U.S. and allied combat and support troops to Southeast Asia during the early buildup of forces in South Vietnam.[7]

American soldiers were transported to South Vietnam on board large "Generals" troopships, APs and APAs; there were no casualties among these ships since the North Vietnamese had little capability to attack these vessels. In March 1965 *General W. A. Mann* (AP-112) delivered the initial segment of two thousand Republic of Korea troopers to South Vietnam.[8] During the last half of the year, sixteen transports supported the second U.S. major troop buildup in Vietnam. *Generals Patch* and *Darby* made the longest troop lift in naval history, sailing from Boston to Vung Tau, South Vietnam, a distance of 12,358 miles. Between 1965 and 1966, two out of every three soldiers arriving in Vietnam came by sea. In August 1966, *Barrett* (AP-196), *Geiger* (AP-197), and *Upshur*

In March 1965 *General W. A. Mann* delivered the initial segment of two thousand
Republic of Korea troopers to join the forces of sixteen nations engaged in the war.
U.S. Navy

(AP-198) transported 18,625 Korean soldiers from Pusan to Da Nang, Qui
Nhon, and Nha Trang.[9] Starting in the mid-1960s troops rotated in and out
of Vietnam by airlift—with few exceptions sealift operations of troops ceased.

THE FALKLAND ISLANDS

On 2 April 1982, the Argentine navy landed four thousand troops on the
British-held Falkland Islands in the South Atlantic. A small contingent of Royal
Marines fought a brave but futile battle against overwhelming forces and were
finally ordered to surrender by Rex Hunt, governor of the islands.[10]

A thousand miles to the east of the Falklands were the associated islands
of South Georgia and the South Sandwich group, which were also attacked
and captured by an Argentine task group. Before capitulating, Royal Marines
on the island heavily damaged a helicopter, killed four Argentine soldiers, and
damaged the Argentine corvette *Granville*. Taking possession of the islands,
the Argentines lowered the Union Jack and raised their country's flag. Gen.
Mario Menendez was proclaimed governor of the islands. During late April,

Queen Elizabeth II was converted into a troopship with a helicopter pad added to her stern deck during the Falkland Islands war. She was loaded with three thousand troops of the 5th Infantry Brigade. *Steamship Historical Society of America*

Other troop carriers included the RFA *Stromness,* which embarked men of 45 Commando Royal Marines. *Imperial War Museum*

The RFA tanker *Tidespring* transported M Company of 42 Commando Royal Marines.
Imperial War Museum

The ro-ro ferries *Europic* and *Norland* (shown here) embarked the 2nd Parachute Battalion.
Imperial War Museum

Canberra returns from the Falklands. *Imperial War Museum*

using conscripts, the occupying Argentine force on the Falklands was increased to ten thousand troops.[11]

On 25 April a small task force that included the destroyer HMS *Antrim* and frigates HMS *Brilliant* and HMS *Plymouth* landed Royal Marines, SAS, and SBS forces on South Georgia and retook the island. Meanwhile the British had assembled a task force that sailed to a staging base at Ascension Island in the South Atlantic. The task force, which consisted of the British carriers HMS *Hermes* and HMS *Invincible*, forty-two warships, twenty-two Royal Fleet auxiliaries (RFAs), and forty-five merchant ships, proceeded further south to retake the Falkland Islands. Included in the force was *Queen Elizabeth II*, which was requisitioned and converted into a troopship with a helicopter pad added to her stern deck. She was loaded with three thousand troops of the 5th Infantry Brigade. Other troop-carrying ships were RFA *Stromness*, which embarked men of the 45 Commando Royal Marines; the converted cruise ship *Canberra* that carried men of the 40 and 45 Commando Royal Marines and the 3rd Parachute

Battalion; the RFA tanker *Tidespring* with M Company of 42 Commando Royal Marines aboard, and the ro-ro ferry *Elk*, which transported two troop elements of the Royal House Guards. Last, ro-ro ferries *Europic* and *Norland* embarked the 2nd Parachute Battalion.[12]

On 2 May the British nuclear submarine HMS *Conqueror* sank the Argentine cruiser *General Belgano* taking four hundred men down with her. This major loss and the sinking of the Argentine submarine *Santa Fe* on 26 April by British helicopters essentially caused the Argentine navy to withdraw from the war zone. However, on 4 May the British suffered the loss of destroyer HMS *Sheffield* when it was attacked by Argentine French-built Super Etendard fighter planes using Exocet air-to-surface missiles. The ship could not be saved, and the order to abandon ship was given; twenty of the ship's crew were lost in the attack. Other Royal Navy losses were to follow.[13]

On 21 May British troops successfully made an amphibious landing near Port San Carlos on the northern coast of East Falkland. They captured Darwin and Goose Green before advancing on the capital city of Port Stanley.[14] The large Argentine garrison at Port Stanley was subsequently attacked by British ground, sea, and air forces and defeated on 14 June 1982. A total of 10,254 Argentine officers and men surrendered. The retaking of the Falklands was costly for the British. Six ships were sunk and ten damaged. Two dozen aircraft were lost to operational accidents, air combat, and enemy ground fire. Two hundred and fifty British soldiers were killed and 777 were wounded. Argentine ground losses were 652 dead and missing. Thirty-one aircraft were downed by British Harrier fighters and thirty more were destroyed on the ground or captured.[15]

For the British to successfully fight an enemy eight thousand miles from its home island and secure all of its objectives was a remarkable feat, but it was also a reminder that a strong navy was vital to a country that is dependent on the seas to protect its interests and, in time of war, critical for its survival.

THE END OF AN ERA

The advent of air trooping that began during the Vietnam War and the subsequent use of airlifts of massive troop movements during later wars, such as Desert Storm, appeared to spell the end of U.S. troop transports by sea. In fact, the last of the navy's AP troopships have been retired, and colleges and univer-

The advent of transporting troops by airlift appeared to spell the end of troop movements by sea. Most of the Navy's troopships were retired, and some have been transferred to colleges and universities as training vessels, including *State of Maine* (ex–AP *Upshur*), which is in the service of the Maine Maritime Academy. *U.S. Maritime Administration*

sities have used some as training vessels. *Texas Clipper* (ex–AP *Chauvenet*) is at Texas A&M University at Galveston; *Golden Bear* (ex–AP *Maury*) is being used by the California State University Maritime College at Vallejo; *State of Maine* (ex–AP *Upshur*) is in the service of the Maine Maritime Academy; *Empire State* (ex–AP *Barrett*) found a home at the State University of New York Maritime College; and *Patriot State* (ex–AP *Geiger*) was assigned to the Massachusetts Maritime Academy. *Patriot State* suffered an engine room fire and was replaced by the former Grace/Prudential passenger cargo liner *Santa Mercedes,* and *Empire State* has been replaced by the former freighter *Mormactide.*[16]

The British troopships *Nevasa* and *Oxfordshire* were launched in 1956 and 1957. At the conclusion of their last trooping voyage from the Far East in 1962, the practice of transport by sea of the British Regular Army in peacetime came to an end after three hundred years of service.[17]

However, as we have witnessed, world events still dictate the movement of troops by sea to quell warring factions within or between nations and to evacuate civilian personnel and refugees in perilous environs. For example, in early 1994 *Empire State* and the Greek-flagged *Mediterranean Sky* sea-lifted the last two thousand U.S. troops from Mogadishu, Somalia. The sealift was used to

There have been instances where old timers have been brought out of mothballs and used again for carrying U.S. troops. The New York State Maritime Academy's *Empire State* (ex-AG-11) saw duty as one of two ships that sealifted the last of two thousand U.S. troops from Mogadishu, Somalia. *Steamship Historical Society of America*

eliminate the danger of enemy fire against U.S. aircraft using the Mogadishu airfield and air space.[18] In 1999 the United Nations sanctioned Operation Stabilize, wherein twenty-eight hundred Royal Australian troops were transported by sea to Timor to stop the violence and atrocities being committed during Timor's turbulent transition to independence. The soldiers were carried aboard the Royal Australian Navy's sealift catamaran *Jervis Bay.*[19]

IRAQ

As the United States began its buildup of forces in the Persian Gulf in early January 2003, troopships were called upon to once again support the country's war effort. During subsequent movements a mix of naval ships carried ten thousand sailors and Marines to the Gulf. Transporting the force were the landing ships USS *Comstock, Anchorage,* and *Pearl Harbor;* amphibious assault ships USS *Boxer* and *Bonhomme Richard;* and the amphibious transport docks USS *Cleveland* and *Dubuque.* At the same time, three thousand Marines with the 2nd Marine Division and four thousand from the 2nd Force Service Support Group departed Wilmington, Delaware, for the Middle East aboard several navy ships. The 4th Army Infantry (seventeen thousand soldiers) embarked aboard troopships from Texas ports. Many thousands of army soldiers were airlifted to the impending war zone.

When the war began in March, U.S. airpower and a "lightning" ground attack from the south to the capital in Baghdad ended the war for all practical purposes. By April enemy resistance appeared to cease, and controlling civil unrest became a major problem for U.S. and British military personnel in the country. However, at the time of this writing (August 2003), American and British soldiers continue to face a number of former regime fighters who have adopted the tactics of guerrilla warfare, which hinder the stabilization and rebuilding of the country.

Obviously, there is still much to be done in Iraq and Afghanistan that will require perhaps a long-term presence of Coalition forces in the country, and troop-carrying transports could be utilized again in the months and years to come. However, the era of the troopship as we know it, especially in World War II, has truly come to an end. The world will never again witness those proud vessels that had to fight the elements of angry seas, attacks by undersea "gray wolves," enemy aircraft, surface raiders, and mines. In spite of these hazards, troopships sailed on, loaded with young fighting men to distant shores and the horrors of war, where "America's best" changed the course of history.

Appendix 1: Other Lost Troopships

Name	Nationality	Troop Casualties (100+)	Date (day/month/ year)	Cause
India	British	160	8/8/15	U-boat
Franconia	British	314	4/10/16	*UB-47*
Invernia	British	120	1/1/17	*UB-47*
Mendi	British	636	21/2/17	collision
Arcadian	British	277	15/4/17	U-boat
Cameronia	British	210	15/4/17	*U33*
Transylvania	British	414	4/5/17	*U63*
Aragon	British	610	30/12/17	U-boat
Tuscana	British	166	5/2/18	*UB-77*
Glenart Castle	British	153	26/2/18	*UC-56*
Djemnah	French	442	15/7/18	U-boat
Warilda	British	123	3/8/18	U-boat
Otranto	British	431	6/10/18	collision
Rawalpindi	British	275	23/11/39	*Gneisenau/ Scharnhorst*

Name	Nationality	Troop Casualties (100+)	Date (day/month/year)	Cause
Rio de Janeiro	British	150	9/4/40	U-boat
Slamat	Dutch	193	27/4/41	Luftwaffe
Anselm	British	250	5/7/41	*U96*
Bahia Laura Donau	German	1700	30/8/41	HMS sub
Taiyo Maru	Japanese	Unknown	5/8/42	USS *Grenadier* (SS-210)
Brazil Maru	Japanese	300+	5/8/42	USS *Greenling* (SS-213)
Abosso	British	172	27/10/42	*U575*
Excaliber	USA	128	11/11/42	*U173*
Nova Scotia	British	650	28/11/42	*U177*
Buyo Maru	Japanese	282	26/1/43	*Wahoo* (SS-238)
Kyokusei Maru	Japanese	1203	2/3/43	air attack
Oigawa Maru	Japanese	1324	3/3/43	air attack
Teiyo Maru	Japanese	1923	3/3/43	air attack
Shinai Maru	Japanese	1052	3/3/43	air attack
Taimei Maru	Japanese	200	3/3/43	air attack
Aiyo Maru	Japanese	252	3/3/43	air attack
Yoma	British	451	17/6/43	U-boat
Timothy Pickering	USA	130	13/7/43	air attack
Cape San Juan	USA	130	11/11/43	I-21
Aikoku Maru	Japanese	unknown	17/2/44	air attack
America Maru	Japanese	unknown	6/3/44	USS *Nautilus* (SS-168)
Miike Maru	Japanese	unknown	21/4/44	USS *Trigger* (SS-237)

Name	Nationality	Troop Casualties (100+)	Date (day/month/year)	Cause
Yoshida Maru No.1	Japanese	900+	26/4/44	USS *Jack* (SS-259)
Hakusan Maru	Japanese	unknown	4/6/44	USS *Flier* (SS-250)
Aki Maru	Japanese	unknown	26/7/44	USS *Crevalle* (SS-291)
Fuso(Huso) Maru	Japanese	unknown	31/7/44	USS *Steelhead* (SS-280)
Yoshino Maru	Japanese	unknown	31/7/44	USS *Steelhead* (SS-280); USS *Parche* (SS-384)
Teia Maru	Japanese	unknown	18/8/44	USS *Rasher* (SS-269)
Mizuho Maru	Japanese	unknown	21/9/44	USS *Redfish* (SS-395)
Arabia Maru	Japanese	unknown	18/10/44	USS *Bluegill* (SS-242)
Asama Maru	Japanese	unknown	1/11/44	USS *Atule* (SS-403)
Gokoku Maru	Japanese	unknown	10/11/44	USS *Barb* (SS-220)
Donau	Germany	unknown	17/1/45	mine

Name	Nationality	Troop Casualties (100+)	Date (day/month/ year)	Cause
Hakozaki Maru	Japanese	unknown	19/3/45	USS *Balao* (SS-285)
Nikko Maru	Japanese	unknown	9/4/45	USS *Tirante* (SS-420)

1. Research of official U.S. documents such as Chief of Naval Operations "Crane" Translations of Radio Intelligence 1940–46, Japanese "Orange" Translations archived at NARA, the Records of the Japanese Navy and Related Documents (1940–60) Collection held at the Naval Historical Center Operational Archives, and various other sources reveal little information regarding casualties suffered by Japanese troopships and naval troop transports during World War II.
2. The eight Japanese ships sunk on 3 May 1943 carried sixty-nine hundred soldiers of the Japanese Eighteenth Army to reinforce their base at Lae, New Guinea. The convoy, which included eight escort destroyers, was destroyed by aircraft of the 5th Army Air Force. B-25s attacking at mast level using "skip bombing" tactics with five-second-delay fuzes proved to be devastating. The encounter was known as the Battle of the Bismarck Sea.

Appendix 2: Letter from Midshipman Drewry to His Father during the World War I British Gallipoli Campaign

The following is a printed copy of a handwritten letter from Midn. G. L. Drewry, R.N.R., VC, to his father from Sedd-el Bahr during the World War I British Gallipoli campaign in Turkey.

HMS River Clyde
Sedd-el Bahr
May 12th 1915

Dearest Father,

I'm awfully afraid I've made you anxious by missing the last two mails, I did write a letter on the 21st April but tore it up again. In my last letter I think I told you that two RN midshipmen were joining the *Hussar* to help me.

Well they came, and we worked in three watches for two days until I got tired of doing nothing so asked the Captain for more work, well I got it with a vengeance.

He took me onboard this ship and gave me thirty Greeks and told me to clean her. Well she was the dirtiest ship I've seen. She was in ballast and had just brought French mules up from Algiers, they had built boxes and floors in the tween decks and carried the mules there without worrying about sanitary arrangements.

We knocked the boxes up and cleaned her up for troops and painted the starboard side P&O colour. A large square port was cut on each side of each hatch in the tween decks and from the No. 2 ports I rigged stages right around the bow. A party of the Armoured Car people came on board and rigged small huts of plates and put maxims in them, 11 altogether. After two days delay on account of weather we put to sea on the 23rd of April at 1.0 pm towing three lighters and a steam boat along our port side and a steam hopper on the starboard side. As soon as we cleared the shipping we dropped the lighters astern. Now I will tell you of our crew. Capt.-Commander Unwin RN (retired supplementary) 1st Lieut:— Mid. Drewry R.N.R., and Warrant Eng. Horend, R.N.R., nine seamen and nine stokers, one carpenter's mate, the original ship's steward and the Captain's servant.

Can you imagine how proud I felt as we steamed down the line, I on the forecastle head.

The flagship (no longer the *Hussar*) wished us luck as we passed. As soon as the tow was dropped I took the bridge until the Captain had lunch then I had mine and carried on with the work for there were many things to do.

At dusk we anchored off Tenedos and that night we had pheasant for dinner, a present from the Captain of the *Soudan*.

Next morning things looked bad a nasty breeze made us afraid our show would not come off, but it died down quickly. At about 6.0 am a signal came to us telling us we were in someone's berth so we had to weigh and for an hour we wandered among the ships with our long tail just scrapping along ship's sides and across their bows. We were nobodies dog nobody loved us. Finally we tied up to the stern of the Fauvette and we put the last touches to the staging on the bow. About 4.0 pm the sweepers came alongside with the troops. At 11.30 pm all was ready and the Capt. told me to snatch some sleep. At midnight we proceeded in this fashion: three lighters and a small steam pinnace hopper towed from No. 1 boom.

At 2.0 am or thereabouts the Capt turned the ship over to me, and I found myself on the bridge very sleepy with only the helmsman, steering towards the Turkish searchlights on a calm night just making headway against the current, shadowy forms of destroyers and battleships slipping past me.

Visions of mines and submarines rose before me as I thought of the 2 and a half thousand men in the holds and I felt very young. Between 3 and 4 am the Capt took over again and I went to sleep again being called at 5.0 am. "Capt says you are to take over the hopper." So I climbed over the side across the lighters into the hopper and then came an anxious time, we steered straight toward Cape Helles and in a few minutes the bombardment commenced. Dad it was glorious! Dozens of ships, battleships, cruisers, destroyers and transports. The morning mist lay on the land, which seemed to be a mass of fire and smoke as the ships raked it with shell. Straight into the sun past battleships roaring with their 12 inches, the noise was awful and the air full of powder. Shells began to fall around us thick but did not hit us. We were half a mile from the beach and we were told not yet, so we took a turn around two ships, at last we had the signal at 6.0 am and in we dashed Unwin on the bridge and I at the helm of the hopper with my crew of six Greeks and one sailor, Sampson. At 6.10 am the ship struck, very easily she brought up and I shot ahead and grounded on her port bow. Then the fun began, picket boats towed lifeboats full of soldiers inshore and slipped them as the water shoaled and they rowed the rest of the way, the soldiers jumped out as the boats beached and they died almost all of them wiped out with the boats' crews. We had a line from the stern of the hopper to the lighters and this we tried to haul in, the hardest haul I've ever tried. Then the Capt appeared on the lighters and the steam pinnace took hold of the lighters and plucked them in until she could go no closer. Instead of joining up to the hopper the Capt decided to make the connection with a spit of rock on the other bow. Seeing this we let go our rope and Sampson and I tried to put a brow out over the bow, the Greeks had run below and two of us could not do it, so I told him also to get out of the rain, and I jumped over the bow and waded ashore, meeting a soldier wounded in the water we (I and another soldier from a boat) tried to carry him ashore but he was again shot in our arms, his neck in two pieces nearly, so we left him and I ran along the beach towards the spit, I threw away my revolver, coat and hat and waded out to where the Captain was in the water with a man named Williams wading and towing the lighters towards the spit. I gave a pull for a few minutes and then climbed aboard the lighters and got the brows lowered onto the lighter. The Capt still in the water sang out for more rope so I went aboard and brought a rope down with the help of a man called Ellard, as we reached the end of the lighters the Capt was wading towards us carrying Williams and we pulled him onto the lighter and Ellard carried him onboard the ship on his shoulders, but he spoilted the act by not coming down again.

Williams was dead. However I got a rope from the lighter to the spit and then with difficulty I hauled the Capt onto the lighter, he was nearly done and I was alone.

He went onboard and the doctor had rather a job with him. All this time shells were falling all round us and into the ship one hitting the casing of one boiler but doing no further damage. Several men were killed by two shells in the No. 4 hold.

I stayed on the lighters and tried to keep the men going ashore, but it was murder and soon the first lighter was covered with dead and wounded and the spit was awful, the sea round it for some yards was red. When they got ashore they were little better off for they were picked off, many of them before they could dig themselves in. They stopped coming and I ran onboard into No. 1 and saw an awful sight: dead and dying lay around the ports where their curiosity had led them. I went up to the saloon and saw the Capt being rubbed down. He murmured something about the third lighter so I went down again and in a few minutes a picket boat came along the starboard side and gave the reserve lighter a push that sent it as far as the hopper (the lighters had drifted away from the spit) with Lieut Morse and myself on it. Just as we hit the hopper a piece of shrapnel hit me on the head knocking me down for a second or two and covering me with blood. However, we made the lighter fast to the hopper and then I went below in the hopper and a Tommy put my scarf round my head and I went up again.

Now we wanted a connection to the other lighters so I took a rope and swam towards the other lighters but the rope was not long enough and I was stuck in the middle. I sang out to Mid. Malleson (Morse &

Malleson arrived in the picket boat) to throw me a line but he had no line except the one that had originally kept the lighters to the spit, he stood up and hauled this line (almost half a coil) and then, as I had drifted away he swam towards the lighter I had left and made it alright.

Then I made for home but had a job climbing up the lighters for I was rather played out. When I got onboard the doctor dressed my head rubbed me down, I was awfully cold. He would not let me get up and I had to lay down and listen to the din.

Then I heard a cheer and looking out of the port I saw the Capt standing on the hopper in white clothes, a line had carried away and by himself he had fixed it.

Then I went to sleep and woke at 3.0 pm to find the hopper's bow had swung round and there was no connection with the shore. I got up and found that nothing was going to be done until dark. At dusk the firing seemed to cease, and the connection was made to the spit again.

During the time I was asleep the Captain and one or two volunteers had taken seven loads of wounded from the lighters to No. 4 hold by the starboard side, a great feat which everyone is talking about. About 8.0 pm the troops commenced to land again and things went well as far as firing goes. While the troops were going out I had a party getting wounded from the hopper and lighters and putting them onboard a trawler laying under our quarter. An awful job, they had not been dressed at all and some of the poor devils were in an awful state, I never knew blood smelt so strong before.

About 11.30 pm the trawler had left and almost all the troops were ashore and the Turks gave us an awful doing, shell, shrapnel and every other nasty thing, but everyone laid low and little harm was done. They finished about 2.0 am. All through the night the village was burning and gave us too much light to be pleasant. Next day was not pleasant, early in the morning our people worked up the right & took the fort and then worked slowly into the village and took it house by house. Then Col. Doughty-Wylie led a charge up the ridge and was killed just as he led his men into the old fort on top of the ridge. All this we saw quite plainly from the ship. I had a run ashore across the spit and took a photo from the beach but the bullets began to fly so I ran back.

It was not until the next day that all the snipers were cleared from the ridge & village.

Samson my hopper man did well on the Sunday afternoon, two or three times he took wounded from the beach to his hopper. On the second day he was severely wounded while sniping from the fore deck. Nothing happened much that night except that a dog frightened one Tommy, he fired at it and so did the rest for nearly an hour.

I won't follow up the soldiers or the censor would tear this up, ten minutes walk and I can see the men in our trenches, in the Straits I can see the enemy shells falling round our ships and always the roar of guns go on. We have been bombarded by aeroplanes but no damage done. I've seen a German chased by two of our planes.

My Capt has just left us for another job and soon I expect to be back to the *Hussar* again.

By the next mail I hope to send you some photos taken here some of them I believe will be of interest and I'm wondering if you could send them to the papers for me.

As we came away I received a letter from the company about the bonus to be given this I have lost, also the forms for the difference of pay. Could you speak to Mr. [name blanked out] in our department and see if he would fix it for me.

The Admiral sent for me on the 28th and gave me a shift of clean clothes & the use of his bath, some luck.

There is lots yet I could tell you but I must not so will send my love & close.

Your affectionate son,
George

N.B. have just received yours of the 15 & 22, glad you are keeping so well.

Appendix 3: List of Equivalent Commissioned Officer Ranks during World War II

German Navy	Royal Navy	U.S. Navy
Grossadmiral	Admiral of the Fleet	Admiral of the Fleet
Generaladmiral	No equivalent	No equivalent
Admiral	Admiral	Admiral
Vizeadmiral	Vice admiral	Vice admiral
Konteradmiral	Rear admiral	Rear admiral
Kommodore	Commodore	Commodore
Kapitän zur See	Captain	Captain
Fregattenkapitän	Captain (junior)	Commander
Korvettenkapitän	Commander	Lieutenant commander
Kapitänleutnant	Lieutenant commander	Lieutenant
Oberleutnant zur See	Lieutenant (senior)	Lieutenant (junior grade)
Leutnant zur See	Lieutenant (junior)	Ensign
Oberfähnrich zur See	Sublieutenant	Senior midshipman
Fähnrich zur See	Midshipman/cadet	Midshipman

Appendix 4: Hospital Ships Used as Troopships

The following has been taken from the Commander in Chief, U.S. Pacific Fleet and Pacific Ocean Areas, document "Operations in the Pacific Ocean Areas during the Month of August 1945."

CAPTURE OF JAPANESE HOSPITAL SHIP

127. A special mission performed by CHARETTE and CONNER (DDs) is of interest. The two destroyers left Morotai on 31 July with the mission of intercepting and searching the TACHIBANA MARU, a Japanese hospital ship which had been reported by air patrols en route through the Banda Sea from the Kai Islands (southwest of New Guinea) to Celebes and Soerabaja.

128. Contact with the ship was made by radar at 2035 on 2 August, after which CHARETTE and CONNER trailed 15 miles astern of her until daylight. At 0637 the target was closed and signalled to stop. During the approach, a number of weighted bags were seen to be thrown overboard. A visit and search party was put on board, and discovered arms and ammunition stored below in boxes marked with red crosses and labelled medical supplies. On receipt of this information, a prize crew was directed to take over the vessel, and she was taken to Morotai for examination.

129. Over 1500 "patients" were found on board, but a visiting doctor considered the majority of them to be in good health, although all feigned illness. Most of the more senior Japanese officers were transferred to destroyers, which probably helped to forestall trouble with the enemy troops, many of whom were later found to have been sleeping on rifles, machine guns, ammunition, and hand grenades. The prompt and well-planned action by the prize crew, totaling only 80 Marines and Bluejackets, evidently had been effective in discouraging resistance.

Notes

CHAPTER 1. THE EVOLUTION OF TROOPSHIPS

1. In writing *The Evolution of Troopships* it was decided to use the contents of E. B. Potter's *Sea Power: A Naval History* in order to establish a timeline of naval operations from man's first use of waterways and seas through the 1970s. In this manner we were able to track the various sea wars, determine when primitive navies first used troopships, and trace their evolution through the centuries. A myriad of source materials, including archival documents (foreign and domestic), official records, and personal memoirs, were then used to fully tell the story of the troopship. Further reading on the Birkenhead includes Thubron, *The Ancient Mariners,* and Rogers, *Troopships and Their History.*
2. Dando-Collins, *Caesar's Legion, The Epic Saga of Julius Caesar's Elite Tenth Legion and the Armies of Rome,* 30–49.
3. Wernick, *The Vikings,* 14–66.
4. Child, Kelly, and Whittock, *The Crusades,* 3.
5. Rice, *Life during the Crusades,* 4.
6. Potter, *Sea Power: A Naval History,* 8–9.
7. Ibid., 11–21.
8. Rogers, *Troopships and Their History,* 1–23. One of the few books which deal with the history of troopships; however, Colonel Rogers focuses on the evolution of British troopships.
9. Ibid., 55–72.

10. Ibid., 103–14.
11. Ibid., 115–28, 160–61.
12. Ibid., 166–77.
13. Harding, *Great Liners at War*, 85–98.
14. Wise, "Gallipoli: World's First Modern Amphibious Assault," *Sea Classics* 3, no. 5.
15. Harding, *Great Liners at War*, 30–50, 68–84.
16. Rogers, *Troopships and Their History*, 178–85.
17. Maddocks, *The Great Liners*, 80–89.
18. Ibid., 72–79.
19. Potter, *Sea Power: A Naval History*, 236.
20. Ibid.
21. Rogers, *Troopships and Their History*, 186.
22. Williams, *Wartime Disasters at Sea*, 142.
23. Giese and Wise, *Shooting the War*, 15–35.
24. Harding, *Great Liners at War*, 20.
25. Williams, *Liners in Battledress*, 130–34.
26. Whipple, *The Mediterranean*, 12.
27. Ibid., 21.
28. Potter, *Sea Power: A Naval History*, 250.
29. Whipple, *The Mediterranean*, 60–87.
30. Potter, *Sea Power: A Naval History*, 251–53; Roskill, *The War at Sea* 1:144–46.
31. Morison, *History of United States Naval Operations in World War II* 1:110–13.
32. Charles, *Troopships of World War II*, 1–2.
33. Bragadin, *The Italian Navy in World War II*, 70–71.
34. Whipple, *The Mediterranean*, 132–33.
35. Young, *Rommel: The Desert Fox*, chapter 10.
36. Bragadin, *The Italian Navy in World War II*, 354–69.
37. Potter, *Sea Power: A Naval History*, 254–56.
38. Cooper, *Liberty Ship: The Voyages of the John W. Brown, 1942–1946*, 1–32.
39. Arness and Wise, *James K. Arness: An Autobiography*, 31–32.
40. Elphick, *Liberty: The Ships That Won The War*, 256–58.
41. Roskill, *The War at Sea: 1939–1945* 3:209–10.
42. Andrade, *SS Leopoldville Disaster—December 24, 1944*, 53–113.
43. Browning, *U.S. Merchant Vessel War Casualties of World War II*, 417.
44. Harding, *Great Liners at War*, chapters 6, 7, 8.
45. Morison, *History of United States Naval Operations in World War II* 10:363.
46. Potter, *Sea Power: A Naval History*, 287–94.
47. The following year *President Coolidge* struck a mine off Espiritu Santo and sank

in twenty fathoms of water. Most all of the five thousand officers and men on board were saved. *Hugh L. Scott* participated in the Allied invasion of North Africa on 8 November 1942, but was sunk in port by enemy action in that campaign.

48. Morison, *History of United States Naval Operations in World War II* 3:209–14.

49. Michno, *Death on the Hellships*, 1–87, 133–39.

50. Smith, "Tragic Voyage of Junyo Maru," *World War II*, 40–44.

51. Browning, *U.S. Merchant Vessel War Casualties of World War II*, 375–76, 481.

52. Potter, *Sea Power: A Naval History*, 296–301.

53. Ibid., 302–9.

54. Roscoe, *United States Submarine Operations in World War II*, 209–16.

55. Potter, *Sea Power: A Naval History*, 318–19.

56. Roscoe, *United States Submarine Operations in World War II*, 527–63.

57. Morison, *History of United States Naval Operations in World War II* 3:15–26.

58. Ibid., 20–21.

59. Hezlet, *HMS Trenchant: From Chatham to Banka Strait*, 134–52.

60. *United States Submarine Losses World War II*, 151.

61. Wheeler, *War under the Pacific*, 187.

62. Potter, *Sea Power: A Naval History*, 351–53.

CHAPTER 2. THE NINETEENTH CENTURY

1. Addison and Matthews, *A Deathless Story: The Birkenhead and Its Heroes*. This 368-page book written in 1906 is considered to be the most comprehensive study of the *Birkenhead* story. Coauthor Matthews was the son of one of the ship's survivors and Addison wrote numerous articles and another book on the subject. They introduce the book as "Being the only full and authentic account of the famous shipwreck extant, founded on collected official, documentary, and personal evidence, and containing the narratives and lives of actors in the most glorious ocean tragedy in history."

    Note: The Birkenhead story was prepared without footnotes inasmuch as few books and documents relating to the incident could be found in either British or U.S. military archives. The above-cited Addison/Matthews book is, as far as our researchers could determine, the most definitive writing on the subject. Further Birkenhead reading includes Kerr, *Unfortunate Ship: The Story of H.M. Troopship Birkenhead;* Rogers, *Troopships and Their History;* and Watts, *The Royal Navy: An Illustrated History.*

2. Roberts, *Andersonville Journey*, 12–16.

3. Elliott, *Transport to Disaster*, 38–42.

4. Salecker, *Disaster on the Mississippi: The Sultana Explosion, April 27, 1865,* 13–21.

5. Elliott, *Transport to Disaster,* 47–51.

6. Potter, *The Sultana Tragedy: America's Greatest Maritime Disaster,* 49–51.

7. Salecker, *Disaster on the Mississippi: The Sultana Explosion, April 27, 1865,* 27–40.

8. Salecker, "A Tremendous Tumult and Uproar: The Tragic Sinking of the Sultana," *America Civil War Magazine* 15, no. 2 (May 2002), 28–30.

9. Elliott, *Transport to Disaster,* 55–95.

10. Potter, *The Sultana Tragedy: America's Greatest Maritime Disaster,* 81–111.

11. Elliott, *Transport to Disaster,* 146–96.

12. *The War of the Rebellion: A Compilation of Official Records of the Union and Confederate Armies,* series I, vol. XLVIII, part II, Reports, Correspondence, etc., 233.

13. Ibid., part I, 212.

14. Ibid., part II, 440.

15. Ibid., part I, 213–17.

16. Elliott, *Transport to Disaster,* 210–11.

17. *The War of the Rebellion: A Compilation of Official Records of the Union and Confederate Armies,* series I, vol. XLVIII, part I, Reports, Correspondence, etc., 217.

18. Elliott, *Transport to Disaster,* 212–15.

19. Salecker, *Disaster on the Mississippi: The Sultana Explosion, April 27, 1865,* 65.

20. Ibid., appendix A.

21. "The Proceedings and Report of the Court Martial of Captain Frederick Speed," Case MM 3967. RG 152, Entry 15, (NARA), M1878 (Roll 2).

22. *The War of the Rebellion: A Compilation of Official Records of the Union and Confederate Armies,* series I, vol. XLVIII, part I, Reports, Correspondence, etc., 220.

23. Salecker, *Disaster on the Mississippi: The Sultana Explosion, April 27, 1865,* 203–15.

24. Rule, "Sultana: A Case for Sabotage," *North & South Magazine* 5, no. 1 (December 2001), 76–87.

CHAPTER 3. WORLD WAR I

1. Smith, *Passenger Ships of the World Past and Present.*

2. *Loss of the SS Royal Edward.* Essex Regimental Museum, London, England; Williams, *Warship Disasters at Sea,* 23–24; "Transport *Royal Edward* Lost." United States Naval Institute *Proceedings* 41, no. 159 (Sept.–Oct. 1915), 1755.

3. Imperial War Museum Document Reading Room, Memoirs of Dr. C. J. G. Taylor, Medic on the Hospital Ship *Soudan.* Extract from chapter 36, 144–45.

4. Snelling, *VCs of the First World War—Gallipoli,* (Introduction).

5. Potter, *Sea Power: A Naval History,* 212.

6. Haythornthwaite, *Gallipoli: 1915,* 6–7.

7. Potter, *Sea Power: A Naval History,* 213.

8. Penn, *Fisher, Churchill and the Dardanelles,* 110–22.

9. Ibid., 134–63.

10. Potter, *Sea Power: A Naval History,* 214–19.

11. Steel, *Battleground Europe: Gallipoli,* 27–29.

12. Snelling, *VCs of the First World War—Gallipoli,* 29–64; Haythornthwaite, *Gallipoli 1915,* 44–45; Moorehead, *Gallipoli,* 140–44; *The First World War Letters of Lieutenant G. L. Drewry RNR VC,* Imperial War Museum Document Reading Room, 216.

13. Williams, *Wartime Disasters at Sea,* 18.

14. Ibid., appendix 2A.

15. Gray, *The Killing Time,* 211.

16. Williams, *Wartime Disasters at Sea,* 34.

17. Ibid., 34; Hocking, *Dictionary of Disasters at Sea during the Age of Steam,* 262.

18. Gray, *The Killing Time,* 210–11, 218.

19. Williams, *Wartime Disasters at Sea,* 30; Halpern, *The Naval War in the Mediterranean, 1914–1918,* 325.

20. Williams, *Wartime Disasters at Sea,* 42; Halpern, *The Naval War in the Mediterranean, 1914–1918,* 325.

21. Botting, *The U-Boats,* 36.

CHAPTER 4. WORLD WAR II, 1940–1943

1. Report of the *Arandora Star* inquiry conducted by the Right Honorable Lord Snell, 24 October 1940. Public Record Office, London.

2. Ibid.

3. Fehle, The Sinking of the SS *Arandora Star.* http://www.rossespoint.com/arandora star.html.

4. Report of the *Arandora Star* inquiry conducted by the Right Honorable Lord Snell, 24 October 1940, Public Record Office, London.

5. Ibid.

6. McClure, The Last Voyage of the *Arandora Star.* http://www.carndonagh.com/arandora/index.html.

7. Report of the *Arandora Star* inquiry conducted by the Right Honorable Lord Snell, 24 October 1940, Public Record Office, London.

8. McClure, The Last Voyage of the *Arandora Star.* http://www.carndonagh.com/arandora/index.html.

9. Darling, *Blue Star Line at War 1939–1945,* 40–45.

10. Blue Star Lines website, SS *Arandora:* http://www.bluestarline.org/arandora.html.

11. Ibid.

12. Darling. *Blue Star Line at War 1939–1945,* 40–45.

13. Ibid.

14. Ibid.

15. Ibid.

16. Ibid.

17. The Blue Star Lines website and Taprell's Blue Star Line at War give these figures, as does a letter from the Reichminister Des Auswartigen, Berlin, dated 19 October 1940, "German Misc. 67," Document Reading Room, Imperial War Museum, London. Capt. F. J. Robertson, an interpreter aboard *Arandora Star,* places the number at 528 Germans and 734 Italians, or 1,262 total. Lord Snell's inquiry stated the number as 473 Germans and 717 Italians for a total of 1,190 (but it's possible that his figures didn't include the 86 German POWs; if this was true than the number of Germans would increase to 559 or 1,276 total internees. Fehle figures are 740 Italians and 476 Germans, or 1,216 internees.

18. Robertson, Report of *Arandora Star*—Conditions on Board and the Disaster. Public Record Office, London.

19. Some sources list about 7 A.M. as the time of impact, but with the ship sailing west, they may not have taken into account the time difference.

20. Tolaini, *The Second World War Memoirs of Victor Tolaini,* Document Reading Room, Imperial War Museum, London.

21. Ibid.

22. Darling, *Blue Star Line at War 1939–1945,* 40–45.

23. Ibid.

24. Ibid.

25. BBC Website, Lancastria, http://www.bbc.co.uk/history/war/wwtwo/lancastria1.html.

26. The History Place, World War Two in Europe timeline: http://www.history-place.com/worldwar2/timeline/ww2time.htm#1.

27. Scislowski, "The Sinking of the *Lancastria*": http://carol_fus.tripod.com/army_hero_lancastria.html.

28. McCart, *Atlantic Liners of the Cunard Line—From 1884 to the Present Day,* 138.

29. Ibid., 139–40.

30. Ibid., 140.

31. BBC Homepage, *Lancastria—A secret sacrifice:* http://www.bbc.co.uk/history/war/wwtwo/lancastria 1.shtml.

32. McCart, *Atlantic Liners of the Cunard Line—From 1884 to the Present Day,* 141.

33. Although most contemporary accounts like the *Daily Telegraph* and *London Times* list the figure aboard the *Lancastria* at between 5,200 and 5,300, other sources indicate the total number of passengers was close to 5,500. However, the Association of Lancastria Survivors contends that there may have been as many as 9,000 on board.

34. Great Shipwrecks website, RMS *Lancastria:* http://www.greatshipwrecks.com/lancastria.html.

35. Scislowski, "The Sinking of the Lancastria": http://carol_fus.tripod.com/army_hero_lancastria.html.

36. Wikipedia, web encyclopedia, RMS *Laconia:* http://www.wikipedia.org/wiki/RMS_Lancastria.

37. Great Shipwrecks website, RMS *Lancastria:* http://www.greatshipwrecks.com/lancastria.html.

38. Whipple, *The Mediterranean,* 132.

39. Ibid., 132.

40. Williams, *Wartime Disasters at Sea,* 134.

41. Ibid., 136–39.

42. Preston, *The Royal Navy Submarine Service,* 124, 126, 131.

43. Compton-Hall, *The Underwater War, 1939–1945,* 81–83

44. Preston, *The Royal Navy Submarine Service,* 131.

45. Imperial War Museum, Document Reading Room, J. H. Biggs, captain of the *Strathallan:* Report of Sinking of SS *Strathallan.*

46. Williams, *Wartime Disasters at Sea,* 173.

47. Auxiliary Ships in World War II—The *Strathallan* website: http://britishforces.com/rtw/ships/auxww2/ww2-troopships.html.

48. War Service, *Strathallan* P&O, National Maritime Museum, Greenwich, England.

49. Golberg, *Margaret Bourke-White: A Biography,* 241, 242, 257–61.

50. Summersby, *Past Forgetting,* 9–17, 99–105.

51. U-boat.net, U562: http://uboat.net/boats/u562.html.

52. Imperial War Museum, Document Reading Room, J. H. Biggs, captain of the *Strathallan:* Report of Sinking of SS *Strathallan.*

53. Ibid., 1.

54. Ibid., 2.

55. Ibid.

56. U-boat.net, U562: http://uboat.net/boats/u562.html.

57.   Correspondence with Pvt. Harry Ball, 110th Army Troops Co., Royal Engineers, 2001.

CHAPTER 5. WORLD WAR II, 1943–1945

1.   Mulligan, *Lone Wolf: The Life and Death of U-Boat Ace Werner Henke*, 113.
2.   Ibid., 114; Williams, *Wartime Disasters at Sea*, 172–73.
3.   Wise, *Sole Survivors of the Sea*, 51–52.
4.   Mulligan, *Lone Wolf: The Life and Death of U-Boat Ace Werner Henke*, 115–16.
5.   Ibid., 116.
6.   *War Diary of U515*, NARA II, College Park, Md.
7.   PRO Adm 199/176, Report of an Interview with Sapper Eric E. Munday, Royal Engineers, 14 August 1945.
8.   *War Diary of U515*, NARA II, College Park, Md.
9.   PRO Adm 199/176, Report of an Interview with Sapper Eric E. Munday, Royal Engineers, 14 August 1945.
10.   *War Diary of U515*, NARA II, College Park, Md.
11.   PRO Adm 199/176, Report of an Interview with Sapper Eric E. Munday, Royal Engineers, 14 August 1945.
12.   *War Diary of U515*, NARA II, College Park, Md.
13.   PRO Adm 199/176, Report of an Interview with Sapper Eric E. Munday, Royal Engineers, 14 August 1945.
14.   Mulligan, *Lone Wolf: The Life and Death of U-Boat Ace Werner Henke*, 122–28.
15.   PRO Adm 199/176, Report of an Interview with Sapper Eric E. Munday, Royal Engineers, 14 August 1945.
16.   Ibid.
17.   Mulligan, *Lone Wolf: The Life and Death of U-Boat Ace Werner Henke*, 41–53.
18.   Ibid., 128.
19.   Ibid., 130–33.
20.   Rohwer, Axis Submarine Successes 1939–1945, 122–25, 135, 140, 153, 161, 164, 166, 175.
21.   Morison, *History of United States Naval Operations in World War II* 10:282.
22.   Gallery, *Twenty Million Tons Under the Sea*, 263–66.
23.   Ibid., 267–69.
24.   Mulligan, *Lone Wolf: The Life and Death of U-Boat Ace Werner Henke*, 208–13.
25.   Browning, *U.S. Merchant Vessel War Casualties of World War II*, 270.
26.   Ibid.
27.   Thornton, *Sea of Glory*, 27–28.

28. Ibid.

29. Ibid., 41.

30. Ibid., 43–44.

31. Ibid., 60.

32. Chapel of the Four Chaplains website: http:// www.Fourchaplains.org.

33. Ibid.

34. Ibid.

35. Ibid.

36. Browning, *U.S. Merchant Vessel War Casualties of World War II*, 270–71.

37. Parachin, "Four Chaplains' Courage: Example for All to Live By." *American Legion Dispatch,* October 2002.

38. Ibid.

39. U-boat.net, *U233:* http://UBoat.Net/Boats/U223.html.

40. Parachin, "Four Chaplains' Courage: Example for All to Live By." *American Legion Dispatch,* October 2002.

41. Ibid.

42. Ibid.

43. Ibid.

44. Ibid.

45. Browning, *U.S. Merchant Vessel Casualties of World War II,* 271.

46. Roskill, *The War at Sea* 3:312; The Hunt for *U223:* http://users.erols.com/sepulcher/U223.html.

47. Waters, *Bloody Winter,* 31. The shipboard HF/DF worked by determining the bearing of a transmitted radio signal, but not the range, unless two ships plotted the point of intersection.

48. Ibid., 23.

49. U-boat.net, U-boat operations, convoy battles: http://www.uboat.net/ops/convoys/sc-118.html.

50. Mooney, *Dictionary of American Naval Fighting Ships* 3:306.

51. Ibid.

52. Roland, *Troopships of World War II,* 193.

53. Mooney, *Dictionary of American Naval Fighting Ships* 3:306.

54. Ibid., 2.

55. Secret Memorandum OP-12-2-EH, Office of the Chief of Naval Operations, 30 April 1941, Subject: Requirements of the Navy for Merchant Vessels for Immediate Conversion.

56. Roland, *Troopships of World War II,* 193.

57. Waters, *Bloody Winter,* 152.

58. Ibid., 152.

59. Ibid., 141.

60. U-boat.net, U-boat operations, convoy battles: http://www.uboat.net/ops/convoys/sc-118.html.

61. Waters, *Bloody Winter*, 142. The captain and chief engineer were picked up and taken to Germany as POWs.

62. Ibid., 145.

63. Ibid., 266. Of the four von Forstner brothers, only Wolfgang survived the war when he was taken prisoner after his boat, *U472*, was sunk southeast of Bear Island, Norway, on 4 March 1944.

64. Timelines differ in different accounts.

65. Waters, *Bloody Winter*, 148.

66. Ibid., 155–56. Times differ in different accounts. Bunker's *Heroes in Dungarees* gives the time 3:52 A.M. The *Dictionary of American Naval Fighting Ships* lists the time as 5:38 A.M. Browning's *U.S. Merchant Vessel War Casualties of World War II* gives the time as 4 A.M. The *Bloody Winter* chronology seems most consistent with convoy timelines.

67. Ibid., 152–53. Again numbers differ; however, most accounts agree that there were 34 Armed Guards aboard and 383 passengers, but differ as to the number of crewmen. The confusion as to the number rescued or lost has to do with the fact that 5 of the 227 rescued subsequently died.

68. Ibid., 157. However, Robert M. Browning Jr., author of *U.S. Merchant Vessel War Casualties of World War II*, contends on page 273 that an order to "abandon ship" was given, but only after the ship began to list.

69. Mooney, *Dictionary of American Naval Fighting Ships* 3:306.

70. Waters, *Bloody Winter*, 275.

71. Morison, *History of United States Naval Operations in World War II* 10:161.

72. Elphick, *Liberty—The Ships That Won The War*, 32–34.

73. Ibid., 13–15.

74. Ibid., 15–16.

75. Ibid., 36–39.

76. Ibid., 52.

77. Project Liberty Ship website, What is a Liberty Ship: http://www.liberty-ship.com.

78. Bunker, *Liberty Ships: The Ugly Ducklings of World War II*, Merchant Marine website: http://www.usmm.org.

79. Elphick, *Liberty—The Ships That Won the War*, 359.

80. Edited Appleton's Encyclopedia: http://www.famousamericans.net/benjamin-contee.

81. Davies, Liberty Cargo Ships: http://www.wwiitechpubs.com/dock/na-usa/nv-usa-ss-liberty-ship/nv-usa-ss-liberty-ship-ftr.html.

82. Browning, *U.S. Merchant Vessel War Casualties of World War II,* 354.

83. WWII U.S. Navy Armed Guard website: http://www.armed-guard.com/ag81.html.

84. Browning, *U.S. Merchant Vessel War Casualties of World War II,* 355.

85. Merchant Marine website, Citations for Distinguished Service Medal during World War II: http://www.usmm.org/heroes.html.

86. Browning, *U.S. Merchant Vessel War Casualties of World War II,* 355.

87. Elphick, *Liberty—The Ships That Won The War,* 311.

88. Merchant Marine website, chronological list of U.S. ships sunk or damaged during 1944: http://www.usmm.org/sunk44.html.

89. The greatest single loss aboard a U.S. naval vessel was the 1,177 officers and men lost aboard USS *Arizona* (BB-39) during the attack on Pearl Harbor on 7 December 1941. Source: USS *Arizona* Memorial.

90. Jackson, *Forgotten Tragedy: The Sinking of HMT Rohna,* 3–4.

91. Waddington, *Rajula* history website: http://www.btinternet.com/˜7Eaf-aditel/rhistory.html.

92. Jackson, *Forgotten Tragedy: The Sinking of HMT Rohna,* 3–4.

93. Ibid.

94. Ibid., 9–13.

95. Sources include U.S. Army Corps of Engineers website: http://www.hq.usace.army.mil; Jackson's *Forgotten Tragedy;* Duncan's *Maritime Disasters of the Second World War;* and sources for World War II troopship crossings website: http://members.aol.com/troopship/shipsrc.html.

96. Jackson, *Forgotten Tragedy: The Sinking of HMT Rohna,* 16.

97. Ibid., 24–26.

98. Strafield, Air Commodore Charles. Report on Air Attack on Convoy Annex HQ, Northeast African Coastal Air Force, 30 November 1943.

99. Ibid. Two of the enemy aircraft were splashed by antiaircraft fire from *Frederick C. Davis.* The ship was later sunk by *U546* in the western Atlantic on 24 April 1945, *Dictionary of American Naval Fighting Ships* 2:447.

     The *Herbert C. Jones* downed one enemy bomber and along with *Davis* collected performance characteristics of the German glider bombs while under fire, which resulted in the two ships being fitted with powerful radio-jamming sets the following month. This new electronic warfare capability proved most effective in countering German glider bombs directed at the Allied naval force off Italy in January 1944 when Allied troops stormed ashore to establish the Anzio beachhead. *Dictionary of American Naval Fighting Ships* 3:310.

100. Jackson, *Forgotten Tragedy: The Sinking of HMT Rohna,* 47.

101. Ibid., 82.

102. The *Rohna* Survivors Association and the article "Pioneer to the Rescue" by Don Fortune of *VFW* magazine, October 2000, both give the figure as 1,138, but fail to take into account the 11 gunners on board. The U.S. Army Corps of Engineers' figures are 1,152 (1,015 U.S. troops, 3 Red Cross volunteers, and 134 crewmen).

103. Jackson, *Forgotten Tragedy: The Sinking of HMT Rohna,* 120.

104. Bennett, *The Rohna Disaster: World War II's Secret Tragedy:* http://Expage.com/page/Rohna.

105. Tom Brokaw. *NBC Nightly News,* 27 December 2000.

106. Ships of the Merchant Marine, SS *Paul Hamilton:* www.ibiblio.org/Hyperwar/USN/Ships/MM/SS PaulHamilton.html.

107. Ibid.

108. Ibid.

109. Morseburg, *The Night the S.S. Paul Hamilton Vanished:* http://www.howardsviews.com/howardssviews2.html.

110. USS *Lansdale* (DD-426: http://www.Destroyers.org/NL-histories/dd426-NL.html.

111. Dailey, *Joining the War at Sea 1939–1945,* 426.

112. Mooney, *Dictionary of American Naval Fighting Ships* 7:35.

113. U.S. Coast Guard website, USS *Roger B. Taney* http://www.USCG.mil/hq/q-cp/history/Taney-1936.html; USS *Laning* (DE-159): http://www.members.dsl-only.NET/USSLaning/beginning.html.

114. Mooney, *Dictionary of American Naval Fighting Ships* 7:35.

115. Ships of the Merchant Marine, SS *Paul Hamilton:* http://www.ibiblio.org/hyperwar/USN/Ships/MM/SSPaulHamilton.html.

116. Ibid.

117. Dailey, *Joining the War at Sea, 1939–1945,* 426.

118. Ibid.

119. Ibid.

120. Hoyt, *The Invasion Before Normandy: The Secret Battle of Slapton Sands,* 53–59.

121. Lt. Eugene E. Eckstam, MC, USNR, (Ret.), Recollections of a Medical Officer on LST-507, Naval Historical Center website: http://history.navy.mil/faqs/faq87-3g.html.

122. Hoyt, *The Invasion Before Normandy: The Secret Battle of Slapton Sands,* 82–84.

123. Ibid., 86–90.

124. Ibid., 96–97.

125. Lt. Eugene E. Eckstam, MC, USNR, (Ret.), Recollections of a Medical Officer on LST-507, Naval Historical Center website: http://history. navy.mil/faqs/faq87-3g.html.

126. Hoyt, *The Invasion Before Normandy: The Secret Battle of Slapton Sands,* 85.

127. MacDonald, "Operation Tiger," (extracted from Army 38, no. 6 [June 1988], 64–67), Naval Historical Center website: http://www.sartori.com/ nhc/frames/faqs/faq20-1.html.

128. Ramsey, "The Other D-Days," *After the Battle,* no. 44, 15.

129. Hoyt, *The Invasion Before Normandy: The Secret Battle of Slapton Sands,* 101.

130. Ibid.

131. Ibid., 103.

132. Ibid.

133. MacDonald, "Operation Tiger," (extracted from Army 38, no. 6 [June 1988], 64–67), Naval Historical Center website: http://www.sartori.com/nhc/frames/ faqs/faq20-1.html.

134. Lt. Eugene E. Eckstam, MC, USNR, (Ret.), Recollections of a Medical Officer on LST-507, Naval Historical Center website: http://history.navy. mil/faqs/faq87-3g.html.

135. Hoyt, *The Invasion Before Normandy: The Secret Battle of Slapton Sands,* 101.

136. MacDonald, "Operation Tiger," (extracted from Army 38, no. 6 [June 1988], 64–67), Naval Historical Center website: http://www.sartori.com/nhc/rames/ faqs/faq20-1.html.

137. MacDonald, "Slapton Sands: The Cover-up That Never Was," (extracted from Army 38, no. 6 [June 1988], 64–67), Naval Historical Center website: http://www.sartori.com/nhc/frames/faqs/faq20-2.html.

138. Ibid.

139. Michno, *Death on the Hellships,* 317.

140. Roscoe, *United States Submarine Operations in World War II,* 147–48; Michno, *Death on the Hellships,* 29.

141. Michno, *Death on the Hellships,* 26–27.

142. Ibid., 26–29.

143. Ibid., 202–5.

144. Roscoe, *United States Submarine Operations in World War II,* 353–54, 537, 546, 553.

145. Ibid., 358.

146. Michno, *Death on the Hellships,* 206–10.

147. Ibid., 211–21.

148. Smith, "Tragic Voyage of Junyo Maru," *World War II Magazine* (March 2002), 40–44.

149. Michno, *Death on the Hellships,* 249–58; Alden, *U.S. Submarine Attacks during World War II,* 146.

150. Sanders, *A Night Before Christmas,* 15. Note: This section on the *Leopoldville* relies heavily on information from Jacquin Sanders' *A Night Before Christmas,* which, when published in 1963, was a pioneering work of investigation into an event, the knowledge of which was suppressed by three governments. Subsequent work by others, and most recollections, are consistent with his account of the event and his conclusions. Some Admiralty reports remain "unavailable" at this writing.

151. Ibid., 27–28. This is confirmed numerous times in survivors' recollections. One survivor in Roberts's book recalls the company boarding one ship and the First Sergeant, with the roster, boarding the other.

152. Ibid., 29–30.

153. Ibid., 54.

154. Ibid., 54.

155. U-boat net: http://uboat.net/history/leopoldville.html.

156. Sanders, *A Night Before Christmas,* 46–47, 207–8.

157. Ibid., 54.

158. Sgt. Hank Anderson, E Company, 262nd Regiment, Interview with author, July 2002.

159. History Channel, *The Sinking of the Leopoldville:* http://www.historychannel.com. Numerous family members recounted receiving notifications from the government reporting their loved ones as "Missing in Action."

160. Sgt. Hank Anderson, E Company, 262nd Regiment, Interview with author, July 2002.

161. Sanders, *A Night Before Christmas,* 83. The Belgians do not corroborate Captain Bowles's account.

162. Ibid., 108.

163. Ibid., 95.

164. Ibid., 97–98.

165. Ibid., 138.

166. Ibid., 139.

167. Roberts, *Survivors of the Leopoldville Disaster,* account of S.Sgt. Frank I. Robinson, 127–28.

168. Sanders, *A Night Before Christmas,* 191–92.

169. Ibid., 244–45.

170. Ibid., 314.

171. Roberts, *Sequel to Survivors of the Leopoldville Disaster,* account of Pfc. William F. Beran, 19.

172. Sanders, *A Night Before Christmas,* 311.

173. U-boat net: http://uboat.net.

174. Sanders, *A Night Before Christmas,* 7–9, 303–4.

175. Raymond Roberts, T/5 766th Ordnance Co., Interview with author, July 2002.

176. Andrade, *S.S. Leopoldville Disaster—December 24, 1944,* 53–113.

177. Roberts, *Sequel to Survivors of the Leopoldville Disaster,* (Dedication).

178. Sanders, *A Night Before Christmas,* 7–9, 303–4.

179. Keegan, *Rand-McNally Encyclopedia of World War II,* 157. Lingayen Gulf, located on the west coast of Luzon, was ideal for amphibious operations. Shallow in depth, it led to a broad plain stretching all the way to Manila, 120 miles to the south.

180. Benford, *The WWII Quiz and Fact Book* 2:80.

181. Sulzberger, *American Heritage New History of World War II,* 548.

182. *Time-Life Books History of the Second World War,* 389–91.

183. Benford, *The World War II Quiz and Fact Book,* 2:136.

184. *Time-Life Books History of the Second World War,* 389–91.

185. Browning, *U.S. Merchant Vessel War Casualties of World War II,* 481.

186. Ibid., 407.

187. Ibid., 481.

188. Ibid., 481.

189. Ibid., 481. Other sources cite 6:37 P.M. Others list only "after dusk."

190. U.S. Navy Armed Guards website: http://www.armed-guard.com/ag78.html.

191. Browning, *U.S. Merchant Vessel War Casualties of World War II,* 481.

192. Elphick, *Liberty: The Ships That Won the War,* 378.

193. U.S. Navy chronology, 1945: http://www.ibiblio. org/hyperwar/USN/USN-Chron/USN-Chron-1945.html.

194. Sulzberger. *American Heritage New History of World War II,* 587.

195. Ibid., 548.

196. Eastern Front, 1941–45, The Vistula-Oder Operation: http://www.geocities.com/sonzabird/majorops.html#uranus.

197. Ibid.

198. U-boat.net. Soldier to the Last Minute, Grossadmiral Karl Dönitz and the Nuremberg Trial: http://uboat.net/men/nuremberg1.html.

199. Williams, *Wartime Disasters at Sea,* 232.

200. U-boat.net. Soldier to the Last Minute, Grossadmiral Karl Dönitz and the Nuremberg Trial: http://uboat.net/men/nuremberg1.html.

201. Ljungstrom, *Robert Ley, 1939–1947:* http://www.greatoceanliners.net/robert-ley.html.

202. Pipes, *A Memorial to the Wilhelm Gustloff:* http://www.feldgrau.com/wilhelm-gustloff.html.

203. Ibid.

204. Ibid.

205. Ibid.

206. Williams, *Wartime Disasters at Sea,* 227.

207. Letter of Oberbootmannmaat Karl Hoffman, survivor of the *Gustloff, The Sinking of the Wilhelm Gustloff:* http://www.cybercreek.com/cybercity/WIIps/gust.html.

208. Ibid.

209. Pipes, *A Memorial to the Wilhelm Gustloff:* http://www.feldgrau.com/wilhelm-gustloff.html.

210. Duncan's *Maritime Disasters of World War II* places the number at 4,658 passengers. Mark Weber of the Institute for Historical Review indicates that the number was as high as 10,000. Lloyd's figures indicate that she had 5,000 refugees and 3,700 U-boat personnel besides her crew aboard. Williams in his *Wartime Disasters at Sea* puts the number lost at between 5,196 to in excess of 7,800. Uboat.net places the losses at over 6,000, as does Sellwood in *The Damned Don't Die.* Historian Mackenzie Gregory states that more recent research puts the number closer to 10,000 aboard with a loss of life exceeding 7,000.

211. Williams, *Wartime Disasters at Sea,* 228; author Heinz Schon in his book, *SOS Wilhelm Gustloff,* published in 2002 contends that the loss of life when the *Gustloff* went down was 10,582.

212. Pipes, *A Memorial to the Wilhelm Gustloff:* http://www.feldgrau.com/wilhelm-gustloff.html.

213. Sellwood, *The Damned Don't Drown: The Sinking of the Wilhelm Gustloff,* 42.

214. Ibid, 61–62.

215. Letter of Oberbootsmannmaat Karl Hoffman, survivor of the *Gustloff, The Sinking of the Wilhelm Gustloff:* http://www.cybercreek.com/cybercity/WIIps/gust.html.

216. Pipes, *A Memorial to the Wilhelm Gustloff:* http://www.feldgrau.com/wilhelm-gustloff.html.

217. Letter of Oberbootsmannmaat Karl Hoffman, survivor of the *Gustloff, The Sinking of the Wilhelm Gustloff:* http://www.cybercreek.com/cybercity/WIIps/gust.html.

218. Williams, *Wartime Disasters at Sea,* 228.

219. Great Ships—Steuben website: http://www.greatships.net/steuben.html.

220. *Wartime Losses of Non-Combatant Ships.* RMS Titanic History Project: http://www.rmstitanichistory.com/steuben/steuben.html.

221. Great Ships—Steuben website: http://www.greatships.net/steuben.html.

222. Williams, *Wartime* Disasters at Sea, 228.

223. Duncan, *Maritime Disasters of World War II:* http://www.iinet.net.au/˘7Egduncan/maritime-1b.html; other sources place the number aboard as high as five thousand.

224. *Wartime Losses of Non-Combatant Ships:* RMS Titanic History Project: http://www.rmstitanichistory.com/steuben/steuben.html.

225. Williams, *Liners in Battledress,* 113.

226. Gregory, *Tragedy at Sea,* 8. Website: http://members.tripod.coom/Tenika/tragedy.html.

227. Ibid.

228. Dobson, *The Cruelest Night,* 163, 165–69.

229. Ibid.

230. Williams, *Wartime Disasters at Sea,* 232–33.

231. Robertson, *The Cap Arcona, the Thielbek and the Athen.* University of Hamburg. Website: www.rrz.uni-hamburg.de/rz3a035/arcona.html.

232. Ibid.

233. Ibid.

234. Duncan, *Maritime Disasters of World War II:* http://members.iinet.net.au/~Egduncan/maritime-1b.html.

235. Robertson, *The Cap Arcona, the Thielbek and the Athen.* University of Hamburg. Website: www.rrz.uni-hamburg.de/rz3a035/arcona.html.

236. Ljungstrom, *Cap Arcona II 1927–1945.* Website: http://www.greatoceanliners.net/index2.html.

237. Williams, *Liners in Battledress,* 113.

238. Robertson, *The Cap Arcona, the Thielbek and the Athen,* University of Hamburg. Website: www.rrz.uni-hamburg.de/rz3a035/arcona.html.

239. Ibid.

240. Ibid.

241. Ibid.

242. Ibid.

243. Ibid.

244. Jacobs, *The Dentist of Auschwitz,* chapter 18.

245. Robertson, *The Cap Arcona, the Thielbek and the Athen,* University of Hamburg. Website: www.rrz.uni-hamburg.de/rz3a035/arcona.html.

246. Accounts differ as to which squadrons attacked which targets in what order. What follows is a compilation of several sources.

247. Duncan, *Maritime Disasters of World War II:* http://members.iinet.net.au/~Egduncan/maritime-1b.html.

248. Some sources give Celle as the base of the 197th Squadron.

249. Duncan, *Maritime Disasters of World War II:* http://members.iinet.net.au/~Egduncan/maritime-1b.html.

250. The Great Ocean Liners website, *Robert Ley:* http://greatoceanliners.net/robertley.html.

251. Williams, *Wartime Disasters at Sea,* 229.

252. Williams, *Liners in Battledress,* 130.

253. Tarrant, *The Last Year of the Kriegsmarine: May 1944–May 1945,* 225.

254. Lacroix and Wells, *Japanese Cruisers of the Pacific War,* 97–98, 149, 354.

255. Morison, *History of United States Naval Operations in World War II* 3:178–80; McCombs and Worth, *World War II: Strange and Fascinating Facts,* 301.

256. Hezlet, *Trenchant at War: From Chatham to the Banka Strait,* 171–72; Lacroix and Wells, *Japanese Cruisers of the Pacific War,* 275.

257. Morison, *History of United States Naval Operations in World War II* 3:332–73.

258. Lacroix and Wells, *Japanese Cruisers of the Pacific War,* 313–14, 318.

259. Dull, *A Battle History of The Imperial Japanese Navy (1941–1945),* 313–16; Lacroix and Wells, *Japanese Cruisers of the Pacific War,* 336, 344.

260. Ibid., 354.

261. Ibid., 358–59.

262. Hezlet, *HMS Trenchant at War: From Chatham to the Banka Strait,* 1–22; *HMS Trenchant Summary of Service, 1942–1963,* Imperial War Museum, Document Reading Room, London.

263. Hezlet, *HMS Trenchant at War: From Chatham to the Banka Strait,* 134–70.

CHAPTER 6. 1950–2003

1. Frank, "Farewell to the Troopship, The AP Troopships Chronology 1945–1973," *Naval History Magazine,* (January/February 1997), 44.

2. Ibid.

3. Cagle and Manson, *The Sea War in Korea,* 190–93.

4. Frank, "Farewell to the Troopship, The AP Troopships Chronology 1945–1973," *Naval History Magazine,* (January/February 1997), 45.

5. Rogers, *Troopships and their History,* 210–11.

6. Frank, "Farewell to the Troopship, The AP Troopship Chronology 1945–1973," *Naval History Magazine,* (January/February 1997), 45.

7. Summers, *The Vietnam War Almanac,* 249–50.

8. Frank, "Farewell to the Troopship, The AP Troopship Chronology 1945–1973," *Naval History Magazine,* (January/February 1997), 45.

9. Ibid.

10. Watts, *The Royal Navy: An Illustrated History,* 234.

11. Hastings and Jenkins, *The Battle for the Falklands,* 74.

12. Watts, *The Royal Navy: An Illustrated History,* 234–35.

13. Ibid.

14. Ibid. 236–37.

15. Hastings and Jenkins, *The Battle for the Falklands,* 17–36.

16. Frank, "Farewell to the Troopship," *Naval History Magazine,* (January/February 1997), 41.

17. Rogers, *Troopships and their History,* 212–15.

18. Frank, "Farewell to the Troopship," *Naval History Magazine,* (January/February 1997), 45.

19. Polson, *Navy Goes Down Under,* explores future of amphibious warfare: Australian catamaran gives possible glimpse of next generation gator." Website: http://www.c7f.navy.mil/news/2000/09/16.html.

Glossary

ABDA	American, British, Dutch, Australian Command
AKA	U.S. Navy attack cargo ship
ANZAC	Australian and New Zealand Army Corps
AP	U.S. Navy transport
APA	U.S. Navy attack transport
Armed Guard (Naval)	U.S. Navy personnel who protected merchant ships and their cargo, acting as gunners, radio operators, signalmen, and medics
ASDIC	British abbreviation for the Allied Submarine Detection Investigation Committee, which developed an antisubmarine echo-ranging device used to detect submerged submarines; the U.S. Navy term for the gear was Sonar, Sound Navigation and Ranging.
ASW	antisubmarine warfare
bareboat charter	the charter of a bare vessel from the owner, without crew, fuel, stores; all such items being furnished by the charterer at the latter's expense
barque, barquentine	a sailing ship of three or more masts with the foremost square-rigged and the others fore- and aft-rigged
B.d.u.	Befehlshaber der Unterseeboote (commander in chief for German U-boats)
B.I.	British shipping line: British India Steam Navigation Company
Bibby	British shipping line
bireme	ancient galley with two tiers of oars

corvette	British lightly armored warship usually assigned as convoy escort ship
DCM	British Distinguished Conduct Medal
DE	destroyer escort
D.E.M.S.	Defensively Equipped Merchant Ship, British counterpart of U.S. Navy Armed Guard
DD	destroyer
DSC	British Distinguished Service Cross
DSO	British Distinguished Service Order
Exocet	French-built air-to-surface missile (AM.39)
Fliegerkorps	German Air Force (Luftwaffe) Squadron/Group
Harrier	vertical takeoff and landing strike aircraft
HMIT	His/Her Majesty's India passenger liner
HMNS	His/Her Majesty's New Zealand Ship
HMT	His/Her Majesty's Troopship
hopper	small steam-powered vessel
Huff-Duff	High-Frequency Direction-Finder (HF/DF)
Kaffir	South African Tribe/Nation
KBE	Knight Commander of the (Order of the) British Empire
Kriegsmarine	German navy (1935–45)
larboard	port side of a ship
Lascar	Indian sailor (Nation of India)
LCP(L)	Landing Craft personnel (Large)
LCT	Landing Craft, Tank
lighter	large, open, flat-bottomed barge
LPH	Landing Platform Helicopter
LSD	Landing Ships, Dock
LST	Landing Ships, Tank
Luftwaffe	German Air Force
MSC	U.S. Military Sealift Command
MSTS	U.S. Military Sea Transportation Service
MTB	Motor Torpedo Boat (German: Schnellboote; U.S.: PT boat)
Oerlikon	20mm Swedish-designed antiaircraft cannon
pinnace	light sailing ship, used in attendance on a larger ship
plinth	stablelike member beneath the base of a column or pier
POW	prisoner of war
quinquereme	ancient vessel with five banks of oars
RAF	Royal Air Force

RCN	Royal Canadian Navy
RFA	Royal Fleet Auxiliary
RMS	Royal Mail Steamship
RN	Royal Navy
RNR	Royal Navy Reserve
sapper	Royal engineer
SAS	Special Air Service
SBS	Royal Boat Service
Seabees	U.S. Navy Construction Battalions
skiff	small boat adapted for sailing or rowing, usually attached to a ship and used for communications, transport, towing, etc.
SOE	Senior Officer Escort
SS	Schutzstaffel/Elite Guard. German troops formed to serve as bodyguards for Hitler and later expanded to take charge of intelligence, central security, policing action, and extermination of undesirables. Branches include the Gestapo and combat units.
SS	steamship
stoke hole	ship's compartment that contains boilers, where the stokers tend the furnaces
Super Etendard	French-built strike fighter aircraft
trireme	ancient galley with three banks of oars
USAAC	United States Army Air Corps
USAAF	United States Army Air Force
USAT	U.S. Army Transport
VC	Victoria Cross (Britain's highest military award)
WAC	Women's Army Corps
WAVES	Women Accepted for Voluntary Emergency Service (U.S. Navy)
WSA	War Shipping Administration
yawl	a ship's small boat, rowed by a crew of four to six

Bibliography

GENERAL

Addison, A. C., and W. H. Matthews. *A Deathless Story: The Birkenhead and Its Heroes.* London: Hutchinson & Co., 1906.

Alden, John D. *U.S. Submarine Attacks during World War II.* Annapolis, Md.: Naval Institute Press, 1989.

Andrade, Allen. *SS Leopoldville Disaster—December 24, 1944.* Orlando, Fla.: Tern Book Company, 1997.

Arness, James K., with James E. Wise Jr. *James K. Arness: An Autobiography.* Jefferson, N.C.: McFarland & Company, Inc., Publishers, 2001.

Benford, Timothy. *The World War II Quiz and Fact Book.* New York: Harper & Row Publishers, 1984.

Bennett, James G. *The Rohna Disaster—World War II's Secret Tragedy.* Philadelphia: X-libris Corporation, 1999.

Botting, Douglas. *The U-Boats.* Alexandria, Va.: Time-Life Books, Inc., 1979.

Bourke-White, Margaret. *Portrait of Myself.* New York: Simon & Schuster, 1963.

Boyd, Carl, and Akihido Yoshida. *The Japanese Submarine Force and World War II.* Annapolis, Md.: Naval Institute Press, 1995.

Bragadin, R. Marc' Antonio. *The Italian Navy in World War II.* Annapolis, Md.: U.S. Naval Institute, 1957.

Browning, Robert M., Jr. *U.S. Merchant Vessel War Casualties of World War II.* Annapolis, Md.: Naval Institute Press, 1996.

Bunker, John. *Heroes in Dungarees: The Story of the American Merchant Marine in World War II.* Annapolis, Md.: Naval Institute Press, 1995.

Bunker, John. *Liberty Ships: The Ugly Ducklings of World War II.* Annapolis, Md.: Naval Institute Press, 1972.

Cagle, Malcolm W., and Frank A. Manson. *The Sea War in Korea.* Annapolis, Md.: U.S. Naval Institute, 1957.

Catton, Bruce. *Grant Takes Command.* New York: Little Brown & Co., 1968.

Charles, Roland W. *Troopships of World War II.* Washington, D.C.: The Army Transportation Association, 1947.

Child, John, Nigel Kelly, and Martyn Whittock. *The Crusades.* New York: Peter Bedrick Books, 1994.

Churchill, Winston S. *The Second World War,* Vols. 1 and 2. New York: Time Incorporated, 1959.

Compton-Hall, Richard. The Underwater War, 1939–1945. Dorset, England: Blandford Press, 1982.

Cooper, Sherod. *Liberty Ship: The Voyages of the John W. Brown, 1942–1946.* Annapolis, Md.: Naval Institute Press, 1997.

Dailey, Franklyn, Jr. *Joining the War at Sea, 1939–1945.* London: Dailey International Publishing, 1999.

Dando-Collins, Stephen. *Caesar's Legion: The Epic Saga of Julius Caesar's Elite Tenth Legion and the Armies of Rome.* New York: John Wiley & Sons, Inc., 2002.

Darling, H. Taprell. *Blue Star Line at War, 1939–1945.* London: Foulsham Publishing, 1973.

Dobson, Christopher. *The Cruelest Night.* Boston: Little, Brown & Company, 1980.

Dull, Paul S. *The Imperial Japanese Navy (1941–1945).* Annapolis, Md.: Naval Institute Press, 1978.

Eckstam, Eugene E. "Recollections of a Medical Officer on LST-507." Naval Historical Center website: http://www.history.navy.mil.

Elliott, James W. *Transport to Disaster.* New York: Holt, Rinehart and Winston, 1962.

Elphick, Peter. *Liberty: The Ships That Won The War.* Annapolis, Md.: Naval Institute Press, 2001.

European War Notes—Transport Royal Edward Lost. U.S. Naval Institute *Proceedings* 41, no. 159 (1915).

Foote, Shelby. *The Civil War: A Narrative (Red River to Appomattox).* New York: Random House, Inc., 1974.

Frank, Winn B. "Farewell to the Troopship: The AP Troopships Chronology, 1945–1973." *Naval History* (January–February 1997).

Gallery, Daniel V. *Twenty Million Tons under the Sea.* Chicago: Henry Regnery
    Company, 1956.

Giese, Otto, and James E. Wise Jr. *Shooting the War.* Annapolis, Md.: Naval
    Institute Press, 1994.

Gould, Emerson W. *Fifty Years on the Mississippi: Gould's History of River Navigation.*
    St. Louis, Mo.: Nixon-Jones Printing Company, 1889.

Gray, Edwyn. *The Killing Time.* New York: Charles Scribner & Sons, 1972.

Greene, Ralph C., and Oliver E. Allen. "What Happened Off Devon?" *American
    Heritage* 36, no. 2 (February/March 1985).

Halpern, Paul G. *The Naval War in the Mediterranean 1914–1918.* Annapolis, Md.:
    Naval Institute Press, 1986.

Harding, Stephen. *Great Liners at War: The Military Adventures of the World's Largest,
    Fastest and Most Famous Passenger Steamships.* Osceola, Wisc.: Motorbooks
    International Publishers and Wholesalers, 1997.

Hastings, Max, and Simon Jenkins. *The Battle for the Falklands.* New York: W. W.
    Norton & Company, 1983.

Haythornthwaite, Philip Jr. *Gallipoli 1915.* Oxford, England: Osprey Publishing, 1992.

Hezlet, Arthur. *HMS Trenchant: From Chatham to Banka Strait.* South Yorkshire,
    England: Leo Cooper, 2001.

Hocking, Charles F. L. A., *Dictionary of Disasters at Sea during the Age of Steam:
    Including Sailing Ships and Ships of War Lost in Action, 1824–1962.* London:
    Lloyd's Register of Shipping, 1969.

Hoyt, Edwin P. *The Invasion before Normandy: The Secret Battle of Slapton Sands.*
    New York: Stein and Day, 1985.

Jackson, Carlton. *Forgotten Tragedy—The Sinking of HMT Rohna.* Annapolis, Md.:
    Naval Institute Press, 1997.

Jacobs, Benjamin. *The Dentist of Auschwitz.* Lexington: University Press of
    Kentucky, 1995.

Keegan, John. *An Illustrated History of the First World War.* New York: Alfred A.
    Knopf, 2001.

Keegan, John. *Rand-McNally Encyclopedia of World War II.* Chicago: Rand-McNally
    Co., 1977.

Kerr, J. Lennox. *The Unfortunate Ship: The Story of H.M. Troopship Birkenhead.*
    London: George G. Harrap & Co., 1960.

Labourdette, Jean-Philippe Dallies. *S-Boote: German E-boats in Action (1939–1945).*
    Paris: Histoire & Collections, 2003.

Lacroix, Eric, and Linton Wells III. *Japanese Cruisers of the Pacific War.* Annapolis,
    Md.: Naval Institute Press, 1989.

Lloyd's War Losses: *The Second World War, 3 September 1939–14 August 1945*. Vols. 1 and 2. London: Lloyd's of London Press Ltd., 1991.

MacDonald, Charles B. "Operation Tiger." (Extracted from *Army*, no. 6, June 1988: 64–67). Naval Historical Center website.

MacDonald, Charles B. "Slapton Sands: The Cover-up That Never Was." (Extracted from *Army*, no. 6 [June 1988], 64–67). Naval Historical Center website: http://www.history.navy.mil.

Madden, Thomas. *A Concise History of the Crusades*. New York: Rowman & Littlefield Publishers, Inc. 1999.

Maddocks, Melvin. *The Great Liners*. Alexandria, Va.: Time-Life Books, Inc., 1978.

Mason, John T. Jr. *The Atlantic War Remembered: An Oral History*. Annapolis, Md.: Naval Institute Press, 1990.

McCart, Neil. *Atlantic Liners of the Cunard Line—From 1884 to the Present Day*. New York: Harper Collins, 1990.

McCombs, Donald, and Fred L. Worth. *World War II: Strange and Fascinating Facts*. New York: Greenwich House, 1983.

Michno, Gregory F. *Death on the Hellships: Prisoners at Sea in the Pacific War*. Annapolis, Md.: Naval Institute Press, 2001.

Moorehead, Alan. *Gallipoli*. New York: Harper and Row Publishers, Inc., 1956.

Morison, Samuel Eliot. *History of United States Naval Operations in World War II*. Vols. 1–15. Boston: Little, Brown and Company, 1975.

Mulligan, Timothy P. *Lone Wolf: The Life and Death of U-Boat Ace Werner Henke*. Westport, Conn.: Praeger Publishers, 1993.

"The Other D-Days." *After the Battle Magazine*, no. 44, 1984.

Parillo, Mark P. *The Japanese Merchant Marine in World War II*. Annapolis, Md.: Naval Institute Press, 1993.

Pearson, Judith L. *Belly of the Beast: A POW's Inspiring True Story of Faith, Courage, and Survival Aboard the Infamous WWII Japanese Hellship Oryoku Maru*. New York: Penguin Putnam, Inc., 2001.

Penn, Geoffrey. *Fisher, Churchill and the Dardanelles*. South Yorkshire, England: Leo Cooper, 1999.

Pope, Stephen, and Elizabeth-Anne Wheal. *The Dictionary of the First World War*. New York: St. Martin's Press, 1995.

Potter, E. B. *Sea Power: A Naval History*. Annapolis, Md.: Naval Institute Press, 1981.

Potter, Jerry O. *The Sultana Tragedy: America's Greatest Maritime Disaster*. Gretna, La.: Pelican Publishing Co., 1992.

Preston, Antony. *The Royal Submarine Service*. London: Conway Maritime Press, 2001.

Rice, Earle, Jr. *Life during the Crusades*. San Diego, Calif.: Lucent Books, Inc., 1998.

Roberts, Edward F. *Andersonville Journey.* Shippenburg, Pa.: Burd Street Press, 1998.

Roberts, Raymond J. *Sequel to Survivors of the Leopoldville Disaster (Dedication).* Bridgman, Mich.: Raymond Roberts, 1999.

———. *Survivors of the Leopoldville Disaster.* Bridgman, Mich.: Roberts Publications, 1997.

———. *Survivors of the Leopoldville Disaster II.* Bridgman, Mich.: Raymond Roberts, 1999.

Rodgers, W. L. *Naval Warfare under Oars.* Annapolis, Md.: Naval Institute Press, 1967.

Rogers, H. C. B. *Troopships and Their History.* London: Seeley Service & Co. Ltd., 1963. (One of the few books that deals with the history of troopships; however, Colonel Rogers focuses on the evolution of British troopships.)

Rohwer, Jurgen. *Axis Submarine Successes, 1939–1945.* Annapolis, Md.: Naval Institute Press, 1983.

Roscoe, Theodore. *United States Submarine Operations in World War II.* Annapolis, Md.: U.S. Naval Institute, 1949.

Rule, D. H. "Sultana: A Case for Sabotage." *North & South Magazine* 5, no. 1 (December 2001).

Salecker, Gene Eric. *Disaster on the Mississippi: The Sultana Explosion, April 27, 1865.* Annapolis, Md.: Naval Institute Press, 1996.

———. "A Tremendous Tumult and Uproar: The Tragic Sinking of the Sultana." *America Civil War* 15, no. 2, (May 2002).

Sanders, Jacquib. *A Night Before Christmas.* New York: G. P. Putman & Sons, 1963.

Satchell, Alister. *Running the Gauntlet: How Three Giant Liners Carried a Million Men to War, 1942–1945.* London: Chatham Publishing, 2001.

Schon, Heinz. *SOS Wilhelm Gustloff—Die grosse Schiffekatastrophe der Geschichte.* Stuttgart, Germany: Motorbuch Verlag, 2002.

Sellwood, A. V. *The Damned Don't Drown—The Sinking of the Wilhelm Gustloff.* London: Allan Wingate Publishers, 1973.

Slader, John. *The Fourth Service: Merchantmen at War, 1939–1945.* London: Robert Hale, 1994.

Smith, Eugene W. *Passenger Ships of the World Past and Present.* Boston: George H. Dean Company, 1963.

Smith, Robert Barr. "Tragic Voyage of Junyo Maru," *World War II Magazine* (March 2002).

Snelling, Stephen. *Gallipoli.* Gloucestershire, England: Alan Sutton, 1995.

Snelling, Stephen. *VCs of the First World War—Gallipoli.* Gloucestershire, England: Sutton Publishing Ltd., 1999.

Steel, Nigel. *Battleground Europe: Gallipoli.* South Yorkshire, England: Leo Cooper, 1991.

Sulzberger, C. L. *American Heritage New History of World War II.* New York: Viking Press, 1997.

Summers, Harry G. Jr. *The Vietnam War Almanac.* Novato, Calif.: Presidio Press, 1999.

Summersby Morgan, Kay. *Past Forgetting: My Love Affair with Dwight D. Eisenhower.* New York: Simon & Schuster, 1975.

Tarrant, V. E. *The Last Year of the Kriegsmarine, May 1944–May 1945.* Annapolis, Md.: Naval Institute Press, 1994.

———. *The U-Boat Offensive, 1914–1945,* Annapolis, Md.: Naval Institute Press, 1989.

Thornton, Francis Beauchesne. *Sea of Glory: The Magnificent Story of the Four Chaplains.* New York: Prentice-Hall, Inc., 1953.

Thubron, Colin. *The Ancient Mariners.* Chicago: Time-Life Books, Inc., 1981.

Waters, John M. *Bloody Winter.* Annapolis, Md.: Naval Institute Press, 1984.

Watts, Anthony J. *The Royal Navy: An Illustrated History.* Annapolis, Md.: Naval Institute Press, 1999.

Wernick, Robert. *The Vikings.* Alexandria, Va.: Time-Life Books, Inc., 1979.

Wheeler, Keith. *War under the Pacific.* Chicago: Time-Life Books, Inc., 1980.

Whipple, A. B. C. *The Mediterranean.* Chicago: Time-Life Books, Inc., 1981.

Williams, David. *Liners in Battledress.* London: Vanwell Publishing Ltd., 1989.

———. *Wartime Disasters at Sea.* Somerset, England: Patrick Stephens Limited, 1997.

Wise, James E. Jr. "Gallipoli: World's First Modern Amphibious Assault." *Sea Classics* 3, no. 5.

———. *Sole Survivors of the Sea.* Mount Pleasant, N.C.: The Nautical & Aviation Publishing Company of America, Inc., 1994.

Young, Desmond. *Rommel: The Desert Fox.* New York: William M. Morrow and Co. Inc., 1950.

TELEVISION MEDIA

"Cover-Up! The Sinking of the S.S. Leopoldville," The History Channel, 25 October 2001.

Tom Brokaw, NBC Nightly News, 27 December 2000.

UNPUBLISHED SOURCES

Abbreviations

Adm   Admiralty Records

Air   Air Ministry Records
Cab   Cabinet Office Papers
IWM   Imperial War Museum
LOC   Library of Congress
NARA   National Archives and Records, Washington, D.C.
NARA II   National Archives and Records II, College Park, Md.
NHC   Naval Historical Center, Washington, D.C.
NMM   National Maritime Museum
PRO   Public Record Office (Kew)

Correspondence with Pvt. Harry Ball, 110th Army Troops Co., Royal Engineers, regarding the sinking of the *Strathallan,* 1002.

IWM Document Reading Room—*Royal Edward*—Memoirs of Dr. C. J. G. Taylor, PP/MCR/126, medic on Hospital Ship *Soudan,* Extract from Chapter XXXVI, 144–45—*Soudan* rescued survivors of *Royal Edward.*

IWM Document Reading Room—First World War Letter of Lt. G. L. Drewry, VC, RNR, to his father. Letter written on board HMS *River Clyde* at Sedd-el Bahr, Turkey, 12 May 1915. Letter describes landing of British, Australian and New Zealand troops at Cape Helles, Gallipoli on 25–26 April 1915.

IWM Document Reading Room—Memoirs of Dr. C. J. G. Taylor, medic on the hospital ship *Soudan.* Extract from chapter 36, 144–45.

IWM Document Reading Room—L. F. Humphrey letter outlining his career during World War II, including service aboard SS *Strathallan,* which was sunk in December 1942, his passage to England working on the *Duchess of Richmond* after being picked upon the beaches of Oran.

IWM Document Reading Room—Nurse M. Ward (10 pp.) dated March 1943 while serving with Queen Alexandria's Royal Naval Nursing Service (QARNNS) in which she describes her rescue after the torpedoing of SS *Strathallan* by a German sub forty miles north of Oran in December 1942.

IWM Document Reading Room—J. F. Sweeny account of his experiences during the sinking of the SS *Lancastria* near St. Nazaire in a collier.

IWM Document Reading Room—Account of Victor Tolaini, Italian internee, on board *Arandora Star,* which was sunk by German submarine *U47* in June 1940. Tolaini describes scenes aboard ship as it was abandoned by internees and Allied soldiers.

IWM Document Reading Room—HMS *Trenchant* Summary of Service, 1942–63.

IWM Document Reading Room—Capt. J. H. Biggs, captain of the *Strathallan:* Report of Sinking of SS *Strathallan*

"Loss of the SS Royal Edward." Essex Regimental Museum. London, England.

NMM—War Service of SS *Strathallan.*

NARA II, United States. Kriegstagebuch (KTB) War Diary of U515.

PRO Adm 1/17669, Action with the enemy (3): Steam ship *Ceramic* sunk by U-boat: report of interview with sapper, Royal Engineers, 1945.

PRO Adm 1/30262, U.S. Legion of Merit, Degree of Commander, awarded to Comdr. A. R. Hezlet, D.S.O., D.S.C., Royal Navy.

PRO Adm 1/30399, H.M.S. *Trenchant* Log/Attack on Japanese Cruiser *Ashigara.*

PRO Adm 1/14269, Merchant Navy (64) SS *Strathallan* sunk by enemy action: awards to personnel of HM ships for rescue operation.

PRO Adm Secret W.P. (40) 432/Ref #HO 213/1834, Report of the *Arandora Star* Inquiry conducted by the Right Honorable Lord Snell, 24 October 1940.

PRO Adm #HO 213/1722, Summary of Lord Snell's Report.

PRO Adm #HO 213/1722, Capt. F. J. Robertson Report of *Arandora Star*— Conditions on Board and the Disaster.

PRO Air 51/259, Intelligence Section . . . SS *Rohna* sunk by HS 293 glider bomb in November 1943.

PRO Air 2/4593 1940–42. Ships and Shipping. General (code B. 74/1) Sinking of SS *Lancastria* in June 1940.

PRO Adm 199/176 (7534) Vols. 2130–48: U.K. Shipping Casualties Section, Trade Division: Report of an Interview with Sapper Eric E. Munday, Royal Engineers, 14 August 1945.

U.S. Department of the Navy, Office of the Chief of Naval Operations Secret Memorandum OP-12-2-EH, 30 April 1941, Subject: Requirements of the Navy for Merchant Vessels for Immediate Conversion.

OFFICIAL WORKS—PUBLISHED

American Naval Fighting Ships (nine volumes). Washington, D.C.: Naval History Division, Department of the Navy, 1959–81.

Roskill, Capt. S. W. *The War at Sea.* Vols. 1–3, parts 1 and 2. London: Her Majesty's Stationery Office, 1961.

United States Naval Chronology, World War II. Naval History Division, Office of the Chief of Naval Operations. Washington, D.C.: U.S. Government Printing Office, 1955.

United States Submarine Losses: World War II. Naval History Division, Office of the Chief of Naval Operations. Washington, D.C.: U.S. Government Printing Office, 1963.

U.S. War Department. *War of the Rebellion: A Compilation of the Official Records of the Union and Confederate Armies.* (70 volumes.) Washington, D.C.: U.S. Government Printing Office, 1880–1901.

INTERNET SOURCES

Website sources for HMS *Upholder, Neptunia,* and *Oceania:* http://www.warships.net/royalnavy/rnshiptypes/submarines/ww2/upholder.html;http://web.ukonline.co.uk/chalcraft/sm/upholder.html;http://shiplover2.virtualave.net/Italy/Neptunia.html.

Merchant Navy Officers website: http://www.merchantnavyofficers.com/rohna2.html.

World War II troopship crossing website: http://members.aol.com/troopship/leopoldv.html

History of the 66th Infantry Division: http://www.grunts.net/army/66thid.html

Leopoldville website: http://www.Leopoldville.net

Index

About the Authors

James E. Wise Jr. became a naval aviator in 1953 following graduation from Northwestern University. He served as an intelligence officer aboard USS *America* (CVA-66) and later as the commanding officer of various naval intelligence units.

Since his retirement from the Navy in 1975 as a captain, Wise has held several senior executive posts in private sector companies. In addition to *Stars in Blue: Movie Actors in America's Sea Services, Stars in the Corps: Movie Actors in the United States Marines,* and *Stars in Khaki: Movie Actors in the Army and Air Services,* he is the coauthor with Otto Giese of *Shooting the War: The Memoir and Photographs of a U-Boat Officer in World War II* and most recently contributed to *James Arness: An Autobiography.* Wise is also the author of many articles published in naval and maritime journals. He lives in Annapolis, Maryland.

Scott Baron, a U.S. Army veteran of the Vietnam War and graduate of California State University–Northridge, worked in law enforcement for a decade and then taught at the police academy and community college in Aptos, California. He lives in Watsonville, California, where he teaches U.S. history at a middle school. He is the author of *They Also Served: Military Biographies of Uncommon Americans,* among other books and articles, and a contributing writer for *Stars and Stripes.*